Social Policy and International Interventions in South East Europe

Social Policy and International Interventions in South East Europe

Edited by

Bob Deacon

University of Sheffield, UK

and

Paul Stubbs

The Institute of Economics, Zagreb, Croatia

IN ASSOCIATION WITH THE SOUTH-EAST EUROPEAN
RESEARCH CENTRE

Edward Elgar
Cheltenham, UK • Northampton, MA, USA

© Bob Deacon and Paul Stubbs, 2007

Published by
Edward Elgar Publishing Limited
Glensanda House
Montpellier Parade
Cheltenham
Glos GL50 1UA
UK

Edward Elgar Publishing, Inc.
William Pratt House
9 Dewey Court
Northampton
Massachusetts 01060
USA

A catalogue record for this book
is available from the British Library

Library of Congress Cataloguing in Publication Data

Social policy and international interventions in South East Europe/edited by
    Bob Deacon and Paul Stubbs.
        p. cm.
    'In Association with the South-East European Research Centre.'
    Includes bibliographical references and index.
    1. Balkan Peninsula—Social policy. 2. Balkan Peninsula—Foreign
relations. 3. Social policy—International cooperation. I. Deacon, Bob.
II. Stubbs, Paul, 1959–   .
HN613.5.S62   2007
320.609496—dc22

                                                            2007011685

ISBN 978 1 84720 096 9

Printed and bound in Great Britain by MPG Books Ltd, Bodmin, Cornwall

Contents

List of figures and tables   vii
List of contributors   ix
Preface   xiii
List of abbreviations   xv

1   Transnationalism and the making of social policy in
South East Europe   1
Bob Deacon and Paul Stubbs

2   Europeanization of social policy? Prospects and challenges
for South East Europe   22
Noémi Lendvai

3   Slovenia   45
Mojca Novak and Katja Rihar Bajuk

4   Bulgaria and Romania   62
Dimitri A. Sotiropoulos and Luana Pop

5   Croatia   85
Paul Stubbs and Siniša Zrinščak

6   Turkey   103
Burcu Yakut-Cakar

7   Macedonia   130
Maja Gerovska Mitev

8   Bosnia and Herzegovina   149
Reima Ana Maglajlić Holiček and Ešref Kenan Rašidagić

9   Serbia   167
Mihail Arandarenko and Pavle Golicin

10 Albania   187
Arlinda Ymeraj

11 Kosovo   203
Fred Cocozzelli

Contents

12 Conclusions   221
     Bob Deacon, Noémi Lendvai and Paul Stubbs

Index   243

Figures and tables

FIGURE

8.1 Map of BiH, outlining the two entities   151

TABLES

1.1 South East Europe: main indicators   12
1.2 Other data on South East Europe   13
2.1 EU initiatives and policy frameworks influencing national
     welfare issues   34
2.2 Road map to the European Union   37
2.3 Contrasting accession and integration   39
4.1 The evolution of public social expenditure as percentage
     of GDP in Bulgaria, 1996–2003   66
4.2 International actors in Bulgaria: main areas of social policy
     advice and assistance   68
4.3 The evolution of public social expenditure as percentage of
     GDP in Romania, 1997–2004   73
4.4 International actors in Romania: main areas of social
     policy advice and assistance   74
5.1 Real GDP and inflation: Croatia, 1989–95   87
5.2 Main trends in the Croatian pension system   92
5.3 Actors and their positions in the Croatian pension reform 95
6.1 Social security coverage in Turkey   106
6.2 Sectoral distribution of employment: gender breakdown
     in Turkey   108
6.3 Distribution of employment according to status at work in
     Turkey   109
6.4 Non-monetary human development indicators: selected
     Turkish provinces, 2000   112
7.1 Social expenditures as percentage of budget in Macedonia
     comparing 1991 with 1996   132
7.2 International governmental organizations in Macedonia,
     1991–96   133

9.1   Interplay of international and local actors and sectoral
      outcomes in the social policy arena in Serbia   183
12.1 International actor presence and significance in the region 224
12.2 European Union and World Bank modes of influence
      compared   229
12.3 Significance of four major factors influencing social policy 235

Contributors

Mihail Arandarenko is Associate Professor of Labour Economics at the Faculty of Economics of the University of Belgrade. He is Chairman of the Board of the Foundation for the Advancement of Economics in Belgrade. He has consulted long and short term to the United Nations Development Programme (UNDP), World Bank, European Agency for Reconstruction (EAR), International Labour Organization (ILO), United States Agency for International Development (USAID) and other international agencies. He has published extensively on labour markets, employment programmes, industrial relations and social policy in Serbia and the region of South East Europe.

Fred Cocozzelli is a member of the Department of Government and Politics at St. John's University in New York City. He completed his master's in international affairs at Columbia University's School of International and Public Affairs in 1999 and his doctorate in political science at the New School for Social Research in 2007. He worked in Kosovo in 1999 and 2000 as a senior field officer in humanitarian assistance and as a consultant on the social assistance scheme.

Bob Deacon is Professor of International Social Policy at the University of Sheffield, UK. He is Director of the Globalism and Social Policy Programme (www.gaspp.org) and founding editor of the journals *Critical Social Policy* and *Global Social Policy*. He has contributed through consultancies and advisory board to the work of the UNDP, United Nations Children's Fund (UNICEF), ILO, World Health Organization (WHO), United Nations Department of Economic and Social Affairs (UNDESA), World Bank, European Union (EU), Council of Europe and some national governments. His most recent book is *Global Social Policy and Governance*, published by Sage.

Maja Gerovska Mitev is Assistant Professor at the Institute of Social Work and Social Policy, Faculty of Philosophy, Ss. Cyril and Methodius University in Skopje, Macedonia. She is also a part-time PhD student at the South East European Research Centre, a collaboration between the University of Sheffield, UK, and City College, Thessaloniki, Greece. Her research interests focus on European social policy, international organizations, and comparative social policy.

Pavle Golicin is Programme Officer of the Poverty Reduction and Economic Development Cluster at the UNDP Country Office in Belgrade, Serbia. He has previously worked at the UNDP Regional Bureau for Europe and the Commonwealth of Independent States in Bratislava, Slovakia. He completed his master's in European political and administrative studies at the College of Europe in 2002.

Noémi Lendvai studied social policy and social work at ELTE University Budapest, before she took an MA in Political Science at Central European University. Her doctoral research at the University of Bristol looked at the impact of EU accession on social policy-making in Hungary, Croatia and Slovenia, and later as a postdoctoral Fellow, she continued to work on the role of the EU in the transformation of welfare in Central and South Eastern Europe.

Reima Ana Maglajlić Holiček has just completed her PhD at Anglia Ruskin University, Cambridge, England. She is a freelance consultant in South East Europe for various organizations, specialized in supporting co-operation of different stakeholders and participation of varied marginalized groups in research, policy development and practice that affects their lives.

Mojca Novak is Associate Professor of Sociology and Social Policy. She collaborates extensively with the School of Business and Management, Novo mesto, and with the Faculty of Social Sciences and the Faculty of Social Work at the University of Ljubljana. Her main subjects of teaching and research concern social policy and public administration management.

Luana Pop is Reader at the Faculty of Sociology and Social Work of the University of Bucharest. She has been a research fellow at the Leuven Institute for Central and Eastern European Studies, Belgium (1997) and at the Max Planck Institut fuer Gesellschaftsforschung, Cologne (2004–2005). She has worked as a consultant on several national policy projects in the field of social policy, undertaken by the Romanian government in partnership with the World Bank (WB), ILO, Department for International Development (DFID) and USAID. She has edited and co-authored a *Dictionary of Social Policy* (2000), while her recent publications focus on the institutionalization of social policy in transition countries.

Ešref Kenan Rašidagić is a senior assistant and PhD candidate in the Faculty of Political Science, University of Sarajevo. As a project manager for the Independent Bureau for Humanitarian Issues, he headed two big social welfare restructuring projects. He also works as a freelance consultant for various international and local organizations, mainly in the field of effective governance, social and child protection, and human rights in general.

Katja Rihar Bajuk graduated in political sciences from the Faculty of Social Sciences at the University of Ljubljana in 2002. She continued her studies at the University of Turku and Roskilde University and has specialized in European social policy. She completed her master's programme with the thesis 'Reforms of the pension systems in selected Central and Eastern European countries: case studies of Hungary and Slovenia'. Since 2002 she has been working in the Ministry of Labour, Family and Social Affairs of the Republic of Slovenia and has been involved in various programmes of international co-operation.

Dimitri A. Sotiropoulos is Assistant Professor of Political Science at the Department of Political Science and Public Administration of the University of Athens. He has been Senior Research Fellow at the Hellenic Observatory of the London School of Economics and Political Science and co-ordinating editor of the *Greek Review of Political Science*. He edited (with Thanos Veremis) the volume *Is Southeastern Europe Doomed to Instability?* (London: Frank Cass, 2002). His most recent publication is the edited volume *Democracy and the State in the New Southern Europe*, co-edited with Richard Gunther and P. Nikiforos Diamandouros (Oxford: Oxford University Press, 2006).

Paul Stubbs is a British sociologist working as a Senior Research Fellow in the Institute of Economics, Zagreb, Croatia. His main research interests include: social policy in South Eastern Europe; transnational governmentalities and policy translation; and social movements and computer-mediated communication. He is a member of the international advisory board of the journal *Global Social Policy* and of the editorial board of the *Croatian Journal of Social Policy*.

Burcu Yakut-Cakar is a researcher at the Social Policy Forum at Bogazici University, Turkey and a PhD candidate in the Department of Economics, Marmara University. She received her BA and MA from the Department of Economics at Bogazici University, Turkey, with a thesis on 'The transformation of the Turkish welfare regime'. She has contributed to various research projects on poverty and social exclusion as well as welfare reforms in Turkey, and is currently completing her PhD on a 'Comparative analysis of poverty and inequality in Turkey'.

Arlinda Ymeraj is employed as a Social Policy Officer with UNICEF, Albania. Her doctoral thesis, completed in February 2006, is on the topic of 'The role of social assistance in reducing social exclusion and increasing social capital'. Between 1996 and 1997, she was Minister of Labour and Social Affairs in Albania, following four years as Director of the Department for Social Assistance in the same ministry. Her publications include a chapter on Albania in the book *Civil Society and Social Care* published by the European Institue of Social Services in 2003.

Siniša Zrinščak is a Croatian sociologist and Professor of Social Policy at the University of Zagreb, Croatia (Department of Social Work in the Faculty of Law). His main interests include: religious and social policy changes in post-communism; Europeanization, globalization and social policy; and civil society development. He is president of the Croatian Sociological Association, president of the International Study of Religion in Central and Eastern Europe Association, and editor-in-chief of the *Croatian Journal of Social Policy*.

Preface

The genesis of this book lies in one of the work programmes of the South East European Research Centre (SEERC), a joint enterprise involving the University of Sheffield and City College, Thessaloniki, that we were involved in shaping in 2002. This enabled us to bring together a network of social policy scholars from across the region to a series of workshops funded by SEERC and, later, by the Friedrich Ebert stiftung (FES) office for Croatia and Slovenia in Zagreb. The idea for this book was born at one of these workshops in Stubičke toplice, Croatia in September 2005. Draft chapters from all the countries were prepared for a subsequent workshop held at the same location in September 2006. This workshop generated an outline of the book's conclusions. In this sense the book and its messages regarding the extent to which, and the means by which, international interventions in the region have shaped its social policies is very much a collective project.

The book would not have been possible without the financial support of SEERC and FES. As editors we want to thank all the contributors for accepting in a comradely spirit our suggestions for revisions to drafts. Thanks are due to the University of Sheffield and the Institute of Economics, Zagreb, for supporting our involvement in this project. The support of Denis Redžepagić of the Institute of Economics in Zagreb has been invaluable in preparing the manuscript for publication.

Bob Deacon, Skipwith, UK
Paul Stubbs, Zagreb, Croatia

Abbreviations

AKP	Justice and Development Party
ANAP	Motherland Party
ASEAN	Association of South East Asian Nations
BHAS	BiH Agency for Statistics
BiH	Bosnia and Herzegovina
BK	Bag-Kur
BPK	Banking and Payments Authority of Kosovo
CARDS	Community Assistance for Reconstruction, Development and Stabilization
CARE	Cooperative for Assistance and Relief Everywhere
CAS	Country Assistance Strategy
CCSM	comparative case study method
CCT	conditional cash transfer
CEE	Central East Europe
CLDS	Centre for Liberal and Democratic Studies
CoE	Council of Europe
CPI	Consumer Price Index
CPI	Corruption Perception Index
CRS	Catholic Relief Services
CSW	Centre for Social Work
DFID	Department for International Development
DHSW	Department of Health and Social Welfare
DLE	Department of Labour and Employment
DLSW	Department of Labour and Social Welfare
DOS	Democratic Opposition of Serbia
DS	Democratic Party (in Serbia)
DSP	Democratic Left Party
DSS	Democratic Party of Serbia
DSW	Department of Social Welfare
DTS	Donor Technical Secretariat
DYP	True Path Party
EAR	European Agency for Reconstruction
EBRD	European Bank for Reconstruction and Development
EC	European Commission
ECHO	European Community Humanitarian Office

EIB	European Investment Bank
EPL	employment protection legislation
EPPU	Economic Policy Planning Unit
ES	Retirement Chest
ESF	European Social Fund
EU	European Union
EUR	euro
EUROSTAT	European Union Statistical Agency
FBiH	Federation of Bosnia and Herzegovina
FDI	Foreign Direct Investment
FES	Friedrich Ebert stiftung
FFP	Food for Peace
FI	financial institution
FOS	Federal Office for Statistics (BiH)
FSC	Financial Supervisory Commission
GDP	gross domestic product
GFAP	General Framework Agreement for Peace
GNI	gross national income
GP	general (medical) practitioner
GPRS	Growth and Poverty Reduction Strategy
GTZ	German Association for Technical Assistance
HDI	Human Development Index
HDZ	Hrvatska demokratska zajednica (Croatian Democratic Union)
HIF	Health Insurance Fund
HNI	HealthNet International
HRBA	human-rights based approach
IBHI	Independent Bureau of Humanitarian Issues
IBRD	International Bank for Reconstruction and Development
ICG	International Crisis Group
ICVA	International Council of Voluntary Agencies
ICTY	International Criminal Tribunal for the former Yugoslavia
IDA	International Development Association
IDP	internally displaced persons
IFI	international financial institutions
IGO	international governmental organization
ILO	International Labour Organization
IMF	International Monetary Fund
INGO	international non-governmental organization
INSTAT	National Institute of Statistics
IO	international organization

IP	implementation partner
IPA	Instrument for Pre-accession Assistance
IPS	Integrated Planning System
IR	international relations
IRC	International Rescue Committee
ISC	Initiative for Social Cohesion
ISP	Institute for Social Policy
JAP	Joint Assessment Paper for Employment Priorities
JIAS	Joint Interim Administration Structure
JIM	Joint Inclusion Memorandum
KFOR	Kosovo Force
KLA	Kosovo Liberation Army
KM	Konvertibilna Marka (Convertible Mark, BiH currency)
KSPP	Kosovo Social Protection Project
LDK	Democratic League of Kosovo
LDP	local distribution partner
LDS	Liberal Democrats of Slovenia
LMD	Labour Market Development
LSMS	Living Standard Measurement Survey
MAPAS	Agency for Supervision of the Fully Funded Pension Insurance
MCI	Mercy Corps International
MDG	Millennium Development Goal
MEDA	financial instrument for implementation of Euro-Mediterranean Partnership programme
MHP	Nationalist Action Party
MIG	Medium Income Guarantee scheme
MKD	Macedonian denars
MLSW	Ministry of Labour and Social Welfare
MoLE	Ministry of Labour and Employment
MOLESP	Ministry of Labour, Employment and Social Policy
MOP	Material Support to Family
MoSA	Ministry of Social Affairs
MoLFSA	Ministry of Labour, Family and Social Affairs
MoH	Ministry of Health
MoLSS	Ministry of Labour and Social Security
MTDS	Medium-Term Development Strategy
MTS	Mother Teresa Society
NATO	North Atlantic Treaty Organization
NAP	National Action Plan, for employment
NGO	non-government organization
NORAD	Norwegian Agency for Development Co-operation

NSDI	National Strategy for Development and Integration
NSSED	National Strategy for Socio-Economic Development
n/a	not available
ODA	official development assistance
OECD	Organisation for Economic Co-operation and Development
OHR	Office of the High Representative
OMC	Open Method of Co-ordination
OSCE	Organization for Security and Co-operation in Europe
PAL	Programme Adjustment Loan
PAYG	Pay-As-You-Go
pc	per capita
PHARE	Pologne Hongarie Assistance à la Reconstruction des Economies (EU, French: Poland and Hungary Assistance for Economic Restructuring programme)
PIO/MIO	penziono/mirovinsko i invalidsko osiguranje (pension and disability funds)
PISG	Provisional Institutions for Self-Government
PPP	purchasing power parities
PRSP	Poverty Reduction Strategy Paper
RS	Republika Srpska
RSIS	Republika Srpska Institute for Statistics
SA	Social Assistance
SAA	Stabilization and Association Agreement
SAP	Stabilization and Association Process
SDA	Stranka demokratske akcije (Democratic Action Party)
SDS	Srpska demokratska stranka (Serbian Democratic Party)
SEE	South East Europe
SEE	state economic enterprise
SEERC	South East European Research Centre
SFOR	Stabilization Force
SFRY	Socialist Federal Republic of Yugoslavia
SHP	Social Democratic Populist Party
SIDA	Swedish International Development Agency
SIF	Social Innovation Fund
SII	Social Insurance Institute
SIPU	Swedish Institute for Public Administration
SIS	State Institute of Statistics
SOK	Statistical Office of Kosovo
SPEAG	Social Protection and Economic Assistance Grant
SRS	Serbian Radical Party
SSND	Social Safety Net Development

SSSP	Support to Social Sector Project
SweBiH	Swedish Psychiatric, Social and Rehabilitation Project for Bosnia-Herzegovina
SSK	Social Insurance Institution
TESEV	Foundation for Economic and Social Studies in Turkey
TÜSİAD	Association for Turkish Businessmen and Industrialists
UK	United Kingdom
UN	United Nations
UNDESA	United Nations Department of Economic and Social Affairs
UNDP	United Nations Development Programme
UNHCR	United Nations High Commission for Refugees
UNMIK	United Nations Interim Administration Mission in Kosovo
UNICEF	United Nations Children's Fund
UNPA	United Nations Protected Areas
UNPREDEP	UN Preventive Deployment Mission
UNPROFOR	United Nations Protection Force
USA	United States of America
USAID	United States Agency for International Development
USD	United States dollars
WB	World Bank
WFP	World Food Programme
WHO	World Health Organization
YAPS	Youth Albanian Parcel Service

1. Transnationalism and the making of social policy in South East Europe

Bob Deacon and Paul Stubbs

INTRODUCTION

This book represents a concerted attempt to understand the role of international actors in the making of social policy in nine countries and one territory in South East Europe. Wherever possible, the chapters have been written by leading scholars from each country. Our aim, throughout the entire process, was to seek to achieve a synergy between the chapters so that the whole would be greater than the sum of its parts. The book reflects our long-term concern with the ways in which 'social policy activities traditionally analysed within and undertaken within one country now take on a supranational and transnational character' (Deacon et al., 1997: 1).

It is this transnational dimension which we revisit in this chapter, concentrating largely on the interventions in national social policies across countries and regions by a variety of international agencies. Chapter 2, authored by Noémi Lendvai, with its focus on processes of Europeanization, offers a complementary introductory chapter. In the concluding Chapter 12, written by three authors, we return to the key questions posed in these introductory texts. The nine chapters in between focus, respectively, on Slovenia; Bulgaria and Romania; Croatia; Turkey; Macedonia (recognized by the United Nations [UN] under the provisional name of the former Yugoslav Republic of Macedonia); Bosnia and Herzegovina; Serbia; Albania; and the territory of Kosovo (a province in Southern Serbia under UN administration since 1999). The chapters in the book were commissioned before Montenegro voted for independence from Serbia, and its recognition as an independent state by the United Nations on 28 June 2006, so there is, unfortunately, no chapter on Montenegro in this book. In addition, some resolution of the status of Kosovo may be achieved in the period between completing this book and its publication.

This chapter first reviews some of the conceptual and analytical frameworks on the transnationalization of policy-making drawn from international relations, policy transfer and politics of scale literatures. We then go on to address how states and their sovereignty need to be reconceptualized before turning briefly to analytical approaches to social policy. The subsequent section focuses on South East Europe and the countries and territories which comprise it, addressing historical legacies, disruptions and continuities, and some of the region's social and economic trends. The final section poses a series of broad questions which we return to in the final chapter in the light of the case studies.

The text is underpinned by a theoretical framework perhaps best described as 'soft' or 'weak' historical institutionalism in so far as we emphasize the importance of macro-context or structural factors, the contingencies of history ('taking time seriously' in Pierson and Skocpol's [2002] formulation), and the importance of 'the combined effects of institutions and processes' (ibid.) which are key features of historical institutionalism in sociology, political science, international relations and economics. Our approach, however, rejects the path dependency of 'strong' historical institutionalism in favour of a more open approach sensitive to the interactions between agents, structures, institutions and discourses (Moulaert and Jessop, 2006). Discourses as 'the intersubjective production of meaning' (ibid.) are, thus, central to the analysis of structure and institutions so that social policies are conceptualized here as both real, having concrete impacts on the well-being of people, and epiphenomena with a logic derived from the interests of those engaged in the process.

Methodologically, the book is based on a refinement of the comparative case study method (CCSM) in which individual case studies are written by researchers with a deep knowledge of the country or territory in question, being given a large amount of autonomy to write about that which they consider important within a broadly agreed framework. As much as testing explicit hypotheses, then, CCSM seeks to formulate, elaborate and refine concepts which can be utilized, later, in more in-depth, primary, research studies in order to further develop theory. The approach explores 'configurations of characteristics' seeing how they fit together in each case and how they differ across cases (Ragin, 1987; 2000). This text addresses ways of studying international actors, states and social policies themselves, before delving deeper into the social policy choices and constraints as a result of the growth of transnational processes.

STUDYING INTERNATIONAL ACTORS, STATES AND SOCIAL POLICIES

International Actors

To begin to understand the international social policy-making process we must draw upon three broad literatures on the transnationalization of policies: international relations and international organization theory; policy transfer, advocacy and diffusion literature; and work on policy assemblages, transnational processes and the politics of scale.

International relations

International relations theorists tend to oscillate between two poles: state-centrism and cosmopolitan transnationalism. For state-centrists, we still live in a world dominated by sovereign states. They use the principal–agent theory to show how international organizations' (IOs) policies are nothing but the products of interstate bargaining. For cosmopolitan transnationalists, international actors enjoy increasing power and autonomy and are shaping the world through an emerging architecture of global governance which includes global institutions and emerging global regulations (Held et al., 1999). Between these poles, international relations theorists pay attention to the ways in which a large number of non-state and often private actors have entered the space we shall call the 'contested terrain of emerging transnational governance'. These non-state actors engage in transnational political spaces, taking on regulatory, policy-making and other kinds of activities not undertaken by traditional intergovernmental organizations. Thus firms evolve private international regimes of self-regulation in many spheres such as labour and environmental standards (Hall and Biersteker, 2002).

Global or transnational social movements from below have become a major force in transnational advocacy, agenda-setting and policy-making (Kaldor, 2003; Scholte, 2005). The term 'complex multi-lateralism' (O'Brien et al., 2000) captures a situation where state–state interaction coexists with a new set of transnational power dynamics within which IOs and the social movements they are confronted by have a degree of policy autonomy at various levels. This framework is useful in explaining some aspects of the ways IOs influence state social policy.

Policy transfer and policy diffusion

The policy transfer and policy diffusion literatures (cf. Dolowitz and Marsh, 2000) reveal accounts of policy transfers across borders where it is clear that 'choices' are being made by some countries to borrow the policy of another. Their list of key questions – Why do actors engage in policy transfer? Who are the key actors involved in the policy transfer process? What is transferred? From where are lessons drawn? What are the different degrees of transfer? What restricts or facilitates the policy transfer process? and How is the project of policy transfer related to policy 'success' or policy 'failure'? – offers a useful entry point (Dolowitz and Marsh, 2000: 8). They focus on push factors (along a continuum from 'coercion' to 'voluntarism'), and on pull factors (a continuum from 'isomorphy' to 'immunity'), suggesting that 'choices' are made often because the country is being coerced by powerful global actors or because the choice is in conformity with its particular ideological goals, or fits better to sets of national cultural assumptions. In other words national social policy choices reflect globalized policy options and contestations about these.

It has been argued that emerging transnational policy advocacy coalitions (Orenstein, 2005), epistemic communities (Haas, 1992) and transnational knowledge networks (Stone and Maxwell, 2005) play a part in shaping transnational processes of policy transfer and implementation. A much discussed example of such a transnational policy advocacy coalition is the global pension policy story (Orenstein, 2005). The agenda-setting was very much in the hands of a global knowledge network based upon economists educated in the Chicago school of neo-liberal economics. This network had a global reach in terms of its links to Milton Friedman, Friedrich von Hayek and others (Valdes, 1995). It then became centred upon work in the World Bank initiated by Larry Summers, then chief economist, which was eventually published in 1994 as *Averting the Old Age Crisis*. A transnational advocacy coalition was then developed to further the adoption of these reforms. This coalition included the World Bank, USAID, the Inter-American Development Bank and other actors (Orenstein, 2005: 193). As will be clear in many of the country case study chapters, this had a considerable, although uneven, impact on national pension policies in South East Europe (SEE).

Meyer et al. (1997), working within the concept of world society theory, argue that cross-border professional associations act to spread policy ideas and practices, which become seen as 'universalistic science'. Education policy and practice, health-care procedures and practices, and by extension other social policies, become technicized and framed in terms of professional standards. In contrast to the literature on coalitions, this theory suggests rather less contestation regarding policy options. A somewhat similar, although more politicized, position is developed by St Clair (2006), who points to the co-production of both 'knowledge' and 'social order' or technologies of practice, by 'transnational expert institutions', particularly the World Bank.

Politics of scale

The politics of scale literature suggests that it is not adequate to attempt to capture the complexity of transnational policy-making by thinking in terms of layers or levels of government or governance. An account of policy-making which talks only in terms of the taken-for-granted hierarchies of sub-national, national, regional and global levels is seen as unable to capture some of the key aspects of policy-making in a globalized world. What is important here is that policy-making is not only taking place at different taken-for-granted levels of governance but that key policy players are transcending each level at any one moment. The policy-making process is multi-sited and multilayered as well as multi-actored coterminously. Within this context, individuals as change agents and policy translators can act in the spaces between levels and organizations (Lendvai and Stubbs, 2006).

Janine Wedel's work, in particular, emphasizes the complexity of transnational encounters, where players know each other, and interact, in a variety of capacities, with multiple identities (which she terms 'transidentities') and in a variety of roles. Her tale is one of shifting and multiple agency, promoted in part by what she terms 'flex organizations', which have a 'chameleon-like, multipurpose character', with actors within them 'able to play the boundaries' between national and international; public and private; formal and informal; market and bureaucratic; state and non-state; even legal and illegal (Wedel, 2004; 167). Policy processes are, then, very much more fluid than either the international relations (IR) or policy transfer literature suggests, leading to new hybrids, complex and overlapping policy assemblages and, indeed, policy accidents and ambiguities.

The 'global is in the local' and the 'local in the global' captures some of this, providing we reassert a notion of power in terms of 'uneven reach', 'differential intensity' of places and spaces and the differential ability to 'jump scale' (Moulaert and Jessop, 2006). Essentially, we would assert that certain policy spaces open up, and others close down, in the encounters between IOs and national governments and that those who are better able to travel between these scales – consultants, international non-governmental organization (INGO) experts, policy entrepreneurs, and so on – are better placed to influence policy. Within this context the national policy-making process can become distorted. Indeed, Jeremy Gould has argued that 'transnational private agencies (find) themselves brokering and, to some extent, supplanting local civil society representation in policy consultation' (Gould, 2005b: 142).

States

Space precludes a revisiting of diverse theoretical approaches to state theory. What is clear is that, in the context of globalization and transnationalism, there is a need to engage with a small, but growing, literature which revisits and revises state theory in contemporary conditions. This is important in order to avoid merely repeating crude typologies which purport to measure variance from an untheorized and taken for granted 'normal' state, as in the concepts, and associated indices, of failed, weak or captured states.

Bob Jessop's earlier (1990) reworking of Poulantzas' (1978) conception of the state as a 'social relation' or as 'the site, generator and product of strategies' (Bratsis, 2002: 259) still offers the most useful starting point. In a sense, this indicates a shift from the state as an 'entity', locked in relationships with other, similarly fixed, universal entities such as 'the market' or 'civil society'. Instead, a more complex notion of interlocking and nested 'aspects of statehood' is needed in which new forms of governance and 'meta-governance' (Jessop, 2004) emerge based on new, complex and contested combinations and recombinations of forces. In this understanding, the 'traditional' dichotomy between 'the state' and 'the market' shared, in fact, by social democracy and neo-liberalism as political projects, needs to be abandoned or, at the very least, understood as unstable and mediated by other realms, notably that deemed 'private' (Clarke, 2004: 77).

Consider classic Weberian notions that the state is that which has a monopoly of the legitimate use of violence and attempt to apply this to Bosnia-Herzegovina or Kosovo. Then consider whether, in terms of the growth of privatized security companies, the definition is completely meaningful anywhere. Taking each of the aspects of statehood in turn, the state as a structured political arena; as a materialized relation of power; as a set of institutions; as a set of functions; as a legal order; and so on (cf. Ougaard, 2004: ch. 4), it is still clear that state theory needs rethinking. Ougaard's solution, in terms of 'the uneven globalization of statehood' (ibid.: 66) seems to offer a way forward, understanding the varying aspects of the internationalization of states in terms of uneven speed, varying degrees and diverse forms.

A similar approach is adopted by Saskia Sassen who points out that the 'frontier zone' of politico-economic interactions between transnational actors and states 'produce new institutional forms and alter some of the old ones' (Sassen, 2000: 164). These interactions need to be set in terms of forms of domination and subordination but also need to be underpinned by an understanding of the spaces for negotiation and the new opportunity structures which come into being as a result. Further, she suggests that it is erroneous to view states as, either, passive victims of, or unchanged by, globalization procesess and politics.

Graham Harrison's concept of the 'sovereign frontier' challenges conventional binary understandings of state sovereignty – either states have sovereignty or they do not – in which the domestic space is seen as discrete and bounded and either resistant to, or overwhelmed by, external actors. His work suggests that many states exist in a sovereign frontier in which the domestic–foreign border becomes porous through a ' "mutual assimilation" of donor and state power' so that donors or, for our purposes here, transnational actors, are more accurately conceived as 'part of the state itself' (Harrison, 2001: 669), or as a kind of 'extended state'. What Gould terms emerging 'new hybrid forms of "global/local linkages" ' (Gould, 2005a: 9) result in a blurring of the boundaries between the internal and the external.

In a sense, understanding the state as a nested set of administrative competences is also relevant, providing we rescue this from traditional public administration theory. In other words, agents and actors in and around state institutions matter, more obviously in transition conditions of supposed 'instability' but, actually, even beyond these cases. Indeed, as other chapters show, the nature of state capacities and their meta-construction matters enormously in terms of the regulatory assemblages accompanying processes of accession to the EU and/or the rolling out of reforms as a condition of World Bank loans.

To this 'extended' concept of the state, we need to add what Wendy Larner has recently termed 'diaspora strategies' which 'not only disrupt conventional distinctions between the domestic and the international, they are also reconfiguring public and private authority as new understandings of nation, state and governance all emerge' (Larner, 2007: 3).

Social Policies

Focusing on one domain of state power and function and one set of state institutions, brings us to social policy and the ways in which transnationalization and globalization have affected the making of social policy. It has been suggested that globalization impacts upon the subject area and practice of social policy in a number of ways, again unevenly in different places at different times (Deacon, 2007). These include: setting welfare states in competition with each other; bringing new players into the making of social policy; raising the issues with which social policy is concerned, those of redistribution, regulation and rights, to a supranational level that has both a regional (EU, Association of South East Asian Nations [ASEAN], and so on) and global dimension; creating a transnational market in social provision and challenging territorial-based structures and assumptions of welfare obligation and entitlement in the context of migration flows. For our purposes what is important from this is that transnationalization in South East Europe multiplies the arenas of social policy discourse and social policy-making.

In terms of social policy understood as sectoral policy (social protection, pensions, health, labour markets and education) this means that international organizations compete to influence national social policy through loans/conditional aid, technical assistance, regulatory frameworks, and so on. In our previous study of the impact of international organizations on the making of social policy in Hungary, Bulgaria, Ukraine and the former Yugoslavia (Deacon et al., 1997) we showed how the World Bank was competing with the ILO to influence pension policy. Since then, as is evident in this volume, the role of the EU has become more important, albeit in complex ways, and the range of actors involved has mutiplied.

In terms of social policy understood as rights accruing to citizenship, this means that migration challenges territorial borders of solidarities and, on the one hand, presages regional and global solidarities and regional and global citizenship but, on the other, reconstitutes solidarities around family, religion and ethnicity. Both of these processes are at work in the context of the forced migrations following the wars and conflicts in South East Europe.

In terms of social policy's identification of a number of diverse worlds of welfare (Esping-Andersen 1990) – market-based liberalism, work-based conservative corporatism and citizenship-based social democracy – globalization poses the question as to whether it is likely to impel countries towards one model. Sykes et al. (2001) noted that while some scholars had argued that neo-liberal globalization would drive countries to adopt liberal or residual social policies, others suggested that developed countries were immune from such global economic pressures. A midpoint position was identified, at least for Western European countries, which concluded that global economic pressures did have some impact on a country's social policy but the nature of this impact was dependent upon the type of institutional welfare state already in existence (Scharf and Schmidt, 2000; Swank, 2002), social democracy being suprisingly resilient and conservative corporatism being most challeneged. Others (Deacon, 2000; Deacon et al., 1997) have argued, focusing on post-communist social policy, that the *politics* of globalization as much as the *economics* of globalization had shaped country thinking about social policy, bringing us back to the influence of the World Bank, the UN and the EU.

However, the welfare regime literature that divides the world into liberal, conservative corporatist, social democratic and perhaps also state-led developmental welfare states begins to unravel in other parts of the world (Deacon, 2007; Gough and Wood, 2004). Rather than attempting to squeeze emerging welfare states and social policy formations into this framework, it may be better to regard emerging welfare settlements as policy assemblages (Clarke, 2004) which are products of the multi-actored and multilayered processes we noted above. Expectations that emerging welfare settlements will follow in the path of earlier Western European trajectories needs to be revised. What is resulting and will result from the complex politics of new welfare settlements will be different, taking place at several levels and involving a proliferation of international actors. This book provides empirical evidence of this in South East Europe.

SOUTH EAST EUROPE: IMAGINING, LIVING IN AND CONSTRUCTING A REGION

Regions are increasingly defined less in terms of physical geography and more in terms of political constructs which create 'imagined communities' at levels beyond that of the nation state (cf. Anderson, 1991). This notion of regions as 'relatively malleable entities contingent on various social practices' (Benchev, 2006: 5) is important, not least in terms of the complex dynamic between notions of identity, nationhood and above all, the spectre of (Western) Europe and its 'Other'. At its most acute in terms of the frozen notion of 'the Balkans' (Todorova, 1997) and only slightly more nuanced in terms of the EU's construction of 'the Western Balkans', the region tends to be defined in negative terms and, in the 1990s, as essentially conflict-prone and underpinned by deep-rooted historical animosities. The difficulty of constructing an antithesis from within, in terms of 'Balkan is beautiful' (Razsa and Lindstrom, 2004) or, more mildly, South East Europe for itself, is reinforced by the real and imagined uneven geopolitics of accession to the European Union, itself constructed in terms of modernity, as states seek to 'join or rejoin Europe'.

Our frame of reference needs to grasp both the heterogeneity of the spaces subsumed within the concept of South East Europe and the historically contingent processes of institution and (nation) state-building which may be relevant in terms of contemporary welfare settlements and in terms of the configurations and forms of international interventions. There is a need to treat notions of 'legacies' extremely cautiously, with Todorova's claim that 'the conclusion that the Balkans are the Ottoman legacy is not an overstatement' (Todorova, 1997: 12) certainly seeming to overstate the case, at least from a social policy perspective. In many of the countries and territories covered in this book, the impact of Ottomanism needs to be set alongside that of the Austro-Hungarian empire in the latter part of the nineteenth century, influenced by Bismarckian ideas and practices on social insurance, which came to frame modern welfare settlements in Croatia, Slovenia, parts of Bosnia-Herzegovina and Serbia. Subsequently, in Turkey, a new reformist social policy was introduced by Kemal Ataturk explicitly attempting to link secularization and modernization.

The period after the Second World War saw all of the countries and territories discussed in this book, with the exception of Turkey, becoming communist or socialist states. Tito's Yugoslavia, at first within the Soviet sphere of influence, adopted an independent path after the break with Stalin in 1948. A number of features of Yugoslav socialism between 1948 and 1990 are important in terms of the themes of this book. First, modernization linked to industrialization and rapid urbanization created a kind of dual social structure, with those employed in the socialist industrial sector having work-based benefits which small farmers did not have. This went alongside mass literacy programmes and extensive efforts in preventive public health. Secondly, formal equality between the republics rested alongside increasing inequalities between the richer northern republics, particularly Slovenia and Croatia, and the rest of the federation, which regional policies appeared powerless to combat. Thirdly, the introduction of participatory socialist self-management also went alongside an increasing recognition of the need to tackle emerging social problems through new centres for social work (CSWs), established in the late 1950s and early 1960s, charged with 'analysing social problems in the municipality, suggesting measures to solve them, undertaking professional guardianship work and solving other social problems' (Šućur, 2003: 8). The corresponding institutionalization of social work education within higher education was, also, unique within the region (cf. Zaviršek, 2005).

Albania, under the leadership of Enver Hoxha, steered an isolationist path after Stalin's death, which meant that progress in health and education in the 1950s were later eroded in the context of repression, technological underdevelopment and a Maoist-inspired cultural revolution, leaving the country as the poorest in Europe by the time the Communist Party lost control in the 1992 elections. The collapse of pyramid savings schemes in 1997, and the influx of refugees from Kosovo in 1999 both threatened the country's stability and highlighted tensions between different regionally based political groupings (cf. Vickers and Pettifer, 2007).

Bulgaria, after initial close links with Tito's Yugoslavia, is perhaps the only example in the region of a classic Soviet satellite state, under the leadership of Todor Zhivkov from 1956 until he was deposed by sections of the Communist Party on 10 November 1989. Parts of the party leadership survived the fall of communism, forming the Bulgarian Socialist Party which has held power in a number of coalition governments. Following a decade of Soviet military presence and economic exploitation, Romania under Gheorgiu-Dej and, even more dramatically, under Nicoleau Ceauşescu from 1965, pursued an independent foreign policy, securing international credits for economic development, creating indebtedness. Later, Romania sought to remove its indebtedness through a systematic policy of exporting produce which resulted in domestic shortages and a sharp decline in living standards in the 1980s. Ceauşescu's demographic policies and major rural and urban programmes also had dramatic impacts on well-being, most notably in terms of the legacy of large numbers of children and adults in appalling conditions in institutional care. The overthrow of Ceausescu did not lead to a dismantling of 'parallel structures' (Gallagher, 2005: 174) but, rather, to uneasy political coalitions between reformed communists and ultra-nationalists.

Turkey, the only regional power except Greece to remain outside of the socialist orbit after the Second World War, joining the North Atlantic Treaty Organization (NATO) in 1952, has experienced periods of multi-party democracy interspersed with periods of military rule. The economic and social effects of liberalization of the economy are discussed in Chapter 6, as is its current status as a candidate country for EU membership.

The impacts of wars and transition on social policies in South East Europe have been documented elsewhere (cf. Deacon et al., 1997; ch. 7), and cannot be addressed in depth here. Nevertheless, the wars of the Yugoslav succession, beginning with the short conflict in Slovenia in 1991, spreading to Croatia from 1991 to 1995 and Bosnia-Herzegonia from 1992 to 1995, as well as the conflict in Kosovo and Serbia in 1999 and the insta-bility in Macedonia in 2001, saw a complex and changing mix of interna-tional humanitarian and security interventions which directly affected processes of social and political change. The concept of 'state-building' is in danger of technicizing the complex social and political engineering which is being attempted in parts of the region. The unfinished nature of this, not least in terms of processes within Bosnia-Herzegovina and the status of Kosovo, are also important factors which need to be addressed within a frame which links social policy with other discourses, notably security, refugee return, and democratization.

The effects of war and transition on well-being have, of course, been dra-matic in all of the countries and territories of the region except Slovenia. Tables 1.1 and 1.2 show the current picture of national income, human development and poverty. Three main data-sets have been used: the World Bank's World Development Indicators (http://devdata.worldbank.org/ data-query/), the UNDP's Human Development Report (http://hdr.undp. org/hdr 2006/statistics/) and the UNICEF TransMONEE database (http:// www.unicef-icdc.org/resources/transmonee.html). These are utilized because they provide reliable and timely comparative data. However, three caution-ary points need to be made. The first is that data is incomplete, particularly for Bosnia-Herzegovina, where the last population census took place in 1991, and for Serbia and Kosovo which are not included in most of the com-parative data bases. Data for Serbia and Kosovo have, therefore, been added

Table 1.1   South East Europe: main indicators

	GNI per capita $ ATLAS method[1]	Under 5 mortality rate (per 1000 pop)	Human Development Index (2004)	Human Development Index rank [2004]	Human Development Index rank minus GDP	Gini index	Population (rounded)	Population in poverty $PPP 2.15 per day per cent[2]	Population in poverty $PPP 4.30 per day per cent[3]
Albania	2 580	19	0.784	73	26	28.2	3 129 680	24	71
Bosnia-Herzegovina	2 440	15	0.800	62	16	26.2	3 907 070	4	35
Bulgaria	3 450	15	0.816	54	12	29.2	7 740 930	4	33
Croatia	8 060	7	0.846	44	7	29.0	4 444 450	n/a	n/a
Serbia	3 280	15	0.772[4]	n/a	n/a	34.4[5]	8 168 410[6]	6	42
Macedonia	2 830	14	0.796	66	16	39.0	2 000 000	4	24
Kosovo	1 600	n/a	0.734[7]	n/a	n/a	n/a	2 400 000[8]	48[9]	n/a
Romania	3 830	20	0.805	60	3	31.0	21 632 150	12	58
Slovenia	17 350	4	0.910	46	1	28.4	1 998 200	n/a	n/a
Turkey	4 710	32	0.757	92	−22	43.6	72 600 000	20	58

Notes:
1. The World Bank's official estimates of the size of economies are based on GNI converted to current US dollars using the ATLAS method. Gross national income (GNI) takes into account all production in the domestic economy (that is, GDP) plus the net flows of factor income (such as rents, profits, and labour income) from abroad. The ATLAS method smoothes exchange rate fluctuations by using a three year moving average, price-adjusted conversion factor.
2. 2002–2004, World Bank (2005).
3. As 2 above.
4. Estimate for 2002 in UNDP (2005: 111).
5. 2002 figure from UNDP (2005).
6. Serbia and Montenegro excluding Kosovo.
7. 2004 estimate UNDP (2004: 14).
8. Source: Organization for Security and Co-operation in Europe (OSCE) based on estimated population.
9. Not comparable, based on $2 per day, 2003 data UNDP (2004: 18).

Table 1.2 Other data on South East Europe

Country	Real GDP growth 2005 (1989=100)	Dependency ratio 2005	Population change 2003–2004	Unemployment rate LFS 2004	Rate of children in residential care 2004 (per 100 000 pop.)
Albania	144.1	63.4	8.1	10.0 (2002)	62.4
Bosnia-Herzegovina	n/a	52.6	n/a	n/a	235.7 (1999)
Bulgaria	93.4	57.8	−5.2	12.0	795.9
Croatia	97.8	61.8	−2.1	13.8	403.9
Macedonia	82.9	54.5	2.7	37.2	175.5
Romania	105.1	54.2	−2.0	8.0	740.3
Serbia and Montenegro	57.7	62.8 (2002)	1.6 (2001)	18.8 (2002)	219.3 (2000)
Slovenia	135.2	53.8	−0.3	6.1	528.0

Source: TransMONEE.

wherever possible based on the most recent Human Development Reports. Secondly, the data has limitations precisely because it has been produced by 'transnational expertised institutions' (St Clair, 2006). The TransMONEE database of countries in transition, which, therefore, does not include Turkey, is more reliant on national statistical offices and is, therefore, subject to the vagaries of their methods, whereas the World Bank tends to work to its own methodologies. Finally, in future all of the countries in the region should be covered by European Union Statistical Agency (EUROSTAT) methodologies – however, thus far only a limited number of countries collect data according to this methodology, so that we have not utilized this data set here.

Tables 1.1 and 1.2 show that all the countries in the region except Turkey have higher Human Development rankings than their gross domestic product (GDP) per capita rankings. What is harder to grasp is the extent of sub-national inequalities and pockets of poverty and exclusion, which mean that nationally aggregated statistical data captures only some of the story. While generalizations regarding social and economic development are fraught with dangers in such a diverse region of some 125.4 million people, with Turkey accounting for 72.6 million and Romania 21.6 million, two key additional trends can be traced:

1. The growth paradox: while real GDP in 2004 remained below 1989 levels in Bulgaria, Croatia, Macedonia, Serbia and, probably in Bosnia-Herzegovina, all the countries in the region have enjoyed annual GDP growth from the year 2000 onwards. Turkey and Albania have enjoyed much longer, but highly volatile, growth over the past 15 years and Slovenia more steady growth over the same period. The paradox throughout the region is that recent growth has not led to improvements in the labour market where total employment levels, and levels of labour force participation have continued to fall or stagnate, and official and standardized unemployment rates have risen, again except in Slovenia and Turkey. Explanations for this vary, from the World Bank's continued concern with labour market 'rigidity', through to a recent ILO text pointing to statistical measurement problems and, crucially, the size of the informal economy in all the countries of the region (cf. Rutkowski and Scarpetta, 2005; Sengenberger, 2006).
2. Mixed picture on poverty and inequality. A recent overview on poverty and social exclusion in the Western Balkans for UNDP (Matković, 2005) covering the countries and territories of this book apart from Slovenia and Turkey, provides a composite picture showing national absolute poverty rates of between 8.4 per cent for Croatia to 25 per cent for Albania and 50 per cent for Kosovo. Again, poverty levels have not fallen

in line with growth. In addition, there is extreme poverty in Albania, Serbia and Kosovo, as well as a large concentration of households just above the poverty line in all countries in the region. Her overview points to significant regional differences and to growing gaps between rural and urban areas, a trend also observable in Turkey (cf. Dansuk et al., 2006). Poverty risks are highest among the unemployed, older people, large families, children, the less well educated, refugees and displaced persons and minorities, particularly Roma. The complexity of ways of addressing poverty reduction, through the Millennium Development Goals (MDGs), the Poverty Reduction Strategy Paper (PRSP) process, and the EU's Joint Inclusion Memorandum (JIM) and Joint Assessment Paper for Employment priorities (JAP) structure, is a theme which recurs throughout the book. Income inequality as measured by the Gini coefficient, gives a mixed picture, being high in Turkey and Macedonia, apparently low in Bosnia-Herzegovina and moderate in all the other countries of the region (Table 1.1 and Sengenberger, 2006: 17).

In addition, a number of factors further complicate the making of social policy in SEE. First, the region as a whole has seen large migration flows in recent years, including outmigration and forced migration as large numbers of people have become refugees or displaced persons. In addition, wider diasporization has also contributed to a partial deterritorialization of social policy in some of the region. The fact that many areas of South East Europe have large numbers of persons who feel connected to the locality and/or nation state, but who are resident abroad and who send remittances home, is relevant for social policy, not only in terms of the need to account for this in studies of household income, poverty and inequality. Taking only offical remittances recorded through banks, recent statistics suggest that these amount to 22.5 per cent of GDP in Bosnia-Herzegovina, 17.2 per cent of GDP in (then) Serbia and Montenegro and 11.7 per cent of GDP in Albania (Sengenberger, 2006: 21). In addition, the role of diasporas in wider politics and, sometimes, as mediators in a variety of international agencies, is also a phenomenon which has been remarked upon, but very little studied. Also, the ways in which minority groups in one state may adopt a kind of 'enclave welfare' system in which they develop their own welfare provisions and/or rely on cross-border support and transfers from a neighbouring country, is an under-researched aspect of the social policy mosaic of South East Europe.

Alongside the informal economy, it is also important to recognize the presence of what Solioz has termed 'parallel power networks' (Solioz, 2005: 80), based on the interweaving of formal and informal social practices. Throughout the region, the concentration of power locally rather than centrally, through a circularity of elites in politics, business, and in some cases in organized crime, working through patronage, is relevant in terms of the need for international agencies to find counterparts and partners for their projects. Again, this is an under-researched issue in the making of social policy in SEE, relating to the territorialization of social control and the extra-institutional nature of welfare in parts of the region. Hence, returning to our earlier discussion of statehood in sovereign frontiers, the complex nature of state forms in SEE has to be understood including, but going beyond, reference only to the protectorate like United Nations Interim Administration Mission in Kosovo (UNMIK) and the role of the Office of the High Representative (OHR) in Bosnia-Herzegovina, in the context of a weak central state and two, de facto three, ethnicized entities with a great deal of autonomy.

Throughout the region, as evidenced in the case studies, with the possible exception of Slovenia, international actors appear to be scrambling for position, with co-ordination itself little more than another 'mandate' to be added on. Hence, even though the World Bank and the European Union have had a joint office in Brussels since 1999 to co-ordinate international assistance for the reconstruction and development of South East Europe (http://www.seerecon.org), the actual impact of this has been minimal, especially in terms of social policy. In addition, the Stability Pact for South Eastern Europe, established at a meeting in Sarajevo in July 1999 as a co-ordinating body aiming to achieve 'lasting peace, prosperity and stability for South Eastern Europe', has also not had a wider impact. The Pact still has a Special Co-ordinator in Brussels and works through a series of working tables and initiatives. Originally conceived, in part at least, as a mechanism for pressuring change in Serbia, excluded until the change in regime, the Pact is now seeking to transform into a more regionally owned initiative (cf. http://www.stabilitypact.org) while still reflecting the influence of some donor countries, notably Germany and Austria.

To borrow from a recent text by John Clarke, South East Europe can be seen in terms of 'the governance of an emergent regional space' whose identity is largely ascribed from outside rather than achieved within, in which political and institutional arrangements have been 'profoundly unsettled', and national spaces and their institutionalizations and interrelationships are still in the process of being worked out. His suggestion that 'governance and the subjects and objects of governing are in process of simultaneous and mutual invention or constitution' but that, paradoxically, 'studies of governance might learn more from such emergent processes than from a focus of "leading examples"' (Clarke, forthcoming), is a leitmotif for this book, applied to the study of the governance of social policy.

THIS BOOK

The book, then, aims to present an overview of the making of social policy in SEE within the context of transnationalism and the complex presence and actions of a range of international actors. In a sense, it is an attempt to test and refine the analytical frameworks set out in this and the following chapter. In the concluding chapter, we revisit a series of questions and outline an agenda for future work. The argument of this chapter has been that the issue of social policy-making in SEE is ripe for collaborative study of the actions of international actors, seeking to address the who, the what, and the how of social policy-making.

Based on the theoretical frameworks elaborated above, a number of substantive questions can be posed regarding the transnationalization of social policy-making in SEE. While not purporting to be exhaustive, they indicate the kinds of research questions which were of interest to the authors:

1. How variable have been and are the social policy choices being made by different countries in SEE in the spheres of social protection, social services, pensions, health and labour market policies?
2. Where, why and how have certain international actors been influential?
3. How have diverse legacies mediated the impact of external actors? How have the specific conditions of post-communist transition impacted on subsequent social policies? Is there a distinct difference between 'normal' post-transition contexts and post-war experiences? Do different confessional practices matter?
4. How complete has the neo-liberal project in social policy been in the region? In what way does the nature of the presence of the EU influence this?
5. How does the 'normal' social policy discourse and disagreement about desirable national social policy get cut across by a social development discourse applied to this region?
6. Which other international actors, in addition to the World Bank, the EU and the UN agencies have emerged as influential in social policy formulation, regulation and provision?
7. What special social policy influences has the Stability Pact, OHR and UNMIK had and what are the likely long-term implications?
8. What are the implications of a policy-making process involving transnational actors for national institutional follow-through? How do variations in state capacity affect this? What are the implications for participation by various publics in policy debate? Are there significant variations in levels of domestic ownership of social policy reforms?

9.   How have traditional domains of social policy been deconstructed and which, if any, new domains have emerged?

10. Are the aid processes that were related to the post-conflict situations of the wars of Yugoslav succession consistent with social policy-making in normal times? If not how might countries now be enabled to own subsequent social policy-making consistent with future European membership?

11. Do international organizations and international NGO interventions enrich the national policy debate and empower local actors or do they disempower them and become substitutes for normal politics?

12. Has the transnationalization of social policy-making led to its depoliticization and technicization in emerging policy spaces?

13. Has the transnationalization of policy-making given rise to cross-border regulation and provision in social policy and what has been the impact of this on national welfare entitlements? What is the significance of the mismatch between citizenship, residence and belonging, particularly in terms of cross-border solidarities and ethnicized claims-making? What might be the significance of 'enclave welfare' and of diasporas?

14. Who are the new intermediaries in policy articulation in SEE and how is their advice rendered accountable and transparent?

15. Is there a mismatch between transnationalized social policy discourses and practices on the ground?

The following chapters report new research informed by these questions. We return in Chapter 12 to these questions and themes to see how far we can now advance our understanding of the content and process of social policy-making in this transnational context.

REFERENCES

Anderson, B. (1991), *Imagined Communities: Reflections on the Origin and Spread of Nationalism*, 2nd edn, London: Verso.

Benchev, D. (2006), 'Constructing South East Europe: the politics of regional identity in the Balkans', *RAMSES Working Paper 1/06*, University of Oxford, European Studies Centre.

Bratsis, P. (2002), 'Unthinking the state: reification, ideology and the state', in S. Aronowitz and P. Bratsis (eds), *Paradigm Lost: State Theory Reconsidered*, Minneapolis: University of Minnesota Press, pp. 247–67.

Clarke, J. (2004), *Changing Welfare, Changing States: New Directions in Social Policy*, London: Sage.

Clarke, J. (forthcoming), 'Governance puzzles', in L. Budd and L. Harris (eds), *eGovernance: Managing or Governing?*, London: Routledge.

Dansuk, E., M. Ozmen and G. Erdogan (2006), 'Poverty and social stratification at the regional level in Turkey', paper presented to the 'Social Policy and Regional Development' conference, Zagreb, November.

Deacon, B. (2000), 'Social policy in Eastern Europe: the impact of political globalisation', *Journal of European Social Policy*, **10** (2), 146–61.

Deacon, B. (2007), *Global Social Policy and Governance*, London: Sage.

Deacon, B., M. Hulse and P. Stubbs (1997), *Global Social Policy: International Organisations and the Future of Welfare*, London: Sage.

Dolowitz, D. and D. Marsh (2000), 'Learning from abroad: the role of policy transfer in contemporary policy-making', *Governance*, **13** (1), 5–24.

Esping-Andersen, G. (1990), *The Three Worlds of Welfare Capitalism*, Cambridge: Polity Press.

Gallagher, T. (2005), *The Balkans in the New Millennium: In the Shadow of War and Peace*, London: Routledge.

Gough, I. and G. Wood (2004), *Insecurity and Welfare Regimes in Asia, Africa and Latin America*, Cambridge: Cambridge University Press.

Gould, J. (2005a), 'Poverty politics and states of partnership', in J. Gould (ed.), *The New Conditionality: The Politics of Poverty Reduction*, London: Zed Press, pp. 1–16.

Gould, J. (2005b), 'Conclusion: the politics of consultation', in J. Gould (ed.), *The New Conditionality: The Politics of Poverty Reduction*, London: Zed Press, pp. 135–51.

Haas, P. (1992), 'Introduction: epistemic communities and international policy co-ordination', *International Organisation*, **46** (1), 1–36.

Hall, R. and T. Biersteker (eds) (2002), *The Emergence of Private Authority in Global Governance*, Cambridge: Cambridge University Press.

Harrison, G. (2001), 'Post-conditionality politics and administrative reform: reflections on the cases of Uganda and Tanzania', *Development and Change*, **32** (4), 657–79.

Held, D., A. McGrew, D. Goldblatt and J. Perraton (1999), *Global Transformations: Politics, Economics, Culture*, Stanford, CA: Stanford University Press.

Jessop, B. (1990), *State Theory: Putting the Capitalist State in its Place*, Cambridge: Polity Press.

Jessop, B. (2004), 'Multi-level governance and multi-level meta-governance', in I. Bache and M. Flinders (eds), *Multi-level Governance*, Oxford: Oxford University Press, pp. 49–74.

Kaldor, M. (2003), *Global Civil Society*, Cambridge: Polity Press.

Larner, W. (2007), 'Expatriate experts: New Zealand's diaspora strategy', in H. Hansen and D. Salskov-Iversen (eds), *Critical Perspectives on Private Authority in Global Politics*, Basingstoke: Palgrave Macmillan, forthcoming, www.open. ac.uk/socialsciences/includes/_cms/download.php?file=1p 1zbqhfofceeawlul.doc& name=expatriate_experts_new_zealands_diaspora_strategy_-_wendy_larner.doc (accessed 3 May 2007).

Lendvai, N. and P. Stubbs (2006), 'Translation, intermediaries and welfare reform in South Eastern Europe, paper presented at ESPAnet Conference, Bremen, September, http://paulstubbs.pbwiki.com/f/Lendvai%20Stubbs%20Bremen.pdf (accessed 3 May 2007).

Matković, G. (2005), 'Overview of poverty and social exclusion in the Western Balkans', paper prepared for Western Balkans Forum on Social Inclusion and the Millennium Development Goals, Tirana, June, website: http://intra.rbec.undp. org/mdg_forum/Overview.htm (accessed 3 May 2007).

Meyer, J., J. Boli, G. Thomas and F. Ramirez (1997), 'World society and the nation state', *American Sociological Review*, **62** (2), 171–90.

Moulaert, F. and B. Jessop (2006), 'Agency, structure, institutions, discourse', paper presented at the European Association for Evolutionary Political Economy Conference, Istanbul, Turkey, 12–14 November.

O'Brien, R., A. Goetz, J. Scholte and M. Williams (2000), *Contesting Global Governance: Multilateral Economic Institutions and Global Social Movements*, Cambridge: Cambridge University Press.

Orenstein, M. (2005), 'The new pension reform as global policy', *Global Social Policy*, **5** (2), 175–202.

Ougaard, M. (2004), *Political Globalization: State Power and Social Forces*, Basingstoke: Palgrave Macmillan.

Pierson, P. and T. Skocpol (2002), 'Historical institutionalism in contemporary political science', in I. Katznelson and H. Milner (eds), *Political Science: The State of the Discipline*, New York: Norton, pp. 693–721.

Poulantzas, N. (1978), *Classes in Contemporary Capitalism*, London: Verso.

Ragin, C. (1987), *The Comparative Method: Moving beyond Qualitative and Quantitative Strategies*, Berkeley, CA: University of California Press.

Ragin, C. (2000), *Fuzzy-Set Social Science*, Chicago, IL: Chicago University Press.

Rasza, M. and N. Lindstrom (2004), 'Balkan is beautiful: Balkanism in the political discourse of Tudjman's Croatia', *East European Politics and Societies*, **18** (4), 628–50.

Rutkowski, J. and S. Scarpetta (2005), *Enhancing Job Opportunities: Eastern Europe and the former Soviet Union*, Washington, DC: World Bank.

Sassen, S. (2000), 'Excavating power: in search of frontier zones and new actors', *Theory, Culture, Society*, **17** (1), 163–70.

Scharf, F. and V. Schmidt (2000), *Welfare and Work in the Open Economy*, Oxford: Oxford University Press.

Scholte, J. (2005), *Globalization: A Critical Introduction*, 2nd edn, Basingstoke: Palgrave Macmillan.

Sengenberger, W. (2006), 'Employment and development in South-East Europe in the context of economic globalization', paper for sub-regional conference on Globalization and Employment, Istanbul, September, http://www.ilo.org/public/english/region/eurpro/ankara/events/istanbul/ist-background.pdf (accessed 3 May 2007).

Solioz, C. (2005), *Turning Points in Post-war Bosnia: Ownership Process and European Integration*, Baden-Baden: Nomos.

St Clair, A. (2006), 'Global poverty: the co-production of knowledge and politics', *Global Social Policy*, **6** (1), 57–77.

Stone, D. and S. Maxwell (eds) (2005), *Global Knowledge Networks and International Development: Bridges Across Boundaries*, London: Routledge.

Šućur, Z. (2003), 'The development of social assistance and social care in Croatia after World War II' (Croatian language text), *Revija za socijalnu politiku* (*Croatian Journal of Social Policy*), **10** (1), 1–22.

Swank, D. (2002), *Global Capital, Political Institutions and Policy Change in Developed Welfare States*, Cambridge: Cambridge University Press.

Sykes, R., B. Palier and P. Prior (eds) (2001), *Globalization and the European Welfare States: Challenges and Changes*, Basingstoke: Macmillan.

Todorova, M. (1997), *Imagining the Balkans*, Oxford: Oxford University Press.

United Nations Development Programme (UNDP) (2004), *Human Development Report Kosovo*, Pristina: UNDP.

United Nations Development Programme (UNDP) (2005), *Human Development Report Serbia*, Belgrade: UNDP.

Valdes, J. (1995), *Pinochet's Economists: The Chicago School in Chile*, Cambridge: Cambridge University Press.

Vickers, M. and J. Pettifer (2007), *The Albanian Question: Reshaping the Balkans*, London: I.B. Tauris.

Wedel, J. (2004), '"Studying through" a globalizing world: building method through aidnographies', in J. Gould and H. Secher Marcussen (eds), *Ethnographies of Aid: Exploring Development Texts and Encounters*, Roskilde, International Development Studies Occasional Paper 24, pp. 149–74.

World Bank (1994), *Averting the Old Age Crisis: Policies to Protect the Old and Promote Growth*, New York: Oxford University Press.

World Bank (2005), *Growth, Poverty and Inequality: Eastern Europe and the Former Soviet Union*, Washington, DC: World Bank.

Zaviršek, D. (2005), 'Between unease and enthusiasm: the development of social work education in Yugoslavia', in S. Hessle and D. Zaviršek (eds), *Sustainable Development in Social work: The Case of a Regional Network in the Balkans*, Stockholm: Stockholm University, Department of Social Work, pp. 26–34.

2. Europeanization of social policy? Prospects and challenges for South East Europe

Noémi Lendvai

INTRODUCTION

Scholarly interest in the Europeanization of social policy has witnessed an unprecedented expansion in the past 15 years. This was probably due not only to the expansion of EU social policy itself, but also to the emerging recognition that the EU might play an important role in the transformation of welfare across Europe. By now, we have an extensive literature on the Europeanization of national welfare systems and on emerging EU social policy governance. Indeed, as South East Europe turns more and more towards the EU through the integration, accession or association of a number of countries, the EU will likely become a more central inter-national actor in the transformation of the region in years to come.

The aim of this chapter is not so much to discuss whether the EU is a strong or a weak player, but rather to focus on how the EU matters. Drawing on a wide range of literature on Spanish, Italian, Greek and Central East European experiences, and utilizing both theoretical and empirical insights, this chapter argues that the EU has a significant influence on a variety of public policies and therefore both directly and indirectly on social policy. The chapter is based on a broad understanding of social policy, in which it is discussed as an assemblage of economic, employment, regional, educational and other policies. This broad public policy framework enables us to discuss not only directly 'social' issues, but also a range of political, economic and cultural issues that are highly rele-vant for social policy.

The chapter is divided into three sections. The first offers a theoretical overview of the Europeanization literature. Here, I differentiate between governance and governmentality approaches and discuss the different argu-ments put forward on how Europeanization works. In the second part, I turn to the Europeanization of social policy and argue that three important issues arise: first, the emergence of multi-level governance; second, the reframing and re-coupling of social policy; and third, the impact of EU on welfare trajectories in terms of the transformation in transitional and post-transitional context. Finally, I discuss some lessons for South East Europe and draw some conclusions.

EUROPEANIZATION: THEORETICAL APPROACHES

Europeanization is one of the most fashionable 'buzzwords' of contemporary scholarship in the field of European studies. Its appeal lies in the multiplicity of the term, as it is used to denote various processes such as the development of institutions of governance at the European level, the penetration of the EU into national and subnational governance, the exportation of the EU as a political organization and governance outside Europe (Olson, 2002), or the transformation of European welfare states induced by the EU (Palier, 2004). Interestingly, while the expansion of the Europeanization literature is considerable and impressive, at the same time more and more methodological concerns are raised, addressing issues such as how to differentiate between globalization and Europeanization (Beyeler, 2003; Graziano, 2003), how to demonstrate causality between EU and domestic policies (Haverland, 2005), whether to use top-down or bottom-up approaches (Radaelli, 2003), and the difficulty in attributing changes to the EU itself, in the context of competing agendas of influential international actors such as the ILO in employment policies, the Organisation for Economic Co-operation and Development (OECD) in terms of benchmarking and best practices (Deacon et al., 1997), or the OSCE and the Council of Europe in terms of gender mainstreaming and minority rights (Hafner-Burton and Pollack, 2002; Lovecy, 2002).

While Europeanization indeed represents a very complex field of inquiry, in this chapter I suggest that we need to differentiate between two fundamentally different, yet complementary, approaches to Europeanization, namely the governance approach and the governmentality approach.

EUROPEANIZATION, GOVERNANCE AND POLICY-MAKING: INSTITUTIONALIST APPROACHES

The overwhelming majority of the Europeanization literature and scholarly thinking applies an institutional approach and casts the process of Europeanization either as 'institutional adaptation' or 'adaptation of policies and policy processes' (Featherstone, 2003). Institutional adaptation refers not only to the importance of institutions and their transformation under the direct or indirect pressure of the EU, but also to the emergence of 'multi-level' and 'network' governance. On the other hand, the adaptation of policies and policy processes refers to the public policy impacts of EU membership. For many institutionalist scholars Europeanization represents an adaptational pressure, which gives way to 'up-loading', 'down-loading' and 'cross-loading' (Howell, 2004), leading to institutional or policy inertia, absorption, transformation (Schmidt, 2002) or retrenchment (resistance) (Radaelli, 2003). Common to these approaches is the notion of 'goodness of fit', which asserts that the adaptational pressure is highest when the distance between the EU and domestic policy is moderate, making institutional or policy change more likely. In case the distance is too big (EU is difficult to digest) or too small (EU policy is already present in domestic policies), adaptational pressure is not likely to induce change.

Another important aspect of institutionalist accounts is the emphasis on the 'logic of consequentialism' and the 'logic of appropriateness'. Rationalist institutionalist scholars argue that because opportunities and constraints of actors within institutions play a key role in the process of domestic changes in response to EU pressures, research on Europeanization needs to focus on the distribution of resources between actors and the existence of multiple veto points in understanding domestic response to EU pressures. In this rationalist approach interest and resources play a key role. Sociological institutionalists, on the other hand, emphasize 'logic of appropriateness', which centres not around interest and power, but instead on ideas, beliefs and various socialization processes which influence the ways in which institutions respond to EU policies, processes and institutions. Here, learning, cognitive shifts and socialization processes are studied as important Europeanization mechanisms. Indeed, many social policy scholars have discussed Europeanization of social policy in similar terms. Guillén and her colleagues (2002; 2004) argued that Spanish and Portuguese social policy is witnessing 'cognitive Europeanization', which refers to the crucial changes that influence the ways policy-makers construct, speak, discuss and act on social issues. Similarly, Sotiropoulos (2004) argues that the Europeanization of Greek social policy meant the emergence of widespread institutionalization that has 'contributed to the socialization of the personnel of related public services and of associations of the social partners into the language and the logic of modern, EU-driven social policies'. Teague (2000) uses the term 'socialisation undercarriage' to characterize the element of EU social policy that evolves through various policy tools, and which builds on commonly developed vocabulary, agendas, policy instruments and new institutions. With an emphasis on soft EU social policy these scholars see the relevance of Europeanization in terms of 'cognitive shifts', 'socialisation', 'policy learning' and 'communicative governance' that induce both direct and indirect changes in the ways social policy is made.

Radaelli (2003) builds a broad and integrated approach by combining different aspects of both rationalist and sociological institutionalism. He argues that Europeanization can be defined as:

> Processes of (a) construction, (b) diffusion, and (c) institutionalization of formal and informal rules, procedures, policy paradigms, styles, 'ways of doing things', and shared beliefs and norms which are first defined and consolidated in the making of EU public policy and politics and then incorporated in the logic of domestic discourses, identities, political structures, and public policies. (Radaelli, 2003: 30)

The institutionalist approach to Europeanization provides us with very important insights into the driving forces of change and resistance and offers a well-developed framework in order to grasp conceptually the complex processes of Europeanization. Both rationalist and constructivist institutionalism have been applied to understand the Europeanization of social policy. Rationalist accounts have argued that 'goodness of fit' is a useful framework to understand European social law, while other institutionalist scholars emphasize learning, socialization and norm-formation as key to the Europeanization process.

However, when the institutionalist approach is applied to Central, East and South East Europe and, indeed, to the field of social policy itself, important caveats need to be made. First, while in institutionalist accounts institutions are seen as stable and established, the institutional landscape in the new member states, candidate countries and aspirant countries are much more fragile, fluid and unstable. Similarly, policy-making processes in Central East Europe (CEE) and SEE are often ad hoc, unsettled and uneven. In this rather complex political and institutional landscape, 'Europeanization involves not so much adaptation but rather the *ab ovo* creation of new actors, institutions and policies' (Dimitrov et al., 2006: 256). Besides, the importance of differentiating between formal and informal institutionalization processes becomes crucial as numerous studies on Europeanization in CEE highlight the problems in terms of the gap between institutionalization and implementation (Sloat, 2004, on gender equality; Fagan et al., 2005, on gender mainstreaming), legal adaptation and institutional adaptation leading to 'shallow Europeanisation' (Czernielewska et al., 2004, on regional policy in Poland), or the problem of learning capacity of domestic institutions (Palne et al., 2004, on regional governance in Hungary). Indeed, framing it in a broad institutional perspective, Dimitrov and others (2006) argue that new members had little incentive to engage in 'deep' Europeanization that would lock-in specific institutional and policy arrangements.

Second, the 'goodness of fit' or 'misfit' thesis may be problematic in terms of their application to social policy for two reasons. First, because EU social policy is far from an ordered, coherent and consistent set of policies on the basis of which we could make claims about Europeanization (Wincott, 2003). It is, rather, very difficult to describe EU social policy as an unambiguous policy out there ready to be downloaded. Secondly, as Paraskevopoulos and Leonardi (2004) argue in the context of cohesion policy, it is not the goodness of fit, but rather *the capacity to undertake significant institutional change* in order to maximize opportunities, that is relevant for the Europeanization process. All in all, one could argue that all the 'variables' of the academic equation (EU policies, domestic policies and many intervening variables) are highly contingent, so that there is a need to take the institutionalist approach less as a static and mechanical, and rather more as a dynamic and differentiated, framework.

EUROPEANIZATION, POLITICS AND GOVERNMENTALITY: POST-STRUCTURALIST APPROACHES

If institutionalist approaches to Europeanization see the process in terms of governance and policy, post-structuralist approaches frame the process more in terms of governmentality and politics. Importantly, while the previous approach would see the EU as an 'already-established supranational arrangement' (Knill, 2001) which 'impacts' in particular ways on domestic structures and processes, post-structuralists hold 'an inessential view of the EU' (Walters and Haahr, 2005: 138), seeing it as a complex constitution in the making, 'locked in as it is between modernity and postmodernity'. For post-structuralist scholars the EU is ambiguous, multiple and contradictory, and innovative and experiential at the same time (Laffan et al., 2000; Rumford, 2003). It is also argued that the EU is located between the international and the domestic, between states and markets, between governments and governance, which constitute a contingent, ever-changing 'in-betweenness'. For this scholarship governance arrangements are not so much about self-evident institutional systems, but more about critical and deconstructive investigation of political-cultural formations (Clarke, 2005) and ways of governing and being governed through language, practices and techniques (Haahr, 2004), and about exerting power by 'constituting interior (state) spaces of social, economic and political forces as knowable domains and utilizing technologies to manipulate these spaces and their processes' (Walters and Haahr, 2005: 137). From a governmentality perspective, Europeanization would be seen not so much in terms of 'impact', but rather as an encounter 'embedding the national in the European and the European in the national' (Laffan et al., 2000: 191).

For post-structuralist scholars, understanding Europeanization starts with the critical interrogation of EU policies, institutions and processes themselves. Instead of seeing EU policies as given, or taken for granted, the governmentality approach emphasizes the multiplicity and the contestation of supranational constructions. In this vein, Walters and Haahr (2005) for example, argue that instead of using the term Europeanization, 'governmentalization of Europe' is preferred since

> the notion of Europeanization implies there is a substance or a core to Europe – a relatively coherent set of values, norms or perhaps institutions. In speaking of governmentalization of Europe we call attention to the production of a plurality of Europes within discontinuous regimes and practices of knowledge. Not Europe but Europes. (Ibid.: 139)

Discursive approaches emphasize the ambiguity of EU policies and the possible hidden political agendas behind them (see Simhandl, 2006, on Roma discourse; Perrons, 2005, and Verloo, 2005, on gender policy; Sasse, 2005, on minority policy). As these scholars emphasize, policies are always multiple and contested and precisely these processes are the ones that are key to understanding the Europeanization process. Above and beyond this, Europeanization is not just about policies, it is also about constructing subjectivities and identities. Unfolding those processes in the field of employment policy, Carmen (2005) demonstrates how the EU regulates and steers social subjects defined overwhelmingly in relation to their employment status. In a similar vein, Mitchell (2006) discusses the ways in which the educational policy of the EU constructs and produces subjects such as 'a fast-paced, mobile, and interchangeable labourer'.

Other critical neo-Gramscian and neo-Marxist scholarship frames Europeanization explicitly in terms of neo-liberal governmentality. For this critical political scholarship what is there to be 'Europeanized' is the neo-liberal restructuring of the social relations of production (Bieler and Morton, 2003), the institutionalization of 'disciplinary neo-liberalism' (Gill, 2001), a new transnational policy paradigm of market-making and market-enabling economic, employment and social policies (van Aperdoorn, 2006), and the regulatory asymmetry between economic and social policies (Holman, 2004). Bohle and Greskovits (2005) go so far as to argue that the weak social dimension of EU integration reflects the interests of Western capital, which is not committed to extending the social model eastwards.

Finally, post-colonial approaches, including a rich literature on South East Europe, argues that EU itself, and in particular accession, is an encounter between the 'colonizer' and the 'colonized' (Böröcz and Kovács,

2001; Kuus, 2004; Rico, 2005). As Böröcz has argued: 'The essence of the European Union's strategy vis-à-vis the Central and East European applicants is *integration without inclusion*: participation in the production systems, and appendance to the consumption markets of EU corporations without the attendant political, economic, social and cultural rights conferred by European Union citizenship' (2001: 108). For post-colonial scholars Europeanization is associated with domination, resistance, objectification and marginality and represents a critical interrogation of EU practices on citizenship, economic relations, and production of subjectivities.

To sum up, post-structuralist approaches bring policy and politics together, and identify critical constitutive practices that may be rendered invisible by institutionalist scholars. However, these critical approaches are based on few, and quite limited, empirical studies about actual practices, and tend to offer a somewhat essentialistic view of the EU.

THE EUROPEANIZATION OF SOCIAL POLICY

Europeanization, Social Policy Governance and Actor Animation

While social policy has historically evolved as a nationally bounded and state-centred policy space, one of the most significant processes that Europeanization fosters is the diffusion of state capacities up, down and sideways (Jessop, 2002) and the proliferation of actors involved in social policy-making (Ferrera, 2005). Importantly, while for many EU countries (referred to by Ferrera et al., 2001), Europeanization signals the emergence of multi-level social policy governance, South East Europe, with its crowded internationalized policy space, as has been shown in many chapters in this book, has had a kind of multi-level social policy governance in place for well over a decade. South East Europe in that sense forms a very special case for Europeanization. However, it may be worth considering the experience of many European countries in terms of the role of the EU in their transformation of welfare.

Both for Spanish and Italian social policy scholars, Europeanization of social policy are strongly associated with regionalization (in the case of Italy) and with decentralization (in the case of Spain). Graziano (2003), for example, by taking social cohesion policy as a point of reference, argues that the EU through its Structural Funds played a crucial role in Italy in facilitating the formation of 'regional interest', in institutionalizing an increasingly open decision-making environment, and rationalizing cohesion policy by progressively separating political parties from administrative structures in the context of the Italian legacy of corrupted and politicized decision-making. In his comprehensive account Ferrera (2005) argues that the EU has indeed promoted a kind of neo-regionalism, which enhanced the institutional and political capacity of meso-governments, and through the substantial resources made available, the EU has fostered a massive region-building exercise. Similarly, Moreno (2003), reflecting on the Spanish experience, frames Europeanization in terms of the regionalization and localization of social policy, with a comprehensive role of regions in the delivery of welfare policies. For Ferrera, however:

> the main novelty is not regional empowerment per se but the complex web of different coalitions that can emerge from the proliferation of levels of governance. Horizontal interregional coalitions and vertical regional-supranational coalitions are the most innovative combinations that can be registered on this front. As far as opportunity structures are concerned, the main novelty is a significant expansion of both 'locality' and 'vocality' options for all actors, but in particular the regions. (Ferrera, 2005: 179)

While there is very little research done on both the horizontal (interregional) and vertical (regional-supranational) coalitions and their role in social policy, there are some research studies on how actors exploit their 'locality' and 'vocality'. However, far from taking an uncritically positive perspective on the increasing vocality of actors in the context of EU integration, many studies point to the difficulties actors face when trying to exploit the opportunity structures for pursuing their own agenda.

Vermeersch (2002), taking the Slovakian Roma mobilization as a case in point, demonstrates insightfully the ambiguity and difficulties of translating pressure exerted by the EU during the accession process into a tool for Roma mobilization. As he argues, based on his interviews with Roma activists, Roma mobilization is ambiguous partly because the EU does not have a coherent view on minority protection to be referenced, and partly because activism was de-mobilized by negative stereotypes in which the Roma were held responsible for hindering the accession of Slovakia to the EU. From this perspective, 'vocality' of actors is understood as both mobilizing and de-mobilizing at the same time. A similar conclusion is drawn by a Hungarian case study on gender equality policies (Krizsan and Zentai, 2006), which argues that while the gender agenda of the EU has clearly facilitated the mobilization of women's non-government organizations (NGOs) and institutionalized, although weakly, the gender agenda in governmental machinery in Hungary, at the same time, the shift in the EU's focus from gender equality to broad equal opportunity policies might contribute to the quiet slipping out of the gender agenda from the public and political discourse in Hungary. On a similar note, Van der Molen and Novikova (2005) argue that the Baltic countries and governments have made the political choice of implementing not a comprehensive gender policy that would enable activism and voicing on behalf of women's NGOs and lobby groups, but rather a narrow, expert-bureaucratic model for gender mainstreaming, framing it as the latest management-equality tool, which pre-empted mobilization. In that sense 'framing strategies' both at the domestic level as well as at the EU level play a crucial role in the actual vocality of actors. Vocality of actors can be seen in terms of both empowerment and disempowerment. On similar grounds, the tension between those competing processes is highlighted by Paraskevopoulos and Leonardi (2004) in the case of Hungarian regional policy where, as they argue, decentralization and regionalization have gone hand in hand with (re)centralization.

To sum up, Europeanization does indeed animate both old and new actors and it is a matter of empirical investigation to unfold the precise mechanisms and technologies for these processes. Importantly, empirical investigations of the vocality (and the silencing) of actors need to go hand in hand with the critical scrutiny of the 'framing process', which provides a strategic and political framework for actors and agencies. As for South East Europe, it is likely that issues around regionalization and decentralization will be enmeshed with issues around nationalization, as many countries in the region emerged as new nation states, which makes those processes even more volatile and contested.

Europeanization: Reframing Social Policy

Following Laffan and others, who argue that the EU is both innovative and experiential and at the same time ambiguous and contradictory, Europeanization could be seen as an 'importation' of those features and tendencies, and their interplay with domestic policy processes. On the one hand, the social dimension of the EU is innovative not only through the introduction of experiential governance techniques such as the Open Method of Co-ordination (OMC), but also through the ways in which the EU as a supranational social policy actor is reframing and re-coupling the notion of 'social policy' itself. Various policy frameworks facilitate different couplings of policy issues. For example, the European Social Fund plays a very important role in re-coupling social policy and employment policy. Since EU social policy is an employment-anchored social policy (O'Connor, 2005), employment comes to the forefront of social policy concerns. This strong link between employment and social policy, however, was not familiar for many new member states. In Estonia, for example, the Ministry for Social Affairs is responsible for health, pensions, social issues and labour market, but as Jakobsson and West (2006) point out, not only does the minister tend to have a background in health with little experience or expertise in dealing with labour market issues, but also 'Estonia has no single document setting out a national employment strategy and . . . most of the strategic goals have been set in papers related to the EU' (Vali, quoted by Jakobsson and West, 2006: 24). Indeed, as the European Commission's *Annual Progress Report on Growth and Jobs* (2006) makes clear, many of the new member states find it difficult to develop a comprehensive strategy to promote an employment policy that provides an integrated framework for macroeconomic policy, employment, education and social policy. Employment in this framework not only means a set of passive and active employment measures, but also a set of macroeconomic and microeconomic policies, lifelong learning strategies, innovation policies and social inclusion measures. Finally, employment issues may well come to the centre of public policy in the current candidate countries, where the employment rate is significantly below the EU average. In 2004 the employment rate for Bulgaria was 54.2 per cent, Romania 57.7 per cent, Croatia 54.7 per cent and Turkey 46.1 per cent (ESSPROS database, 2005).

Another site for the re-coupling is the link between regional policy and social policy encouraged by the European Regional Development Fund or Poland and Hungary Assistance for Economic Restructuring Programme (PHARE) Cross-border Co-operation Funds. Here, social policy, regional policy and development policy come together in a framework that provides substantial financial support for the new member states as part of the Structural Funds, and for candidate countries as a substantial part of the pre-accession funds. However, regional inequalities are addressed in other frameworks too, for example the above-mentioned European Commission report calls on the new member states to take into account the regional aspect of employment and incorporate them into their strategies for growth and job promotion. In Hungary, the impact of the re-coupling of the issues of regional and social policy was not only the establishment of a new institutional network promoting regional social policy programmes, and therefore the quasi-institutionalization of regional social policy as such (non-existent before), but also the recognition of and renewed interest in the territorial, geographic and spatial aspects of social exclusion processes (for example the amplification of the urban–rural divide, the link between exclusion and transportation in terms of remote areas and their lack of social service provision, and inequalities in local social services).

Quintessentially, Europeanization signifies a process where 'national social policy' frameworks are reconfigured, reframed and re-coupled. Social policy, through the OMC, is framed as 'social inclusion', 'lifelong learning', 'fiscal policy', 'gender equality and gender mainstreaming', or 'social protection' in terms of pensions and health care. Social policy becomes 'social cohesion' in the Structural Funds, 'social inclusion' in the OMC and 'social regulation' in the hard laws of the EU. In a number of contexts, social policy is uneasily framed within 'crime and security policy', 'regional policy', 'migration policy' and 'neighbourhood policies'. These different scripts for social policy will necessarily stretch domestic understandings and framing of social policy and, as a result, Europeanization will foster and forge new issue coalitions cross-cutting sectors, organizations and new policy developments.

The EU no doubt works with a dynamic understanding of social policy, which it sees as a productive factor contributing to economic growth and development. In this dynamic framework, activation, social exclusion and inclusion, joined-up policy-making and partnership play important roles. Poverty becomes social exclusion, education becomes learning, and labour markets become employability and activation, which emphasizes the need for a dynamic, adaptive and cross-cutting understanding of social policy in facing contemporary post-industrial challenges. The social dimension of the EU, in a sense, is an assemblage of innovative policy ideas developed in various welfare regimes in Western Europe (gender mainstreaming from Scandinavian countries, activation from Netherlands, social exclusion from France and Britain, and so on). The challenge here for policy-makers both in new member states, candidate and aspirant countries is how to initiate and maintain inter-sectoral and inter-professional co-operation, promote institutional learning and adaptation in order to meet the EU's strategic priorities and objectives, while for the researcher the challenge is to unfold the subtle processes of transformation of social policy meanings, discourses, ideas, policy tools and objectives.

While no doubt EU social policy is very innovative and experiential, many scholars interpret this reframing process not as a benevolent act of 'adaptation and learning' of 'joined-up policies', but more as a political act and discourse to subordinate social policy to economic growth and competitiveness. As I noted above, for neo-Gramscian and neo-Marxist scholars, both the EU accession process as well as EU integration represents a neo-liberal restructuring of economic and social relations. Others emphasize the struggle over different visions of social policy and economic policy at the supranational level (for example, between a Polanyian or Schumpeterian, or neo-liberal versus social democrat version) (Taylor-Gooby, 2003). Yet others argue that a core aspect of EU social policy is the de-coupling of economic integration and social protection issues (Scharpf, 2002) and the asymmetry between economic and social policy regulation, where

(a)symmetric regulation, then, not only refers to the discrepancy between European economic and monetary free market regulation, on the one hand, and the lack of social regulation (or harmonisation) at the European level, on the other, but – more importantly – to the adverse impact of economic and monetary integration at the European level on social cohesion at the national level. (Holman, 2004: 716)

Europeanization, from this point of view could then be seen as the 'importation' of those tensions and imbalances to the new member states as well as to candidate countries. Indeed, the accession process of the eight post-communist countries concluding in the accession in 2004 itself was seen as a highly imbalanced process, in which economic issues, economic liberalization and opening up of markets dominated, while social issues have been marginalized and neglected (Brusis, 2000; Ferge and Juhász, 2004).

Europeanization and the Trajectories of Post-communist Welfare Transformation

In this section, I turn to the experience of the new member states and address some of the issues around the Europeanization of post-communist welfare. While there are ongoing debates on how strong or weak the Europeanization process is in terms of influencing national welfare policies, and in this debate the accession process seems to be on the 'weak' side, the contemporary experiences of new member states seem to suggest that Europeanization is a crucial process, which indeed shapes and shakes the trajectories of their welfare transformation. As such, it may be important to move beyond the accession process and cast an eye on the EU integration process as well. After the 2004 accession, new member states have become part of a number of EU initiatives and policy frameworks, which are directly linked to core welfare issues (Table 2.1).

Through various mechanisms, summarized in Table 2.1, the impact of the EU on domestic welfare developments is very comprehensive. The EU sets out political objectives in almost all aspects of public policies. The EU also monitors and reports progress in member states in meeting specific targets. In that sense, EU social policy is the complex interplay of economic policies (set out by the Stability and Growth Pact and the Convergence Programmes, which provide a road map for countries to join the Euro), as well as employment, education and social inclusion policies (through the OMC, the revised Lisbon Agenda and the Structural Funds).

From this point of view, the crucial question is how Europeanization shapes the welfare trajectories of post-communist Europe. Within this fundamental, yet complex question, I address three issues: one is the contradictory and competing pressures on domestic social policy-makers; the second is the dilemmas faced by new member states in terms of how to transform their welfare states in order to meet contemporary socio-economic

*Table 2.1   EU initiatives and policy frameworks influencing national
welfare issues*

Stability and Growth Pact/Convergence Programme
- sustainable public finances
- public welfare spending
- pressure on pension and health reforms

Lisbon Agenda/National Reform Programme
- revised Lisbon agenda
- comprehensive and integrated market and social reforms

Open Method of Co-ordination
'Soft governance' on
- social protection and social inclusion
- employment and education
- statistical coordination

Structural Funds
- spending strategy/development framework for enhancing economic and
  social cohesion
- programmes for employment, inclusion, gender and regional development

Free movement of goods, persons, services and capital
- migration, harmonisation of social security, related social regulations, labour
  mobility, the mobility of health-care insurance and service organizations, care
  providers and patients and the implication of internal market in that field,
  de-territorialization of citizenship-based social benefits, and other indirect
  pressures for welfare states

---

challenges, and the third is how these two processes are likely to impact on
the future development of post-communist welfare.

First, it is important to note that the EU exerts a number of different,
often contradictory and competing, pressures on policy-makers. For
example, while on the one hand the OMC process promotes social inclusion and the fight against poverty, at the same time, on the other hand, the
EU promotes economic criteria that demand the reduction of public expenditures. The so-called Convergence Programmes for 2005–2009 for example
forecast a 2–3 per cent reduction of public welfare spending throughout the
new member states. There are also competing agendas between the developmental agenda of Lisbon and the Structural Funds, on the one hand,
and the economic restrictions, deregulation and pressures on public
finances and spending, on the other hand. These conflicting processes represent very different claims on public finances, and create very real dilemmas for domestic social policy-makers.

Secondly, Europeanization raises a number of dilemmas faced by politicians and policy-makers in terms of the transformation of welfare states in the context of EU integration. Quintessentially, while welfare states in the new member states face similar demographic, economic, labour and social challenges, the institutional capacities of post-communist welfare states are very different from most of the old member states. While in the West, the post-industrial challenges are faced in response to well-developed Keynesian or post-Keynesian welfare states, with strong notions of social citizenship, labour–capital compromise and a commitment to social justice, equality and solidarity, post-communist Europe is facing similar post-industrial challenges in the context of the absence of the Keynesian post-war welfare development (probably with the exception of Slovenia) and instead has a legacy of 15 years of market- and state-building, weak social citizenship, and imbalanced and distorted labour–capital relations. Consequently, the specific structural conditions that prevail in post-communist Europe need to be considered when we try to unfold the impact of the EU and understand the transformation of post-communist welfare.

Finally, faced with the above-mentioned dilemmas, the third dilemma for post-communist welfare is which welfare model to 'converge' to. While for many scholars the EU represents a workfare agenda, Wincott (2003) argues that 'workfare' takes very different shapes and forms across Europe, ranging from punitive interventionist-neoliberal workfare to inclusive, high-quality training-based activation. The Europeanization of post-communist welfare is not simply an issue of underdevelopment, or catch-up, nor is it simply a modernization story. Europeanization is taking place in the context of very different structural conditions, complex public policy choices, multiple socio-economic trajectories and unique institutional landscapes. However, to be able to capture those complex trajectories we need to go beyond a narrow understanding of what social policy is and locate social policy within a broad public policy framework.

THE EU IN SOUTH EAST EUROPE: PROSPECTS AND CHALLENGES

South East European Road Maps to the European Union

South East European countries have a variable geometry in terms of their distance from and prospects for European Union membership. Of the ten countries and territories discussed in this book, Slovenia joined the EU in May 2004 and Romania and Bulgaria became members in January 2007. While Slovenia had a rather smooth accession process, and has recently joined the Euro zone, Romania and Bulgaria joined the EU on a conditional basis. Serious concerns have been raised regarding both countries in terms of the justice system and the fight against corruption. The next group of countries, labelled by the EU as the 'Western Balkans', come under an EU framework with three key elements: Stabilization and Association Agreements (SAAs), autonomous trade measures and substantial financial assistance. Regional co-operation constitutes a cornerstone of the Stabilization and Association Process. Croatia, which has achieved candidate status, started negotiations and appears to be progressing well, had difficulties with political conditionality based on perceptions of their ambivalent co-operation with the ICTY. Importantly, current accession negotiations in SEE countries differ in three important respects from the previous rounds: first, the number of negotiating chapters is larger, initial benchmarks are set and political conditionalities are taken more seriously in all of the SEE countries. Paradoxically, the likely accession of Croatia to the EU will depend not so much on the Croatian performance itself, but rather on the political situation within the EU, attitudes towards further enlargement and internal reforms within the union. Macedonia's accession, as the newest candidate country in the region, faces an even more unpredictable road map to the European Union (see Table 2.2). In the case of other countries such as Albania, Bosnia-Herzegovina, Serbia and Montenegro, the EU appears to be lacking a comprehensive strategy, beyond a slow process of feasibility studies leading to SAAs. Turkey's candidacy is probably the most politicized issue in the history of the EU. The recent decision to suspend negotiations will have a fundamental impact not only on Turkish accession, but on the accession of other SEE countries as well.

Overall, the accession process for South East European countries takes place in an unusually fragile context, not only with respect to the status of the candidate and aspirant countries, but also, possibly more importantly, with respect to the heightened internal debates about the future direction of the European Union. This will continue to strongly politicize the accession process in all the SEE countries, and is likely to lead to 'stop and starts' in negotiations and result in a kind of 'floating' accession process.

THE LESSONS FROM THE PREVIOUS ENLARGEMENT

So what kind of lessons can be drawn from the latest rounds of enlargement for South East Europe? First, it is important to differentiate between accession and integration. While there is a more or less consensus that the

Table 2.2 Road map to the European Union

Country	Status	Road map to EU	Notes
Albania	Aspirant country	June 2006: SAA signed Jan 2003: Negotiations begin on SAA Jan 2000: Feasibility Report accepted	
Bosnia-Herzegovina	Aspirant country	Nov 2006: Negotiations begin on SAA Nov 2003: Feasibility Report accepted	New High Representative is also EU Special Representative The conclusion of negotiations is contingent on significant overall progress in addressing key priorities, notably police reform, ICTY co-operation, public broadcasting and public administration
Bulgaria	Member of the EU	January 2007: Becomes member of the EU April 2005: Accession treaty signed Feb 2000: Accession negotiations begin Dec 1995: Application for membership submitted	Process of ratification of Accession treaty is ongoing. Safeguard clause allows postponement of entry to 1 January 2008 Conditional entrance to the EU
Croatia	Candidate country	October 2005: Accession negotiations begin June 2004: European Council accepts Croatia as a candidate country Feb 2003: Applied for membership Oct 2001: Signed SAA	Accession negotiations were held up pending full co-operation with ICTY Unclear how long negotiations will take Likely date for membership now seen as 2010 or 2011, provided EU reforms are in place
Kosovo/a	None	No contractual relations with EU	Serbia and Montenegro's Partnership Agreement (adopted June 2004) includes Kosovo Recent EU communications stress EU's commitment to Kosovo/a and to resolving final status
Macedonia	Candidate country	November 2006: Commission's progress report submitted to Council	No prospect of negotiations starting until progress made in meeting

Table 2.2 (continued)

Country	Status	Road map to EU	Notes
		Dec 2005: Granted candidate status March 2004: Submits membership application April 2001: Signs SAA	political, economic and other criteria
Montenegro	Aspirant country	September 2006: SAA negotiations launched June 2006: EU recognizes Montenegro as sovereign state	SAA is adapted from SAA with Serbia and Montenegro
Romania	Member of the EU	January 2007: Membership of the EU Feb 2000: Accession negotiations begin June 1995: Submits application for membership	Conditional entrance to the EU
Serbia	Aspirant country	May 2006: SAA negotiations called off Oct 2005: Negotiations begin on SAA Apr 2005: Feasibility study completed	Currently SAA negotiations on hold pending full co-operation with ICTY
Slovenia	Member of the EU	May 2004: Joins EU Dec 2002: Negotiations concluded March 1998: Began Membership negotiations June 1996: Signed Association agreement	
Turkey	Candidate country	Nov 2006: Partial suspension of negotiations Oct 2005: Accession negotiations begin Dec 2004: European Council defines conditions for opening negotiations Dec 1999: Granted candidate status April 1987: Second application Sept 1959: First application for membership	General agreement that eventual membership is some time away

Source: Based on http://ec.europa.eu/enlargement/countries/index_en.htm, accessed 15 May 2007.

Table 2.3   Contrasting accession and integration

Accession process	Integration
Weak social dimension	Stronger, more contested, more diverse social dimension
Mainly adoption of the social *acquis*	Implementation of the *acquis* plus OMC, Structural Funds and other initiatives
Technocratic process	Political process
Weak networks (NGOs, policy-makers, lobby groups, and so on)	Institutionalized networks
Hierarchical governance, weak participation in, lack of ownership of EU policies	Horizontal governance style, full participation, possible contestation and opt-out

accession process has a weak social dimension in which social policy is marginal, after accession social policy becomes more prominent through a number of different policy frameworks across different policy sectors. Also, while the accession process has been characterized as asymmetrical governance, with no or little participation, lack of ownership and no comprehensive understanding of the EU by candidate countries, integration offers full participation, contestation and a horizontal governance style, where new member states have a legally equal status (although as the latest round of accession of Romania and Bulgaria shows, the EU can retain strong conditions both before as well as after accession). While accession seems an overwhelmingly technical and technocratized process, integration is a deeply political process (Table 2.3).

Secondly, while it is less obvious during the accession process, the EU fundamentally shapes the transformation of welfare development both directly and indirectly. In that sense the key question becomes whether the newcomers take a reactive approach to the EU, with passive adoption of rules and norms, or take a proactive stance in which they aim for an active translation of EU values, norms and policy frameworks and an active search for their own response to the EU. In any case, Europeanization no doubt fosters very diverse responses, rather than any unified and uniform effects, in which local configurations play a fundamental role.

Thirdly, there are broader questions around how the EU will shape the trajectories of welfare transformation in South East Europe. As discussed in Chapter 3, employment and particularly activation came to the forefront of social policy-making in Slovenia. Indeed, in the light of a low employment rate and high unemployment in many South East European countries, the EU's employment-anchored social policy will certainly be an important new public policy focus. Other agendas, such as lifelong learning, gender equality and mainstreaming and social inclusion will also be likely to occupy more space in public debates. However, the EU remains largely silent on a number of core transition agendas such as social insurance schemes, the role of civil society (with the exception of Turkey), social services, housing, developing welfare mixes, decentralization, social work, deinstitutionalization, and many other issues. Apart from specific sectoral issues, another important question will be to what degree South East European actors will be able to participate in European networks, such as trade unions and NGO networks. Finally, institutional capacities will be a key site for Europeanization. The capacity of institutions to learn, to participate in European networks, to shape policy agendas and to implement EU policies and programmes will be crucial in the coming years. In this regard, a particularly important role will be played by civil servants working in ministries, who will have the most intensive and formative relations with the EU and have an important role in how they empower and include other non-governmental actors in this process.

Fourthly, it is very likely that, despite the weakness of the social dimension of the EU Accession process, the EU will become a more and more central international actor in the region in the years to come. In that sense it will be crucial that both policy-makers as well as social policy scholars take a closer look at the EU and its relevance for South East Europe. The lesson from Central and East Europe is that their approach was reactive rather than proactive, formal rather than substantive, and it may well be that they will pay a price for that in terms of their ability to meet tough EU targets in the course of the integration process.

As for theoretical challenges, there is a need for critical accounts in which the EU is not taken for granted, where Europeanization is not just seen as learning and adoption in a seemingly neutral sense, but also seen as a political process. The challenge for institutionalist accounts is to unfold the different types of adoptions, such as formal, behavioural and discursive, and their differential impact on various policy fields. The challenge for governmentality scholars is to frame social policy more broadly as a core public policy that constitutes subjectivities, located between policy and politics and mediating between different discourses, claims and representations.

REFERENCES

Beyeler, M. (2003), 'Globalization, Europeanization and domestic welfare state reforms', *Global Social Policy*, **3** (2), 153–72.

Bieler, A. and A. Morton (eds) (2003), *Social Forces in the Making of the New Europe: The Restructuring of European Social Relations in the Global Political Economy*, Basingstoke: Palgrave.

Bohle, D. and B. Greskovits (2005), 'Capital, labour and the prospects of the European social model in the East', paper presented at the 5th Pan European International Relations Conference 'Constructing World Orders', The Hague, 9–11 September.

Böröcz, J. (2001), 'The fox and the raven: the European Union and Hungary renegotiate the margins of "Europe"', in J. Böröcz and M. Kovács (eds), *The Empire's New Clothes: Unveiling EU Enlargement*, Telford: Central Europe Review, pp. 51–110.

Böröcz, J. and M. Kovács (eds) (2001), *The Empire's New Clothes: Unveiling EU Enlargement*, Telford: Central Europe Review.

Brusis, M. (2000), 'Internal problems of the European Union that might obstruct an enlargement toward the East', in H. Tang (ed.), *Winners and Losers of EU Integration. Policy Issues for Central and Eastern Europe*, Washington, DC: The World Bank, pp. 265–90.

Carmen, E. (2005), 'Governance and the constitution of a European social', in J. Newman (ed.), *Remaking Governance*, Bristol: Policy Press, pp. 39–59.

Clarke, J. (2005), 'What's culture got to do with it? Deconstructing welfare, state and nation', paper for 'Anthropological approaches to studying welfare', research seminar, Arhus University, 16–18 November.

Czernielewska, M., C. Paraskevopoulos and J. Szlachta (2004), 'The regionalisation process in Poland: an example of "shallow" Europeanisation?', *Regional and Federal Studies*, **14** (3), 461–95.

Deacon, B., M. Hulse and P. Stubbs (1997), *Global Social Policy. International Organizations and the Future of Welfare*, London: Sage.

Dimitrov, V., K. Goetz and H. Wollmann (2006), 'Domestic institutions and European governance', in V. Dimitrov, K. Goetz and H. Wollmann (eds), *Governing After Communism*, Lanham, MD: Rowman and Littlefield Publishers, pp. 249–63.

ESSPROS database (2005), available at www.eurostat.eu (accessed 15 May 2007).

European Commission (2006), *Annual Progress Report on Growth and Jobs*, Brussels: European Commission, http://ec.europa.eu/growthandjobs/pdf/2006_annual_report_full_en.pdf (accessed 15 May 2007).

Fagan, C., J. Rubery, D. Grimshaw, M. Smith, G. Hebson and H. Figueiredo (2005), 'Gender mainstreaming in the enlarged European Union: recent developments in the European employment strategy and social inclusion process', *Industrial Relations Journal*, **36** (6), 568–91.

Featherstone, K. (2003), 'Introduction: in the name of "Europe"', in K. Featherstone and C. Radaelli (eds), *The Politics of Europeanization*, Oxford: Oxford University Press, pp. 3–27.

Ferge, Zs. and G. Juhász (2004), 'Accession and social policy: the case of Hungary', *Journal of European Social Policy*, **14**, 233–51.

Ferrera, M. (2005), *The Boundaries of Welfare. European Integration and the New Spatial Politics of Social Protection*, Oxford: Oxford University Press.

Ferrera, M., A. Hemerijck and M. Rhodes (2001), 'The future of social Europe: recasting work and welfare in the new economy', report for the Portuguese Presidency of the European Union.

Gill, S. (2001), 'Constitutionalising capital: EMU and disciplinary neoliberalism', in A. Bieler and A.D. Morton (eds), *Social Forces in the Making of the New*

Europe: The Restructuring of European Social Relations in the Global Political Economy, Basingstoke: Palgrave, pp. 47–69.

Graziano, D. (2003), 'Europeanization or globalization?', *Global Social Policy*, **3** (2), 173–94.

Guillén, A. and S. Álvarez (2004), 'The EU's impact on the Spanish welfare state: the role of cognitive Europeanization', *Journal of European Social Policy*, **14** (3), 285–99.

Guillén, A., S. Álvarez and P. Adão e Silva (2002), 'European Union membership and social policy: the Spanish and Portuguese experiences', paper for the inaugural ESPANET conference (November), Copenhagen.

Haahr, E. (2004), 'Open co-ordination as advanced liberal government', *Journal of European Public Policy*, **11** (2), 209–30.

Hafner-Burton, E. and M.A. Pollack (2002), 'Gender mainstreaming and global governance', *Feminist Legal Studies*, **10** (3/4), 285–98.

Haverland, M. (2005), 'Does the EU cause domestic developments? The problem of case-selection in Europeanization research', *European Integration Online Papers*, **9** (2), http://eiop.or.at/eiop/texte/2005-002a.htm (accessed 15 May 2007).

Holman, O. (2004), 'Asymmetrical regulation and multidimensional governance in the European union', *Review of International Political Economy*, **11** (4), 714–35.

Howell, D. (2004), 'Developing conceptualisations of Europeanization: synthesising methodological approaches', *Queen's Papers on Europeanization*, **3** (2004).

Jakobsson, K. and C. West (2006), 'Europeanisation of Employment policy making in the Baltic States', working paper online, www.wage.wisc.edu/uploads/Events/Work&Welfare/West_Govconf.pdf (accessed 15 May 2007).

Jessop, B. (2002), *The Future of the Capitalist State*, Cambridge: Polity Press.

Knill, C. (2001), *The Europeanisation of National Administrations*, Cambridge: Cambridge University Press.

Krizsan, A. and V. Zentai (2006), 'Gender equality policy or gender mainstreaming? The case of Hungary on the road to an enlarged Europe', *Policy Studies*, **27** (2), 135–51.

Kuus, M. (2004), 'Europe's Eastern expansions and the reinscription of otherness in East-Central Europe', *Progress in Human Geography*, **28** (4), 472–89.

Laffan, B., R. O'Donnell and M. Smith (2000), *Europe's Experimental Union, Rethinking Europe*, London: Routledge.

Lovecy, M. (2002), 'Gender mainstreaming and the framing of women's rights in Europe: the contribution of the Council of Europe', *Feminist Legal Studies*, **10** (3/4), 271–83.

Mitchell, K. (2006), 'Neo-liberal governmentality in the European Union: education, training and technologies of citizenship', *Environment and Planning D: Society and Space*, **24**, 389–407.

Moreno, L. (2003), 'Europeanisation, mesogovernments and "safety nets"', *European Journal of Political Research*, **42**, 271–85.

O'Connor, J. (2005), 'Employment-anchored social policy, gender equality and the open method of coordination in the European Union', *European Societies*, **7** (1), 27–52.

Olson, J. (2002), 'The many faces of Europeanization', *ARENA Working Papers*, WP 01/2.

Palier, B. (2004), 'The Europeanisation of welfare reforms', www.ksg.harvard.edu/inequality/Summer/Summer06/papers/Palier.pdf (accessed 15 May 2007).

Palne, I., C. Paraskevopoulos and Gy. Horvath (2004), 'Institutional "Legacies" and the shaping of regional governance in Hungary', *Regional and Federal Studies*, **14** (3), 430–60.

Paraskevopoulos, C. and R. Leonardi (2004), 'Introduction: adaptational pressures and social learning in European regional policy – cohesion (Greece, Ireland and Portugal) vs. CEE (Hungary, Poland) countries', *Regional and Federal Studies*, **14** (3), 315–54.

Perrons, D. (2005), 'Gender mainstreaming and gender equality in the new (market) economy: an analysis of contradictions', *Social Politics*, **12**, 389–411.

Radaelli, C. (2003), 'The Europeanization of public policy', in K. Featherstone and C. Radaelli (eds), *The Politics of Europeanization*, Oxford: Oxford University Press, pp. 27–57.

Rico, E. (2005), 'Citizenship at Europe's borders: some reflections on the post-colonial condition of Europe in the context of EU Enlargement', *Citizenship Studies*, **9** (1), 3–22.

Rumford, C. (2003), 'Rethinking the state and polity-building in the European Union: the sociology of globalization and the rise of reflexive government', *EurPolCom Working Paper*, 4(03), Centre for European Political Communications.

Sasse, G. (2005), 'EU conditionality and minority rights: translating the Copenhagen criterion into policy', *EUI-RSCAS Working Papers 16*.

Scharpf, F. (2002), 'The European social model: coping with the challenges of diversity', *MPIfG Working Paper*, 02/8.

Schmidt, S. (2002), 'The impact of mutual recognition – inbuilt limits and domestic responses to the single market', *Journal of European Public Policy*, **9** (6), 935–53.

Simhandl, O. (2006), 'Western gypsies and travellers' – "Eastern Roma": the creation of political objects by the institutions of the European Union', *Nations and Nationalism*, **12** (1), 97–115.

Sloat, A. (2004), 'Legislating for equality: the implementation of the EU equality acquis in Central and Eastern Europe', *Jean Monnet Working Paper*, 08(04), NYU School of Law.

Sotiropoulos, D. (2004), 'The EU's impact on the Greek welfare state: Europeanization on paper?', *Journal of European Social Policy*, **14** (3), 267–84.

Taylor-Gooby, P. (2003), 'Introduction: open market versus welfare citizenship: conflicting approaches to policy convergence in Europe', *Social Policy and Administration*, **37** (6), 539–54.

Teague, P. (2000), 'EU social policy: institutional design matters', *Queens's Papers on Europeanization*, 1 (2000), 1–16.

Van Aperdoorn, B. (2006), 'The Lisbon Agenda and the legitimacy crisis of European socio-economic governance: the future of "embedded neo-liberalism"', conference paper presented at the 4th Convention of the Central East European International Studies Association (CEEISA), University of Tartu, Estonia, 25–27 June.

Van der Molen, I. and I. Novikova (2005), 'Mainstreaming gender in the EU-accession process: the case of the Baltic Republics', *Journal of European Social Policy*, **15** (2), 139–56.

Verloo, M. (2005), 'Displacement and empowerment: reflections on the concept and practice of the Council of Europe approach to gender mainstreaming and gender equality', *Social Politics*, **12**, 344–65.

Vermeersch, P. (2002), 'Ethnic mobilisation and the political conditionality of European Union accession: the case of the Roma in Slovakia', *Journal of Ethnic and Migration Studies*, **28** (1), 83–101.

Walters, W. and J. Haahr (2005), *Governing Europe. Discourse, Governmentality and European Integration*, London: Routledge.

Wincott, D. (2003), 'Beyond social regulation? New instruments and/or a new agenda for social policy at Lisbon?', *Public Administration*, **81** (3), 533–53.

3. Slovenia

Mojca Novak and Katja Rihar Bajuk

INTRODUCTION

Slovenia seceded from Yugoslavia in 1991, gaining national sovereignty and political stabilization in terms of international recognition. In fact, this political stabilization did not, at first, lead to economic and social stabilization. The early 1990s saw a period of economic recession and social stagnation, in the context of the loss of the Yugoslav market. The painful reorientation to Western European markets led to many bankruptcies and high levels of unemployment and early retirement. Social security was added to the national agenda, framed in terms of structural unemployment and the instability and unsustainability of the pension fund, both of which became major political and policy issues. Slovenia's social problems resembled those of parts of the developed industrial world, in terms of an ageing population and regressive demographic trends.

Economic growth slowed in the early 1990s. Slovenia's budgetary balance remained relatively constant (0.2 per cent in 1994 and −1.0 per cent in 1999) and stable. The ratio of workers to pensioners of 1.4:1, the effective retirement age (58.5 years), and excessive early retirement which had been widely implemented in the 1980s forced tactical and strategic decisions to be made. Regardless of harsh critiques of the country's economic performance, the economy has shown positive trends since the early 1990s, unlike most of the transition countries of Central and Eastern Europe, although the indicators concerned are far from reaching the top international ranking. They show a moderate and stable increase in the wealth of the country, which is shared by the majority of residents. At the same time, some social groups still live in hardship and experience social exclusion, forming a marginalized subsection of the population, failing to benefit from the fruits of economic growth.

In this chapter we focus on four broad social policy sectors: unemployment and labour market policies; pensions policies; health policies; and policies against poverty and social exclusion. We take a chronological approach to analysing and explaining the uneven impact of international actors in these sectors in social policy reform during the transition and

Slovenia's EU accession process. Slovenia became a full member of the European Union on 1 May 2004 and, on 1 January 2007, became the first new member state to join the European Monetary Union.

It is frequently suggested that certain international actors such as the World Bank, the International Monetary Fund (IMF), the Council of Europe, the United Nations Development Programme, and other aid providers and donors influenced significantly Slovenia's inclusion into the international community, but that their influence was dwarfed by the process of EU accession. Certainly, the EU and the Council of Europe had a significant political impact, providing guiding principles, indicators, measurement methodologies and monitoring tools for the government and the state administration in the process of adopting and adapting professional standards in social policy reform strategies. The government and the political establishment was slower in incorporating national experts and expertise into the political and policy decision-making process, although this is now established as a permanent feature of multi-level governance in Slovenia.

UNEMPLOYMENT AND LABOUR MARKET POLICIES

A slow-down in economic growth in early 2000 had a significant impact on unemployment. While recent years have seen a decrease in the registered unemployment rate, the employment rate has remained virtually stagnant. Since the late 1990s, the ILO Labour Force Survey methodology has become the permanent parallel unemployment rate measurement. Between 2003 and 2004, the ILO unemployment rate was approximately 6 per cent of the active population, while the rate of official, registered, unemployment stabilized at approximately 11 per cent annually. These figures put Slovenia in the middle of the EU25 in terms of unemployment. However, structural unemployment problems remain above the EU average, indicating the importance of the gender employment gap, youth unemployment, long-term unemployment, unemployment of those with lower levels of education, and lower rates of employability of disabled people and Roma, as well as significant differences in regional rates of unemployment. The labour force constraints have been recognized by the government as development challenges, with strategic frameworks produced to make the labour force market more inclusive and to promote employment as a civic right (MoLSFA, 2004).

Unlike most Central and Eastern European countries, apart from Hungary, Slovenia introduced an unemployment scheme in the early 1970s (Wright et al., 2004) in line with the Bismarckian welfare model (Novak, 2001), thus implementing a two-pillar system of unemployment protection, through an insurance-based unemployment benefit and through social assistance (Wright et al., 2004). In the early 1980s, Slovenia had an extremely low unemployment rate (approximately 0.5 per cent of the total labour force), which was mostly due to an insistence on the socialist ideological belief that everybody who is able (and willing) to work should be employed. 'Employed but workless' was a manifestation of this political strategy, which was ended in the early 1990s and which saw a rapid increase in the rate of unemployment over a short period – from 4000 unemployed in the early 1980s to 130 000 unemployed in the early 1990s. In addition, the size of the labour force fell from 800 000 to 640 000 approximately, in part as a result of significant job losses, and partly due to excessive early retirement. Despite its significant impact on pension fund sustainability, the early retirement phenomenon has failed to attract either political or research interest (Novak, 2000). At the same time, harmonization of Slovene employment policy with EU and OECD standards led to the advent of some kinds of labour market activation policies (Wright et al., 2004: 517).

Since the mid-1990s, the unemployment insurance scheme has been severely criticised, both by Slovene experts and by international agencies such as the OECD and the World Bank, as creating poor work incentives within a rigid, bureaucratic and inefficient labour market (Vodopivec, 1996). Overall, employers' contributions to different social insurance funds are approximately 16 per cent compared to 22 per cent rates for employees' contributions. This is said to have made labour costs too high to encourage the creation of low-paid jobs. The unemployment rate was particularly high for poorly qualified and older workers who tend to be over-represented among the long-term unemployed. Apart from this, first-time job seekers and young unemployed experienced similar obstacles in seeking jobs. The activation policy focused first on a reduction in the duration and level of unemployment benefits (allowances and assistance), thus manifesting a 'passive' policy stage. The transition stage from passive to active policy forms then followed by introducing new obligations on those unemployed, such as increasing surveillance and tightening conditions through activity testing. The EU accession process brought active employment measures onto the Slovene unemployment regulation agenda, focusing on individual unemployed persons in terms of increasing their employability and enabling them to be more competitive on the labour market. In 2001, when the social assistance scheme was reformed, a strategy for activity testing of the unemployed was implemented to emphasize the subsidiary nature of cash benefits and to decrease work disincentives (Wright et al., 2004). Regardless of high political support, the activation policy has not yet influenced passive unemployment measures. The focus has been shifted from the demand side to the supply side of the labour market, prioritizing work and employability over social insurance and social security schemes. Such a strategy has led the state administration to focus on raising the employability of individuals through training and retraining (Ignjatovic et al., 2002).

Since then, political efforts in this area have received a new thrust from the international arena in terms of the adoption of social inclusion strategies (Novak, 2005). Framed in this way, activation policy strategies are planned in terms of equalizing opportunities and increasing the independence of persons with disabilities, and are extended to other groups who are frequently excluded from the labour market, such as young people, women, the long-term unemployed, individuals with low levels of acquired education, and Roma. Active labour market policies are also given specific attention in less developed regions where unemployment gaps show greater disparities compared with the rest of Slovenia. In line with this, job preservation schemes were launched primarily in low-skill sectors such as the textile industry with extensive financial support from the state budget and, from 2005, from the EU Structural Social Fund (MoLSFA, 2004).

Unemployment policy reform, therefore, can be seen as one area where the broad policy frameworks of international organizations, particularly the EU and the World Bank, dovetailed with the concerns of Slovenian policymakers regarding the inflexibility of the labour market. Policy transfer processes were largely on the basis of learning from others, with Slovenia's peer group now firmly the OECD member states. Activation policy principles and strategies were adopted from other countries, particularly from Denmark, and applied in accordance with specific national and regional circumstances. The process of drawing up action plans on employment and social exclusion as part of the obligations of EU membership, concentrated attention on various vulnerable groups such as young people and first-time jobseekers, older unemployed, the long-term unemployed, people with disabilities and the Roma population. The process of EU accession and membership meant that the government and state administration began to co-operate consistently with international and national experts to design strategies to decrease unemployment, on the one hand, and to increase the labour-market and social inclusion of marginal social groups, on the other hand. Finally, the ILO was influential in terms of statistical measurements, providing a parallel figure of national levels of unemployment.

PENSIONS POLICY

Reforms of the pension scheme have been, and continue to be, of prime importance on the political agenda in virtually all European countries, largely because the implications of ageing are significant, not only for social but also for fiscal and economic policies. The economies of CEE were facing additional challenges arising from the recent fundamental transformation of their societies and economies calling for a completely new economic and political environment.

As the prevailing public pension system in Slovenia in the 1990s was expected to become unsustainable and thus represented a threat to fiscal stability, the first thoroughgoing reform commenced in 1996. The decisive factor in the government's decision to introduce pension reform, which was concluded in 2000, was the critical demographic situation in Slovenia, together with the projected consequences of this for the sustainability of the pension system in the near future, and the significant difference between the relatively favourable old-age dependency ratio and less favourable system dependency ratio, or the ratio of contributors to pensioners. The falling number of contributors in the early 1990s was also a consequence of high unemployment rates as a result of implemented structural adjustment reforms, caused mainly by closing down ineffective production facilities and withdrawing subsidies to companies. In Slovenia, measures had been adopted to meet the challenge of high unemployment, including generous possibilities for early retirement. Gradually the unemployment rate was decreased, but not the costs of the social security system.

The broadly stable macroeconomic performance of Slovenia throughout the 1990s helped to frame the contours of pensions reform. The government was obliged to make up deficits that arose within the pension system as a result of the unfavourable ratio between contributions and benefits, but it was helped in this regard by the largely stable budgetary balance. Slovenia did not rely heavily on foreign direct investment (FDI) and was not as heavily indebted as some other CEE countries. This made the country more able to resist policy prescriptions of the international financial organizations, such as the World Bank and the International Monetary Fund (Rihar Bajuk, 2004).

The internal politics of pension reform activities in Slovenia are, therefore, particularly relevant. In 1994 the post of the Minister of Labour, Family and Social Affairs was given to a politician from the Liberal Democrats (LDS), and in 1997 a new coalition government, led by the LDS, was formed. The starting points for the reform of the pensions and disability insurance systems had been prepared by July 1996. These were clearly in favour of minimum security provided by the first pillar and a mandatory, fully funded second pillar, as advocated by the World Bank. The work on pension reform continued with the preparation of a White Paper. In fact, largely as a result of a coincidence of circumstances, the drawing up of this White Paper was co-ordinated by a team funded under the EU's PHARE programme (Stanovnik, 2002).

Strong criticism of the plan from the trade unions emerged only after the formation of the tripartite negotiating working group in January 1998. They opposed the pension reform plan, in particular the raising of the pensionable age to 65 years, the proposal for equal retirement age for both genders, the introduction of the mandatory second pillar and the proposed calculation of the pension assessment base from the best 25 years. This led to several demonstrations and, even, to a serious threat of a general strike.

Eventually, most of their arguments held sway. The government abandoned the idea of a mandatory second pillar and, at the same time, proposed the gradual introduction of a voluntary, fully funded supplementary pillar. The main fears of the trade unions were that the transition to the mandatory second pillar would cause a large deficit in the first pillar and thereby seriously reduce the scale of publicly provided pensions. Even the Ministry of Finance opposed this move, arguing that a mandatory fully funded pillar would worsen the fiscal position in the short and medium terms.

The only issue not resolved remained the tax treatment of supplementary pension schemes. Eventually these premiums were given very favourable tax treatment, which can be regarded as an important step towards the universal use of the second pillar and, consequently, as paving the way towards the introduction of the mandatory second pillar. By the end of 2002, one-quarter of all insured persons contributed to the occupational schemes, while by June 2004 the level of coverage had more than doubled to around 51 per cent of the workforce (EC, 2006b).

The adopted pension reform plan in Slovenia thus includes: gradual increase of retirement age; reduction in differences in retirement requirements for men and women; matching indexation of pensionable income with the pension calculation formula; strengthening the link between benefits and contributions; and a combination of various types of pension scheme financing. Through mandatory insurance, insured persons are granted entitlements to old-age, disability, survivor's and work incapacity benefits as well as long-term care and services, on the basis of their work and contributions record, and the principles of reciprocity and solidarity (MoLFSA, 2005).

In terms of international actors, it can be seen that the World Bank played an important role in the intellectual debate on the most appropriate direction of pension reforms. The first engagement of an IMF and the WB team in Slovenia can be traced back to 1995, when they produced a report on new challenges confronting the social insurance system in Slovenia. This document suggested a pension reform in two stages: first, a parametric reform of the first pillar and, later, the development of a multi-pillar system. The report had a significant impact on the draft version of the White Paper on pension reform (Stanovnik, 2002). Despite its strong interest, the WB was not actively involved in preparation of the pension reform, since their loan was not available at the right time. Therefore, technical assistance for the preparation of the White Paper was received through the PHARE programme of the European Union. Nevertheless, in 1997 the WB and the government of Slovenia approved a Country Assistance Strategy (CAS), which forsaw a number of activities regarding pension reform in Slovenia, although eventually not all of them were implemented. The WB has installed two models for pension reform simulation, including staff training. World Bank experts took part in the process by attending and co-financing an international conference on pension reform in November 1997, after the White Paper had already been prepared. Most of the papers at the conference advocated a multi-pillar approach, whereby the second fully funded pillar would be mandatory. In March 1998, the WB prepared and financed a workshop on Second Pillar Issues, where a mandatory second pillar failed to gain full support. After this workshop the idea of a mandatory second pillar was abandoned, and the World Bank and the government agreed to drop plans for a WB loan that would have helped implement the pension system reform (Stanovnik, 2002: 45, 63).

An assessment of the CAS states that, although the new pension legislation fell short of the WB team's recommendation, it did remove projected deficits in the pay-as-you-go (PAYG) system for the next 15 years or so, and introduced a third pillar – a voluntary fully funded system. Nevertheless, progress in the creation of occupational funds by many large employers also on a voluntary basis could, in the WB's opinion, eventually lay the groundwork for a more broadly defined contributory pillar (World Bank, 2000: 7).

While playing a more important role in pension reform in Slovenia than elsewhere in CEE, it is not the case that the EU took a specific stand in the debate. Their advice to Eastern Europe through the PHARE programme has not been systematic in the way that the World Bank's advice has been. Others have noted the uncertainty introduced by competitive tendering and reliance on consultancy firms of unknown or flexible policy persuasion leading to a de-politicization of the global social policy discourse (de la Porte and Deacon, 2002). It is worth noting that Slovenia's decision to use PHARE-programme resources for technical assistance during preparations for the pension reform was not ideologically motivated. Rather, it was simply that the possibility of a PHARE grant appeared just at the right time. The PHARE team started their work with a critical assessment of the starting points for the reform. The final version of the White Paper included only a few of their suggestions: it did not include a great deal of the policy recommendations associated with a European conservative corporatist approach, including the idea about introducing a mandatory fully funded second pillar. The PHARE team in Slovenia represented some kind of counterbalance to the World Bank's proposals (Fultz, 2004), by exposing the most conspicuous weaknesses of a mandatory second pillar.

Concerning harmonization of national legislation with EU legislation, it is important that social security systems are largely under the authority of the member states (Oksanen, 2004: 92), thus having a significant impact on the direction of the future reforms. There is indirectly binding legislation within the framework of co-ordination of economic policies. Namely, any serious imbalance in public finances is dealt with at the EU level, and, since the public pension system represents an important part of public finances, EU pressure can be relevant here. Following the increase in the pension system deficit, higher expenditures for pensions, and the increase in dependency rates in Slovenia after 1991, threatened the sustainability of the fiscal system; therefore, pension reform was necessary to fulfil the conditions for membership set by the EU. An EC report (2006b) demonstrates again that all EU countries are facing serious financial problems as a result of population ageing, whereby the long-term budgetary impact of ageing in Slovenia is among the three largest increases in the EU, augmented notably by a considerable increase in pension expenditure as a share of GDP.

In contrast to the neo-liberal orientation of the World Bank, the International Labour Organization seeks to secure common international labour and social standards. The ILO's activities are anchored in relevant ILO social security standards and in the concept of decent work. According to the ILO's view, establishment of pension systems based on individual savings accounts should not weaken solidarity-based systems, which share risks between all insured persons. The ILO also highlights a crucial role that social partners have to play in this field and a general responsibility of the state for proper administration of the institutions and services concerned in securing protection envisaged in the ILO Convention (Humblet and Silva, 2002). Another important distinction with the World Bank has to be made with regard to the instruments available for influencing national social policies. The ILO can offer technical assistance programmes, but cannot give loans, which could, to some extent, involve social conditionality.

As regards the ILO's technical assistance, there was no funding at that time provided for the programmes aimed at assisting pension system reform in Slovenia. However, advice from ILO experts was not neglected. In addition to informal contacts between individual ILO experts and the Ministry of Labour, Family and Social Affairs (MoLFSA), former ILO officials also participated in the PHARE project dealing with reform of the Slovenian pension system, having a significant impact on the cautious balancing of different ideas (Fultz, 2004). The outcomes of the Slovenian pension reform were eventually very much in line with the ILO's views. Therefore, the ILO often gives it as an example of a successful reform to the countries of South-East Europe that are currently going through the process of reforming their pension systems.

Hence, in terms of pension reform in Slovenia, we can conclude that various policy actors, on the national and supranational level, have influenced the direction of the reform through ideology, interests and power. Recent pension reform developments reflect the controversy between the strategy of scaling down public PAYG schemes on behalf of commercially managed individual savings schemes and the strategy of combining adjustments of the public PAYG system with the development of voluntary supplemental retirement schemes. In this respect the reform process can be divided into two stages.

Looking at the national level, originally, in the first stage, the reform proposal was liberally oriented. This coincided with the period of more intense involvement of the World Bank. The second stage of the process was characterized by the inclusion of various veto actors. A broader compromise was achieved through negotiations between individual political parties and as a result of the considerable influence of the social-democratic ideology of the trade unions. Their informal veto power even caused changes in the proposed basic structure of the pension system and the rejection of the World Bank's proposals. As regards the supranational level, the second stage was marked by the involvement of other international organizations with a different set of policy prescriptions, including the EU and the ILO. The number and diversity of the actors involved considerably limited the degree of change within the pension system.

The consensus view among politicians and researchers is that the implemented changes should ensure the financial sustainability of the pension system for only the next 15 to 20 years, so that further reforms in this field will be necessary in the near future. Due to the gradual introduction of the examined changes, with all the reform measures not due to be completed until 2017, the appropriateness and success of the implemented reforms will only be evident after a decade or two. In the transition period, according to the national strategy report on adequate and sustainable pensions (MoLFSA, 2005), Slovenia succeeded in maintaining a fairly favourable level of social protection. Several indicators considered, it has achieved or even surpassed the average EU15 level. The share of its inactive population is too large, in particular among the elderly and less educated, and lately also among young job seekers. Educational attainment remains too low, and lifelong learning too limited to enable ongoing adaptation to changes in the environment. In the next decade Slovenia will increasingly face economic and social challenges due to the changing population structure, low birth rate and rising longevity, which means that the present model of inter-generational solidarity will place an increasingly heavy burden upon the active population.

In terms of numbers, the ratio of the average old-age pension to the average net wage decreased from 75.3 per cent in 2000 to 70.2 per cent in 2004. The employment rate of older workers remains low and is one of the lowest among the EU25. Incentives in this respect seem to remain insufficient which leads to a low effective retirement age. The share of total expenditure for pensions declined from 11.4 per cent of GDP in 2000 to 10.9 per cent in 2004, although the number of pensioners increased by approximately 2.1 per cent per year in the period 2000–2004 (EC, 2006b). In line with the Report on long-term sustainability of public finances in the EU (EC 2006a: 156) the projected increase in pension expenditure between 2004 and 2050 amounts to 7.3 per cent which is among the highest increases in the EU.

Together with the above-mentioned indicators, one needs to keep in mind that Slovenia is projected to experience rapid ageing in the coming decades. Demographic trends will result in a considerable increase in the old-age dependency ratio, from 21 per cent in 2004 to 56 per cent in 2050. Therefore, the budgetary pressures due to age-related expenditures are stronger in Slovenia than in most other member states.

HEALTH POLICIES

In Slovenia, it is the legal obligation of the state to arrange compulsory social insurance schemes including health insurance, and to control and co-ordinate their operation. Further, the Constitution determines that everybody has the right to health care (Ministry of Health, 2006). According to official data (MoLSFA, 2006), the health system in Slovenia is well organized, but it is also a subject of harsh critiques. In principle, health-care access is primarily provided by public institutions, but private providers are taking progressive steps in competing for patients, both through the concession rule and through direct payments. In practice, access to health services is sufficient with some identified gaps such as long waiting lists for some services and unequal access with regard to regional distribution. Regardless of the universalistic access to basic health care services, persons excluded from voluntary health insurance, about 1 per cent of the population, are eligible only to treatment in the case of emergency. Further, an increasing need for long-term care for elderly patients has been identified, thus putting after-care strategies on the policy agenda.

The late 1990s witnessed increasing demands for health sector reform to renovate the primary health care by implementing more equal health-care service access and more equal health-care funding. In this respect, primary health care and after care continue to remain major milestones for future strategies to be implemented targeting particularly:

1. Some vulnerable groups such as the homeless.
2. Long waiting lists for treatments for patients with cardiovascular and acute diseases, and cancer.
3. Long waiting lists for early warning medical examination especially for women.

To meet the above concerns, Slovenia has intensified international collaboration which had been initiated after gaining political sovereignty in 1991, when direct international contacts and agreements significantly multiplied. Adoption of a high level of public health standards and transfer of related know-how, various training and health promotion programmes, and education activities have been the subject of the majority of these contacts. Since 1993, Slovenia has been a member of the World Health Organization, adopting its strategies and programmes, and participating in its WHO EURO projects such as the Healthy Cities Network, Healthy Schools Network, Food and Nutrition Action Plan, Health Impact Assessment of Agricultural Policy, and so on. The current major topic of collaboration with the WHO is to reform health care in Slovenia with priorities which focus on the development of health system infrastructure, quality in health care, and health-care investment. Up to 2006, Slovenia agreed health promotion arrangements with the Czech Republic, the Slovak Republic, Albania, Israel, Kuwait, the People's Republic of China, the Russian Federation, Romania, and Serbia and Montenegro. Bilateral agreements have been signed also with Flanders, Wallonia, Bavaria and with regions from the Alps-Adria Community.

Health as a key factor of social cohesion was first added to the activities of the Stability Pact for South Eastern Europe in 2000 and was followed up by the Action Plan for the Initiative on Social Cohesion in the following year. In the same year, the health ministers from the concerned countries signed the Pledge on Meeting the Needs of Vulnerable Populations from South-Eastern Europe, which revealed the partnership and co-operation in the health sector and in the provision of health services to vulnerable groups as major subjects of activity. In 2001, seven recipient countries of assistance from the Stability Pact for South Eastern Europe established the South Eastern European Health Network, which was joined by Moldova in the following year. In this framing, Slovenia – in collaboration with Greece and Hungary – turned into a donor country, thus promoting and helping to implement joint activities in recipient countries by providing technical expertise and financial assistance. The projects which have been implemented so far concerned mental health, foodstuffs' safety, communicable diseases, blood safety, tobacco control and an emergency health service (Ministry of Health, 2006).

One may conclude that Slovenia underwent a specific shift in the health sector in the period under consideration; namely, since gaining political sovereignty, she has become a member of various health organizations, adopting not only their strategies and programmes, but also their expertise and training, as well as donations. Ten years later, that is, in the early 2000s, after adopting the agenda and strategies of the Stability Pact for South Eastern Europe, Slovenia has been operating as a donor country in collaboration with Hungary and Greece, thus providing expertise and financial aid to recipient countries. Conversely, intensive international activity has failed to solve the health problems of some marginal groups at home, and particularly of those who have neither a residence permit nor citizenship.

POLICIES AGAINST POVERTY AND SOCIAL EXCLUSION

Slovenia experienced some economic decline during the 1980s, followed by an increase in unemployment in the 1990s, so that social security and standard-of-living issues attracted much criticism. In this context, the major policy breakthrough was made by adopting the Council of Europe and European Commission initiatives on eradicating poverty and social exclusion (Novak, 2005). As a result of these initiatives, various poverty and social exclusion experts, including those at the national statistical office and authors of the UNDP Human Development Report, as well as political party and civil society representatives, collaborated to prepare and comment on the National Programme to Combat Poverty and Social Exclusion. After being endorsed by the government, Parliament adopted it in the year 2000.

The programme's strategic objectives were implemented through co-ordinated action in different governmental departments, thus enabling the development of a common regulatory framework to address complex issues such as poverty and social exclusion. Further, it also constructed a framework for adopting EU standards and provided precise instructions for preparing the Joint Inclusion Memoranda and subsequent National Action Plan (NAP), obliging the government to combat poverty and social exclusion constantly with compatible sets of strategies.

Most commentators agree that Slovenia launched policies to combat poverty several years before the adoption of international initiatives. The fusion of exogenous social inclusion initiatives and indigenous poverty combating policies is evident in the documents mentioned, and can be considered as an efficient outcome of Slovenia adopting the EU standards. After implementation of the strategies in the period 2004–2006, statistical data have revealed the following shifts:

1. A decrease in the rate of registered unemployment (from 13.6 per cent in 1999 to 11.2 per cent in 2003) and the poverty incidence rate (from 13.1 per cent to 11.9 per cent in the same period).
2. An increase in the rate of those receiving social assistance (to 4.7 per cent), social care at home (to 4 per cent) and institutional care for the elderly (to 4 per cent).

Although extreme poverty and hardship have been eradicated in Slovenia, the data prove that various social groups live on the margins of society. According to the official poverty line (of EUR215 per month), approximately 4 per cent of the population is entitled to social benefits, including the homeless and Roma. Unfortunately, sporadic information on the latter prevents us from making more valid and reliable conclusions. Some sources claim that the number of homeless is approximately 700, while others claim it to be approximately 1000, based on their use of soup kitchens, shelters and other in-kind assistance. Further, census data show that approximately 6000 to 7000 Roma live in Slovenia. Additionally, some other vulnerable groups such as the poor, school dropouts, women, people with disabilities and those who live in underdeveloped areas attract also specific public and political concern when considering their living conditions and their access to significant living resources, while those who are excluded from access to residence permit and citizenship are still ignored as a major public concern.

Despite extensive political action, social inclusion policy in Slovenia still faces some key challenges in terms of targeting vulnerable groups through increasing their employability by retraining and empowering them to be more competitive on the labour market, through investment in education and the promotion of lifelong learning, and through access to decent living conditions. These strategies should be complemented by a number of measures including: reducing regional differences in access to significant living resources; improving the provision of social services; and guaranteeing a minimum standard of living by providing a minimum income and proper shelter (MoLSFA, 2004).

Similar to the unemployment sector, joint reform efforts of the government and state administration were extensively related to the EU standards and technical assistance programmes, mostly being framed by the PHARE

Consensus Programmes on family benefits and social assistance. It is significantly due to Slovenia's inclusion in the Council of Europe (CoE) and the EU that the political authorities have been made to communicate with national and international experts on issues of poverty, social exclusion and social inclusion policies. International standards of measuring poverty and social exclusion forced the political authorities and the state administration to elaborate the national circumstances and design political measures to decrease people's hardship. Since the late 1990s poverty and social exclusion, and social inclusion policies, are issues which constantly attract the interest of political actors. Moreover, hardship has finally ceased to be limited solely to poverty and bad material living conditions. Since the late 1990s, but primarily through the adoption of the Joint Inclusion Memoranda and subsequent National Action Plan, it is now considered a complex and complicated social phenomenon which has to be permanently observed and reconsidered in order to improve inclusion strategies.

CONCLUSIONS

In terms of unemployment, pensions, health and social inclusion, the impact of international actors has been somewhat uneven. The government has made a number of attempts to adapt each of these policy domains to international demands and standards when implementing strategies to transcend the economic crisis and enter the European Union. In the 1990s, pension and unemployment schemes were key issues for the government, as well as for all other critical political and civil society actors. They finally found the long-lasting expert appeals and warnings attractive enough to turn them into a subject of permanent political debate and of political bargaining and negotiation; namely, Slovenian social analysts charted negative economic and social trends, also anticipating related policy deadends. Their findings and conclusions were ignored until the mid-1990s. In 1996, the government and state administration launched a series of activities for preparing the reform in the unemployment and pension sector, and in social care and social assistance. It is fair to say that reform of the pension scheme had already started in the early 1990s, but did not gain strong political support at that time. The pension reform project attracted national and international experts, thus creating the conditions for fruitful discussions to blossom. In line with this, pension reform was a major political and social issue in the late 1990s. No other sector and reform attempts attracted national attention to a similar extent nor in comparable depth. Moreover, it proved to be the site where national and international actors found their vital interest to act and intervene. The activities have been accomplished by signing the social agreement after tough negotiations among trade unions, government and employers' representatives (the Chamber of Commerce), and by adopting the Pension Act, labelled by many as a mini-constitution, in late 1999. Its implementation started on 1 January 2000, thus guaranteeing fiscal sustainability in pensions for 15 years.

Some supranational agencies had a major part in this venture, with the most visible being the World Bank and the European Union. The World Bank provided technical assistance for pension reform preparatory works by assisting the organization of conferences, study visits, workshops and seminars for government administration to acquire the necessary expert knowledge and to enhance public awareness of the necessity for pension reform. Significant expert assistance was provided also through PHARE programme technical assistance, which was particularly significant for a critical assessment of the reform initiative. The PHARE experts co-ordinated the pension preparatory works, while operational tasks were left to be executed by the national team. Financial support from PHARE contributed to programmes increasing national awareness and making a breakthrough in adopting the reform strategies on a national scale. Significant technical assistance was provided also by the ILO whose experts closely collaborated with the Slovene state administration.

In the process of adapting the unemployment sector to the EU standards and best international practice, Slovenian political authorities were particularly attracted by the activation policy strategies implemented in Denmark. In line with this, the ILO standards in surveying unemployment matched efficiently the related national standards (registered unemployment) being supported by EU demands on tightening the unemployment policy through increasing re-employment.

In other social policy sectors under consideration, the open and manifest collaboration with international and supranational agents was less evident, being carried out more in terms of adopting programme strategies than changing profoundly the policy prescriptions. In these respects, the standards of international health organizations helped Slovenia to adapt its strategies, programmes, expertise and training, and to begin to be a donor agency. In the framework of the Stability Pact for South East Europe, Slovenia turned from being a recepient country in the 1990s to a donor country ten years later.

The inclusion of Slovenia, first among the member countries of the Council of Europe and then of the European Community, has forced the national political authorities also to accept international standards for combating poverty and social exclusion, thus finally leaving behind their policy of ignorance of these subjects. The CoE and the EU social inclusion policy compelled the Slovene government and its administration to launch a series of activities to elaborate this issue in close collaboration with national and international experts, social partners and civil society. Further, by adopting the EU standards in this field, the government was forced to monitor properly and regularly the impact of social inclusion policies.

Summing up, various international and supranational agencies have had a significant part to play in reforming Slovene social policy strategies and social protection schemes. In this frame, their influence can be described as being that of welcome mentors and consultants who have been obliged to respect Slovene-specific national conditions and relatively high social protection standards. However, some supranational agencies suggested to the political authorities that social expenditures should be radically cut in order to make the national economy's performance more competitive on the global scale. Even though they may have attracted some over-heated followers – particularly among a young generation of neo-liberal economic scholars – these suggestions have never been fully applied to political strategies. As is frequently proved by extensive empirical evidence, political strategies have changed according to new political options and paradigms. Conversely, despite many successful attempts, the social policy paradigm is still dominated by the Bismarckian welfare model, though its fabric may be slowly but constantly fading away.

REFERENCES

De la Porte, C. and B. Deacon (2002), 'Contracting companies and consultants: the EU and the social policy of accession countries', *GASPP Occasional Paper*, Helsinki, www.gaspp.org.

European Commission (EC) (2006a), *The Long-term Sustainability of Public Finances in the European Union*, http://ec.europa.eu/economy_finance/publications/european_ economy/2006/ee406_en.pdf (accessed 23 July 2006).

European Commission (EC) (2006b), *Synthesis Report on Adequate and Sustainable Pensions*, http://ec.europa.eu/employment_social/social_protection/docs/2006/sec_2006_304_en.pdf (accessed 20 July 2006).

Fultz, E. (2004), Authorised personal communication, 3 August.

Humblet, M. and M. Silva (2002), *Standards for the XXIst Century: Social Security*, Geneva: ILO Publications.

Ignjatovic, M., A. Kopac, I. Svetlik and M. Trbanc (2002), 'Slovenia's navigation through turbulent transition', in J. Goul Andersen, J. Clasen, W. van Oorschot and K. Halvarson (eds), *Europe's New State of Welfare. Unemployment, Employment and Citizenship*, Bristol: Policy Press, pp. 195–217.

Ministry of Health of the Republic of Slovenia (2006), 'International co-operation', http://www2.gov.si/mz (accessed 13 April 2006).

Ministry of Labour, Family and Social Affairs of the Republic of Slovenia (MoLSFA) (2004), *National Action Plan on Social Inclusion (2004–2006) – NAP 2004*, Ljubljana: Ministrstvo za delo, druzino in socialne zadeve.

Ministry of Labour, Family and Social Affairs of the Republic of Slovenia (MoLSFA) (2005), *Republic of Slovenia National Strategy Report on Adequate and Sustainable Pensions*, http://ec.europa.eu/employment_social/social_protection/ docs/2005/si_en.pdf (accessed 23 May 2006).

Ministry of Labour, Family and Social Affairs of the Republic of Slovenia (MoLSFA) (2006), *Prvo letno porocilo o izvajanju Nacionalnega akcijskega načrta o socialnem vključevanju 2004–2006 (First Annual Report on National Action Plan on Social Inclusion 2004–2006)* – *NAP Report*, Ljubljana: Ministrstvo za delo, družino in socialne zadeve.

Novak, M. (2000), 'Old social risks in a new light: the old age', *Druzboslovne razprave*, **16** (32–33), 289–303.

Novak, M. (2001), 'Reconsidering the socialist welfare state model', in A. Woodward and M. Kohli (eds), *Inclusions and Exclusions in European Societies*, London: Routledge, pp. 111–26.

Novak, M. (2005), 'Building social inclusion strategies in Slovenia through co-ordinated action: from national poverty and social exclusion Combating Programme to social inclusion National Action Plan', paper presented at UN MDG Conference, Vilnius, Lithuania, April.

Oksanen, H. (2004), 'Fairness across generations requires partial funding', in OECD, *Reforming Public Pensions: Sharing the Experiences of Transition and OECD Countries*, Paris: OECD Publications.

Rihar Bajuk, K. (2004), 'Reform of the pension systems in selected Central and Eastern European Countries: case studies of Hungary and Slovenia', MA dissertation, Roskilde University, Denmark.

Stanovnik, T. (2002), 'The political economy of pension reform in Slovenia', in E. Fultz (ed.), *Pension Reform in Central and Eastern Europe – Volume 2: Restructuring of Public Pension Schemes: Case Studies of the Czech Republic and Slovenia*, Geneva: ILO Publications.

Vodopivec, M. (1996), 'The Slovenian labour market in transition: empirical analysis based on data on individuals', in OECD, *Lessons from Labour Market Policies in Transition Countries*, Paris: OECD, pp. 269–311.

World Bank (2000), *Republic of Slovenia: Country Assistance Strategy – Progress Report*, Washington, DC: World Bank.

Wright, S., A. Kopac and G. Slater (2004), 'Continuities within paradigmatic change', *European Societies*, **6** (4), 511–34.

4. Bulgaria and Romania

Dimitri A. Sotiropoulos and Luana Pop

INTRODUCTION

Bulgaria and Romania share many similarities with other post-communist South East European countries, but also differ from them. In the 1990s neither country experienced war, as ex-Yugoslavia (1991–95), or state collapse, as Albania (1997). Both Bulgaria and Romania share historical legacies and exposure to the neo-liberal model of economic and social reform as the rest of SEE countries. In addition, the two countries were recently subjected to similar pressures in the form of requirements to join the EU. Bulgaria and Romania offer examples of typical problems faced by social policy in post-communist societies where welfare reforms were 'usually "second (or third) generation" reforms in the broad structural adjustment agenda' (Nelson, 2001: 236). This means that in each country such reforms were dependent on the state of the economy as a whole and that they were attempted later in the 1990s (Hausner, 2001; Nelson, 2001). After the watershed of 1989 economic growth plummeted and when it started rising again the 'welfare effort' of these countries did not follow suit. Welfare state retrenchment hit hardest the most vulnerable categories of the population, such as children and ethnic minorities (Deacon, 2000; Kornai et al., 2001; Sotiropoulos et al., 2003). Wages dropped sharply after 1989 and did not start recovering before the beginning of the current decade, a trend which is more visible in Romania than in Bulgaria. Unemployment was on the rise in Bulgaria for most of the 1990s and is still higher than in Romania. Income inequality rose sharply in both countries after 1989, was high in the mid-1990s and remains at high levels today.

Bulgaria and Romania are ahead of the rest of SEE countries in terms of welfare indicators. In terms of the Human Development Index (HDI), Bulgaria ranks third, below Slovenia and Croatia. Romania ranks fifth below Slovenia, Croatia, Macedonia, and Bulgaria. In terms of GDP per capita measured in purchasing power parities (PPP) Bulgaria ranks third, again below Slovenia and Croatia, whereas Romania ranks fourth below Slovenia, Croatia and Bulgaria. Both countries applied for membership in

1995 and started accession negotiations in 2000. Since January 2007, when Bulgaria and Romania joined the EU, they have been under a regime of special governance: as was the case with the ten new members which joined the EU in spring 2004, the EU has kept for itself the right to use safeguard mechanisms in order 'to ensure the smooth accession of Bulgaria and Romania' (European Commission, 2006c). The mechanisms were called 'safeguard clauses' and were included in a June 2005 Protocol of the Treaty of Accession of Bulgaria and Romania. There were three types of clauses: a general clause to cover for economic difficulties, an internal market clause to facilitate adaptation to EU markets, and a justice and home affairs clause to remedy shortcomings in co-operation in civil and criminal matters. In addition, in the case of Bulgaria and Romania, specific provisions included a control on the management of structural funds channelled to the two countries; another control system in regard to payments to farmers and rural development expenditures; and a mechanism to verify progress in judiciary reform and the fight against corruption.

Despite such constraints, it is noteworthy that less than 20 years ago it was unimaginable that one day Bulgaria and Romania would join the EU and experiment with different welfare models. Before 1989 in Bulgaria and Romania the state offered full and free health coverage to all citizens, but the quality of medical and hospital services was very uneven. After 1989 the public health service steadily deteriorated. The downturn of the economy in both countries dampened health expenditures (Deacon, 1992: 6, based on UNDP data). Also before 1989 there was a comprehensive, pay-as-you-go pension system which provided Bulgarians and Romanians with state pensions, which, however, reflected social status inequalities. After 1989 pensions continued to obtain the largest share of social expenditure. Handing out pensions was a practice of post-communist Bulgarian and Romanian governments, aimed to cover the social costs of economic restructuring (closing down or privatization of public enterprises). However, owing to the economic crisis, which became particularly acute in Bulgaria in 1997, pensions lost a lot of their purchasing power.

In the late 1990s under the influence of the IMF and the WB government policy in both countries switched to a three-pillar system in pension provision. The three pillars consist of (a) a mandatory PAYG system, (b) a compulsory, privately managed, social insurance fund based on capitalization and (c) a voluntary system organized along private insurance lines and stimulated by various policy measures. In parallel both governments raised the minimum retirement age in order to address the financial deficits of the pension system.

It is commonplace to argue that in the enlargement process the EU has been much less concerned about welfare development than about other aspects of progress required from candidate countries, including macroeconomic stabilization and justice and home affairs improvement. This trend reflects larger EU priorities, affecting older member states too. For instance, the European Social Model has been under constant attack by both neo-liberal and 'Third Way' European politicians (Vaughan-Whitehead, 2003). European Union assessments of the situation of individual Balkan countries make only a passing reference to the social *acquis*. To some extent, this may be due to the underdevelopment of a common European Social Policy. On the one hand, it can be argued that social policy has been a recurrent concern of the EU, which is integrated in documents ranging from the Treaty of Rome (1957) to the Treaty of Nice (2001) and is evident in the breadth of the relevant legislation (Falkner, 2006: 81–2, 95; Vaughan-Whitehead, 2003: 3–6). However, in EU policy-making there is still an imbalance between the values of economic competitiveness and social cohesion. Both values appear in EU documents, such as the Treaty of Amsterdam (1997). In reality, member states of the EU feel the pressure to keep the balance between the two aforementioned values mostly because of the mobilization of domestic collective actors, such as political parties, trade unions and social movements. Candidate member states do not feel such strong pressure either from their weak civil societies or from the EU (Deacon et al., 1997: 91–2). For example, in 2005 and 2006, the European Commission was concerned only with a few areas of the Bulgarian and the Romanian social protection systems.

In Bulgaria there is visible improvement in only one out of the several sub-areas of social policy monitored by the European Commission (European Commission, 2005; 2006a). This is the sub-area of the management of the European Social Fund (ESF), where the Bulgarian government has been able to recruit staff and train civil servants. In the sub-area of social dialogue there are persisting problems of representation of the social partners, as the impartiality of the government's interlocutors is doubted (European Commission, 2006a). In health services, problems continue and are acute, particularly in the less developed regions and among the poorer social strata. A new commission against discrimination is suffering from lack of staff and administrative co-ordination. And last but not least, the European Commission finds 'the basic conditions in the institutions caring for the elderly, the physically and mentally handicapped and the children appalling' (European Commission, 2006a: 28).

In Romania the European Commission calls for new labour legislation to cover for collective redundancies, part-time and fixed-time work, and the European Works Councils (European Commission, 2006b). In the rest of sub-areas of social policy there is the familiar trend of introducing new institutions. Two institutions created in 2002 were the National Agency for

Employment and the National Anti-Poverty and Promotion of Social Exclusion Plan. New institutions, such as the Social Inspection Agency, have recently been designed. Persisting problems include health and safety gaps, discrimination against the Roma and lack of co-ordination among welfare agencies. People with disabilities do not have equal access either to education or to the labour market and still encounter problems in physically accessing buildings. The Commission also evaluates negatively the treatment of people with disabilities in residential institutions. Last but not least the Commission notes that the situation in the 'equal treatment of women and men has deteriorated' (European Commission, 2006b: 30).

In this chapter we discuss welfare institutions and policies in a framework combining the approach of the school of global social policy actors (Deacon et al., 1997) with the approach of 'soft' historical institutionalism. In the context of this approach, we adopt a broad definition of 'institutions' in order to include not only international and domestic organizations, but also new pieces of legislation, government commissions and reform plans. In the remaining sections of this chapter we present trends in social policy, first for Bulgaria and then for Romania. We emphasize the impact of pressures coming from domestic collective actors and international organizations. Our survey of organizations and policies is not exhaustive. For each country we very briefly present examples of social assistance, child-care, pension, health-care and unemployment policies. We conclude that in both countries international influences and domestic pressures seem to have contributed to a very uneven welfare regime of social protection, containing loopholes and unable to counter the adverse social effects of post-communist capitalism.

BULGARIA

Transition to Democracy and the Formulation of Social Policy in Bulgaria

Since 1989, Bulgaria has gone through a period of transition marked by economic, fiscal and institutional reform. What distinguishes the Bulgarian transition from the Romanian one is the process of social pacts and 'Round Table' discussions. These were introduced in the beginning of the 1990s, took place among political and social collective actors and resulted in a series of political and institutional reforms. However, throughout the 1990s welfare reform was constrained by economic and political conditions. In Bulgaria as in most other post-communist countries many sub-areas of

Table 4.1   The evolution of public social expenditure as percentage of
GDP in Bulgaria, 1996–2003

	Pension system	Unemployment	Social security and assistance	Health
1996	6.9	0.4	1.6	3.1
1997	6.2	0.7	2.6	3.6
1998	8.1	0.7	2.5	3.6
1999	8.2	1.0	3.1	3.9
2000	9.5	0.7	4.0	3.7
2001	9.1	0.8	3.7	4.0
2002	9.1	0.6	3.7	4.4
2003	9.2	1.7	2.5	4.9

Source: Government of Bulgaria and the European Commission (2005), Statistical
Annexes, table 4, p. 53, on the basis of data of the Bulgarian National Statistical Institute
(not compatible with ESSPROS nomenclature). There is no data on expenses in education
in this EU document.

social policy, such as child care, have undergone little change, while other
public policies have experienced considerable transformations (Deacon,
2000; Stubbs, 2001).

After 1989 major traits of the Bulgarian welfare state included the
passage from a de-commodifying to a less de-commodifying system and
from a universalistic social protection system to a system including
assessment-based provisions; the continuing strong influence of the communist elite, which stayed in power under the cover of the Bulgarian
Socialist Party; and the adherence to socialist values within the public
administration. Over time in the 1990s the welfare state proved unable to
provide coverage for the categories of the population hit by privatizations
and rising unemployment. People resorted to their family networks and to
informal care to cover for the lack of a comprehensive welfare system.
When in the late 1990s welfare spending increased, pensions took up an
increasing share of it. As Table 4.1 shows, since the late 1990s public social
expenditure in Bulgaria has been almost equally divided between pension
expenses, on the one hand, and all other social protection expenses, including health, unemployment and social assistance expenses, on the other.
Pensions clearly consumed by far the largest share of welfare state expenses.
Health expenses increased gradually and reached a peak in 2000–2003, but
in proportional terms were always less than half the corresponding pension
expenses. Unemployment and social assistance expenses clearly lagged
behind pension and health expenses.

Before 1989 the state was the only relevant institution in charge of welfare provision. Currently in Bulgaria, as in other post-communist societies, the state is no longer the single welfare decision-maker and provider. International organizations also play a crucial role, primarily in the implementation of projects, but also in policy-making (Table 4.2).

Until the mid-1990s, the IMF, the WB and the ILO competed to gain influence over the shaping of social security and social assistance in Bulgaria. Communist-led trade unions resisted changes promoted by neo-liberal consultants. The country faced a dilemma between post-communist conservatism and antisocial liberalism (Deacon et al., 1997).

Major Trends and Current Situation of Bulgarian Social Policy

Today the dilemma is probably solved in favour of neo-liberalism. Still the situation seems inchoate, as in various policy areas international organizations diffuse their own agendas, while the influence of the EU has grown, as a result of Bulgaria's decision to apply for EU membership. For example, in the area of social assistance, the WB, the UNDP and the EU heavily influenced aspects of Bulgarian policy-making, including poverty measurement, management of relevant funds and the design of poverty alleviation plans (Table 4.2). In the past, international organizations focused on vulnerable groups, women, minorities and underdeveloped regions. Recently, new international pressures have been put on Bulgaria to deal with gaps in social assistance. For instance, there is a new Commission for Protection Against Discrimination, founded in November 2005; and a new National Plan for the Fight Against Poverty and Social Exclusion, drafted in April 2006 (European Commission, 2006a: 28–9). Social assistance became targeted and there was a shift from ad hoc social assistance, characterized by sporadic measures (cash benefits, provision of coal in the winter months) to a more neo-liberal residualist approach (Sotiropoulos, 2005: 283).

Child care was another area where international organizations, such as the WB, UNICEF, the EU and specialized NGOs, played an important role in shaping policy (Table 4.2). These organizations pressed for the reform of institutionalized child care and provided expertise, training and help with the design of alternative schemes. Owing to pressures from local and international NGOs the human rights of children obtained prominence in the child-care discourse (Stubbs, 2001). However, a lot of policy formulation remains 'dead letter'. In this and other policy areas, when an Act is passed in Parliament, there are no accompanying guidelines for its implementation and no accompanying programme of action. The new Public Education Act (adopted in 1991 and amended in 2002), the Social Assistance Act

Table 4.2 International actors in Bulgaria: main areas of social policy advice and assistance

	WB/IMF	EU (EC/EAR)	UN (UNDP, UNICEF)	ILO	Bilateral agencies
Strategic frameworks	Country assistance strategies (until 2004); country partnership strategies (beginning in 2004)	EU *acquis*; Joint Inclusion Memorandum	MDGs, human development approach	Decent work country programme	
Labour market institutions and policies	Labour force survey; design of passive and active labour policies (WB)	Freedom of movement; equal pay for equal work	Capacity-building especially at the municipal and district level; protection of minorities	Labour standards; better working environment for vulnerable groups; strengthening representation by social partners; improvement of social dialogue	Improvement of government and local capacity (DFID)
Child care	WB Child Welfare Reform project; reform of child-care institutions; introduction of alternative child-care schemes	Influence on child-friendly legislation; provision of expertise in child care; training of child-care professionals	Technical assistance with childcare institutions; preventive work (UNICEF)		Projects of the NGO, 'Save the Children UK' in Bulgaria
Social assistance	Poverty measurement;	Assistance with and monitoring of the	Development of policy documents		In view of Bulgaria's EU

				accession, support of a 'pro-poor accession process' (DFID)
	social assistance reforms for minorities; improvement of capacity of ministries and local authorities; technical assistance to absorb EU funds	management of EU's structural funds; help with new plan to fight poverty and social exclusion; and new plan for the equal treatment of women and protection of minorities	and projects aimed at vulnerable groups and economically underdeveloped regions; poverty reduction; equitable local and regional development	
Pensions	Advocacy, design and elaboration of three pillar system			
Health	Financial and logistical support and advice for reform design		Assistance with lowering infant and maternal mortality rates; HIV/AIDS prevention; expansion of health-education curriculum	

(adopted in 1998) and the Child Protection Act (2000) are examples of the pattern of inconsistency between official pronouncements and actual developments (Sotiropoulou and Sotiropoulos, 2007).

In the area of pensions the influence of the IMF and the WB was evident in the design of a new three pillar system (Table 4.2). A new institution, called 'State Insurance Supervision Agency', was created in order to oversee the new system (Sotiropoulos et al., 2003). In 2003 another institution, called the 'Financial Supervisory Commission' (FSC) was created in order to supervise investment and insurance companies as well as pension funds. The FSC was more independent from the government than previous commissions. The new three-pillar system was meant to replace the existing PAYG system which had accumulated a large debt. In 2006, it was estimated that the PAYG system's debt was growing by 0.2 per cent of GDP per year and that the Bulgarian government would be unable to bridge the gap between revenues and expenditures as far as pensions were concerned. The reason for this estimation was that fewer people enter the system than before and that in the new system the private pillar is 11 times smaller than the PAYG system (Stanchev, 2006: 96–7).

In regard to health care, the WB and the IMF played an important role in the design of a new privatized system, while the UNDP promoted policies to lower infant and maternal mortality, to prevent the spread of AIDS/HIV and to change the health-care education curriculum (Table 4.2). The privatization of health care was accompanied by the foundation of a national agency, the National Health Insurance Fund in 1999. The fund was to oversee the management of public hospitals, contract out health services to private companies and negotiate with the medical profession. The reform met with implementation problems and resistance by sectoral interests and was delayed by the lack of political will to push through the new measures.

In regard to unemployment and labour markets, international organizations, such as the WB, the UNDP, the ILO and the DFID, addressed various problems. For example the UNDP focused on capacity-building, while the ILO promoted better working environment of vulnerable groups and representation of social partners in decision-making (Table 4.2). The aim towards which many organizations converged was to facilitate Bulgaria's accession to the EU.

All initiatives in the aforementioned policy areas experienced problems of implementation. In order to understand the seriousness of these problems, which often render new policies 'dead letter', suffice to say that all types of welfare institutions should be co-ordinated by the Ministry of Labour and Social Policy. This ministry is primarily responsible for formulating policy and managing the welfare state in Bulgaria. In practice this is difficult to achieve, owing to the abundance of competent entities. For example, a total of 1256 governmental, local governmental and non-governmental organizations are involved in the delivery of social services. In regard to employment policy, there is a central employment agency which runs 19 national employment projects and oversees nine regional centres, 120 local bureaus as well as municipalities and NGOs working with minorities and people with disabilities (Bulgarian Position Paper, 2006).

Policy Outcomes

The impact of social policy reforms in Bulgaria should be interpreted in the context of the larger picture of Bulgarian society. The Bulgarian population is ageing. In 2000–2005 the average annual population growth was negative (−0.85 per cent), while approximately 22 per cent of the population was aged 60 years and above. Over time a significant part of the Bulgarian labour force was out of work. In 1995–2002 the annual unemployment rate averaged 15.3 per cent (The Economist, 2005: 122). Changes brought about in Bulgarian social policy by international and domestic influences did not amount to a dramatic improvement in social protection. This is evident in the low level of salaries and social assistance benefits. For instance, in 2002 manual workers working at a sewing machine earned on the average 50 euros per month, primary school teachers 110 euros and civil servants 150 euros. Poor families with children, if eligible, received a monthly benefit of 7.5 euros (Sotiropoulos, 2005: 282–3). It is no wonder that in 1996–99 on average, in terms of income inequality, Bulgaria was the most unequal among all Central European and SEE countries (World Bank, 2000: 140, table 4.1). To take another example, since the mid-1990s the condition of children in Bulgaria has improved, but problems remain. In 2003 infant mortality rate was 12.3 per 1000 live births, while in 2002 the mortality rate for children under 5 was 17.1 per 1000 live births (World Bank, 2005). Finally, there is a continuing polarization between high-income and low-income groups. The wealthiest group of the population reaps a large share of the income created in the informal sector of the economy, while in 2005 the share of the population below the poverty line was 13 per cent (World Bank, 2006). Most disadvantaged population categories included low-skill workers and members of minorities.

To sum up the situation in Bulgaria, the state is no longer the single welfare provider. International organizations are coming to play a decisive role, primarily in the implementation of projects and in policy-making. The delayed development of the social policy in post-communist Bulgaria has led to a welfare system containing loopholes and has been accompanied by a burst of local, national and international institutions formulating and implementing welfare measures. Nevertheless, poverty and inequality persist. Currently, the single most important problem is the inadequate implementation of social policy, to which we will return towards the end of this chapter.

ROMANIA

Transition to Democracy and the Formulation of Social Policies in Romania

The institutionalization of social policy in Romania during the transition to democracy, and its impact upon policy outcomes, differed from the rest of former socialist countries. Unlike Bulgaria or other CEE countries, Romania 'did not enjoy a completely non-violent path of transition to a democratic form of government' (Elster et al., 1998: 55). Its extrication path differed from that of other countries mainly because of the lack of any form of social pact or Round Table talks. In Romania presumably the main cause of this different starting point was the personal dictatorship of Ceauşescu (Ibid.: 55). However, we suggest that in the process of policy for-mulation Romania was rather exposed to various contingencies and individual initiatives of policy-makers rather than to major structural con-strains and legitimate constituencies.

As a consequence new social policy legislation was adopted in the context of a 'logic of pressures' rather than as a result of any consistent cal-culation of social needs and risks. Social policies were articulated as a response to internal pressures exerted especially by trade unions (Zamfir, 1999; 2002). Union leaders were selected from among cadres, that is, former enterprise engineers or economists (Flonta, 1999). In the early 1990s their power was particularly enhanced by social movements, such as the trade union movement in the mining sector which also served specific political purposes.[1] Thus in the first years of transition, Romanian governments focused mostly on regulating employment protection and on creating a framework for protecting the unemployed, assisted by the ILO and the IMF. Compared to all other countries in the region, Romania showed a delayed start and a slow rhythm in adopting new legislation in the field of social policy. Until 1995 there was no important new social policy legisla-tion, with the single exception of the universalization of child allowance (in 1993). The same held true for health care and education. New regulations in these policy areas responded to immediate necessities, and legislation was scattered. Since the mid-1990s the significance of trade unions drasti-cally decreased. Workers became the main losers of the transition (Zamfir, 2004), although they preserved to some extent their power to negotiate

Table 4.3   *The evolution of public social expenditure as percentage of GDP in Romania, 1997–2004*

	Pension system	Unemployment	Social assistance	Health	Education	Total
1997	5.4	1.3	1.2	2.6	3.3	15.9
1998	5.8	1.4	1.3	3.5	3.3	17.3
1999	6.9	1.5	0.9	3.8	3.8	18.4
2000	6.4	1.2	0.7	3.7	3.1	17.2
2001	6.5	0.8	0.8	4.0	3.2	18.2
2002	7.3	0.7	1.2	4.0	3.6	18.1
2003	7.0	0.8	1.0	4.1	3.9	18.4
2004*	7.4	0.8	3.3	n.a.	4.1	19.4

Note: * Projection; n.a.=not available; not all types of social expenditure are included.

Source: Government of Romania and the European Commission (2005), Statistical Annexes, table 3, p. 82, based on data from the Romanian Ministry of Public Finances.

policy outcomes. After the mid-1990s expenditures on pensions and health increased (Table 4.3). At the same time external pressures, for example, pressures from international organizations, started gaining more ground.

The impact of various international actors upon policy arrangements has been variable. Some organizations had a direct impact upon specific policy measures (see Table 4.4 for the WB's influence in the field of social assistance, the ILO's contribution to employment policies and UNICEF's involvement in the field of child-care reform in the late 1990s). Other international organizations had a direct impact on framework legislation rather than on specific programmes (for example, the International Bank for Reconstruction and Development [IBRD], EU). Other actors, such as USAID or DFID, international NGOs and consultancy firms, had a higher impact on local expertise than on designing legislation.[2] Most international organizations have refocused their activities towards capacity-building (monitoring, administrative capacity, expertise), while being more reticent regarding changes of the content of policies. Most probably this trend helped with Romania's EU accession process and helped overcome the different points of view of the several agencies involved.

While domestic pressures focused on salary increases and claims regarding various benefits and rights,[3] the consequences of external pressures were more differentiated and can be summarized as follows: (a) in some cases, new laws, which had been adopted under the influence of international organizations, were never enforced, as if they would not exist all,

Table 4.4 International actors in Romania: main areas of social policy advice and assistance

	WB/IMF	EU (EC/EAR)	UN (UNDP, UNICEF)	ILO	Bilateral agencies (DFID, USAID)
Strategic frameworks	Country assistance strategies (until 2004); Country partnership strategies (beginning in 2004)	EU *acquis*; Joint Inclusion Memorandum	MDG/Human Development Framework; UN Development Assistance Framework (based on the Common Country Assessment); UNICEF country programme	Decent Work Country Programme	
Labour market/ unemployment policies	Technical and financial support for development of unemployment mitigation measures in mining areas	Technical and financial support (PHARE) for: – gender equality – incentive measures	Promoting employment generating activities, social dialogue, work condition improvement for vulnerable groups: Roma, rural women, youth, low-income workers; supporting capacity-building at local level	Promotion and technical/ capacity-building support for implementing: – decent work standards – end of child labour – gender equality in work	

Child care	Technical/financial assistance for Early Childhood Education Development for Roma; financial/technical support for the reforms in child care (IBRID)	Development of integrated community services for children; abandonment prevention; and technical assistance for capacity-building at the central level (PHARE)	UNICEF: capacity-building (through spreading out best practice and excellence models) and financial support for de-institutionalization of children; capacity building for monitoring children's rights	Technical support for monitoring child labour; and identification of risks for child labour exploitation	Technical/financial support and expertise for improving the legislation; setting accreditation standards for NGOs and capacity building (DFID); information systems for monitoring child care (USAID)
Social assistance (including family and child benefits and services)	Advocacy and assistance for the adoption, revitalization and improvement of a MIG scheme; advocacy for better targeted family benefits; direct influence on the social legislation regarding financial decentralization through conditionality/triggers	Influence on the legislation concerning the social protection of the elderly; advocacy for the extension of family benefit network; capacity-building at the local level – for social inclusion of Roma; support for social service improvements in the social protection of the elderly	Capacity building; improving local social services for: – vulnerable groups – underserved areas in order to support poverty reduction and equal access to quality services		Support for strategic reforms in the field of energy (heating and electricity) production and distribution (USAID); capacity-building at the local level for delivering of social programmes (DFID)

Table 4.4 (continued)

	WB/IMF	EU (EC/EAR)	UN (UNDP, UNICEF)	ILO	Bilateral agencies (DFID, USAID)
Pensions	Advocacy for additional private-administrated and occupational pension systems; support for enhancing the institutional capacity to correlate formerly awarded pensions in line with those awarded after 2001			Advocacy/ technical support for gender equality within the pension system	
Health	Technical/ financial support for the health reform; direct influence upon the decentralization of health care	Financial support for the reform of the health system (PHARE funds)	Capacity-building and expertise support for: − HIV/AIDS prevention − nutritional awareness − maternal care	Advocacy and support for prevention of HIV/AIDS at the workplace	HIV/AIDS and TBC prevention and social inclusion of infested children (USAID)

whereas in other cases their implementation was delayed;[4] and (b) other laws failed to become operative, owing to the lack of administrative capacity to support the new policy measures.[5] Thus, some pieces of legislation 'died' naturally, while other pieces continued to impose some direction of action on implementing agents, without being supported even by their initiators. The 'luckiest' pieces of the relevant legislation are still functional but run a 'blind' course, as monitoring and assessment capacities are not inbuilt in Romanian welfare institutions responsible for providing services and benefits.

Some important consequences of the aforementioned 'pressure logic' in the process of policy making in Romania were the following: (1) a highly inconsistent legislation, sometimes insensitive to actual local needs, sometimes incompatible with local institutions and unsupported by local administrative arrangements and capacity; (2) the emergence of extra-institutional decision-making channels, functioning in parallel to, if not in conflict with, the corresponding legitimate democratic channels,[6] leading to lack of transparency in policy-making, high exposure to corruption and the further weakening of democratic institutions, and (3) internal and external pressures on policy-making and implementation which favoured the development of a haphazard integration of internal policy networks rather than an integration process which could have supported decentralization and effective policy implementation. The instability of actors and policy networks, due to the incessant abolishing, refurbishing and redefining of the organizations involved in social policy, also had adverse effects on policy implementation (Pop, 2003; 2005).

Major Trends and Current Situation of Romanian Social Policy

In Romania social services developed slowly, since they required not only a high involvement of local actors, but also the emergence of expert systems and complex financial and accountability mechanisms. By contrast, schemes for cash benefits were less problematic to design, and reforms in this area were more easily and widely accepted all over the CEE (Nelson, 2001: 237). Romania was no exception. A first conclusion is that the most underdeveloped areas in social protection are those which mostly rely on social services including child care, social integration of the disabled, community services for the elderly and other disadvantaged groups.

Child care represented one of the most disputed areas of reform. The reform of institutionalized child care began in 1997, by the creation of a national agency assigned to design framework legislation and unify the scattered services provided to institutionalized children. The legislation was mainly the product of pressure exerted by various international agencies and NGOs. It led to the adoption of imported programmes,[7] which brought about the slowing down of reforms. In addition the reform promoted financial and decisional decentralization, although there was not adequate institutional capacity at the local level. Both the content and institutional environment hindered the development of an effective strategy for reforming child-care institutions.

In the area of social security reforms most delays were encountered when policies were highly dependent on the state of the economy and costs were significantly high (for example, in the pension reform). Delays occurred, despite the fact that, under the high pressure of international agencies, acceptance of the need for reform was widespread. The first major step in reforming the Romanian pension system was taken in 2001, when the formula by which the benefit level used to be calculated was modified. The new formula better reflected the correlation between the contribution level during the whole career period of an individual and the level of the pension he or she would receive at the end of his or her career. A first consequence of this step was a substantial lowering of pensions for those to be retired. The introduction of the new system still creates equity problems as it involves a complex mechanism of re-correlation of pensions calculated before 2001.

The law regarding privately administrated public pension funds (second pillar) was passed in 2004 and was followed (in 2005) by a framework legislation regarding the creation, organization and functioning of the Monitoring Commission of the Private Pension Systems. In 2006 a law on individual and occupational pensions was passed (the third pillar). Yet the implementation of both laws has been delayed, as the procedure of accrediting administrators for private pension funds is still in progress. Thus the implementation process of the second and third pillars of the pension system is still in the beginning stage. Overall, however, the Romanian pension system reform fits the CEE reform pattern which has been inspired by the WB. Compared with other categories of the Romanian population, pensioners still have the lowest poverty incidence. However, in the near future the actual problems faced by the traditional pension system (high dependency ratio, low coverage of rural population) will generate insurmountable difficulties.

In 1997 universal health care was replaced by an insurance-based system (financed through a separate fund – the National Health Insurance Fund). In addition, a family, physician-based primary health-care system, comparable to the UK system, was introduced. The purpose of this reorganization was to increase the transparency of health expenditures and to improve accountability for expenditures in the different health-care sectors in order to improve the quality of health services and access to primary health care. The system was based on extended financial decentralization and on the presumption of the separation of medical and management activities. Yet the lack of specific regulations regarding tasks, competences and control over various new institutional actors led to a financial re-centralization of the system, thus making the management of a nationwide, insurance-based, health-care service difficult. Despite the increase in health expenditures over time (Table 4.3), primary health care is still marked by unequal access. In public hospitals the relationship between quantity/quality of services and financing is still lacking transparency.

In Romania, as in the rest of CEE countries, reforms of social assistance and family benefits have followed a neo-liberal logic (Deacon et al., 1997: 91–103). The reforms aimed at offering minimal social protection to beneficiaries, while adhering to an austerity state budget and reducing fiscal burdens. Compared with most former socialist countries, in Romania there were delays in reforms of social assistance and family benefits. The average level of most social benefits decreased in real terms (due to purchasing power erosion), while eligibility was limited and benefits were targeted to lower income deciles. Targeted social assistance benefits were adopted. A mechanism of MIG was put in place in 1995. Its financing and targeting mechanisms improved in 2001 and again in 2006. Categorical family benefits – first introduced in 1997 and directed towards families with two or more children – were limited to low-income families in 2004.

Since 2002 unemployment benefits have been offered on a flat-rate basis and the eligibility period has been made dependent on the length of the contribution period. Trade unions opposed some of these new measures, especially in regard to unemployment, insurance-based benefits. Voices of protest rose against the flat-rate benefit system, as contributions were linked to income. A similar dispute erupted around the flat-rate character of the insurance-based leave allowance provided to employed parents with children until the age of 2, who are part of the social insurance system.[8] Despite some resistance, the reforms eventually went on mainly because many realized the problematic state of the Romanian economy. The direction which such social assistance and social insurance reforms have taken has led to a peculiar form of redistributive policy: categorical benefits, tested through income criteria, coexist with a social insurance system that shows social assistance traits.

On the one hand, the coverage and level of benefits decreased, while social contributions and taxes were maintained at a high level.[9] On the other hand, pressure on social expenditure increased even more, as the employment rate decreased and the number of pensioners increased. Compared with Bulgaria, Romania spent less on pensions (as a share of GDP) and showed a tendency towards targeted benefits. The combination of these patterns with high social contributions and a predominance of social insurance was a rather unpopular combination. It consisted of high net costs as compared to benefits and was made possible by the strength of the government's power over a weak parliament as well as by the combination of pressures exerted by various internal and external actors (Pop, 2003).

Policy Outcomes

The impact of social policy reforms has to be assessed against the occupational structure of Romanian society. During the transition we witnessed a constant decrease of the number of employees from 8.1 million in 1990 to less than 4.5 million in 2003 (Institution Naţional de Statistică, 2004), an increase in the number of pensioners (from a total of 3.6 million in 1990 to 6.3 million in 2003) and a low incidence of salaried work in rural areas, as the share of full-time employees in agriculture decreased from 4.4 per cent in 1998 to 2.7 per cent in 2003 (Pop, 2006).

Since 2000 there has been a high social polarization between low-consumption and high-consumption groups. This polarization is due to a sharp decrease of salary income, combined with a significant increase of social benefits as a share of the total income of the poorest households. Despite the fact that since 2000 overall poverty rates have decreased, the gaps among various risk categories have become deeper. Most disadvantaged population categories include households with three or more children, single-parent households, households with at least one disabled person and households headed by women (Preda et al., 2006). Moreover, Roma communities are characterized by a high incidence of long-term poverty. Finally, despite improvements in most indicators measuring compulsory education services and public/primary health services, high informal costs, almost inexistent housing policies and insufficient community care services tend to further increase social inequalities.

CONCLUSIONS

In this chapter, we have argued that, after the transition to democracy in both Bulgaria and Romania, social policy design and implementation were shaped by domestic pressures. By contrast, after the mid-1990s policies were highly influenced by international actors who either exerted direct pressures or indirect influence by providing expertise and moulding local knowledge and expertise. Most external actors aimed at shaping the content of the policies, according to a neo-liberal ideology. Other actors, such as foreign governments, international NGOs and consultancy firms, had an impact on the development of local knowledge and expertise. During the past few years the WB and the IMF focused on specific policy contents, while the EU offered more guidelines for framework legislation in the field of social policy. Most international organizations refocused their activities on capacity-building instead of influencing the content of policies. In addition, Romanian social policy seemed more exposed to internal and external pressures and to top-down, often unaccountable decision-making, as no legitimate collective actors emerged on the scene during and after the transition period.

The first social policy reforms witnessed in these countries, much like other post-communist countries, were policy measures related to social assistance and family cash benefits, followed by reforms in social insurance systems. The latter reforms mostly followed a neo-liberal logic, justified by budgetary constraints. Any areas of social protection which required the development of social services and a higher synergy of local expertise, funds, capacity and legislative consistence evolved far more slowly. This was partially the result of a former institutional legacy and partially the result of the 'logic of pressures' in the context of which the formulation of social policy took place. The main consequences of the aforementioned external and domestic influences on social policy formulation were inconsistent legislation as well as programmes and policies which could 'in principle' have been effective, but which eventually remained unsupported by administrative, organizational and institutional arrangements. Such outcomes, in turn, generated a back-and-forth legislative and administrative process, which has led to increased costs and lack of legitimacy of most social policies, a cost that by far exceeds the benefits which new policy measures have brought along.

NOTES

1. Examples included protests on 29 January 1990, under the slogan 'death to intellectuals'; rallies on 13–15 June 1990 as a reaction to 'University Place' events; mobilization of September 1991 when unions provoked the fall of the Petre Roman government; mobilization of January and February 1999 against the decision of convicting Miron Cozma, the leader of miners' trade union national confederation since 1992, who had been sentenced to 18 years imprisonment. Even in 2003 the leaders of the largest trade union confederations in Romania (for example, the National Council of Trade Unions 'Frăţia' and the National Block of Trade Unions) supported the release of Miron Cozma from prison.
2. For example, the procedure suggested by the EU for selecting consultants (especially in the case of the PHARE programme) through international bidding among various independent consultancy groups increased the power of the latter and led to the diminishing of EU's influence on the strategic directions of welfare development (Zamfir, 2004: 93).
3. As Zamfir (2004) argues, in Romania the inflationist process initiated by the government, in order to ensure a small (the smallest after the Czech Republic's) average annual budgetary deficit in 1990–2002, was tacitly accepted by the IMF.
4. An example of legislation which was passed in 2000 and was merely neglected until recently concerns the social protection of the elderly. Delayed implementation of legislation

occurred when the law stipulated the initiation of active policy measures (as in the case of unemployment policy) or required specific social services.

5. This is the case of decentralized social assistance programmes, in the context of which, in 2002, means-tested social assistance was transformed into a Minimum Income Guarantee (MIG) scheme.

6. Elster et al. (1998) point to very similar processes and talk about extra-constitutional decision-making; governing through emergency ordinances is not unconstitutional nor is it undemocratic. However, governing through ordinances issued by the central executive means that the government exclusively assumes both executive and legislative functions, leaving little room to the legislature. Decision-makers conflate executive and legislative functions in one.

7. The reason was that value systems and diagnosed needs of these programmes varied significantly from the initial ones.

8. While the leave for parents with children (up to 2 years old) was introduced as part of the social insurance system in 1997, in 2004 it was transformed. Instead of a benefit dependent upon the level of income/contribution, it became a flat-rate benefit.

9. In 2000, in Romania social insurance contributions on average took up about 58 per cent of gross salaries. Compared to OECD countries, this is a very high share, since in 2003 the highest social security contributions – paid jointly by employee and employer – did not exceed 39 per cent (this was the case in France; see taxation database in OECD, 2005).

REFERENCES

Bulgarian Position Paper (2006), 'Bulgaria', briefing paper for the network 'Social Capital Social Policy', presented at the network's meeting, London School of Economics and Political Science, 28 June.

Deacon, B. (ed.) (1992), *The New Eastern Europe: Social Policy. Past, Present and Future*, London: Sage.

Deacon, B. (2000), 'Eastern European welfare states: the impact of the politics of globalization', *Journal of European Social Policy,* **10** (2), 146–61.

Deacon, B., M. Hulse and P. Stubbs (1997), *Global Social Policy. International Organizations and the Future of Welfare*, London: Sage Publications.

Economist (The) (2005), *Pocket World in Figures*, London: Profile Books.

Elster, J., C. Offe and U.K. Preuss (1998), *Institutional Design in Post-Communist Societies: Rebuilding the Ship at Sea*, Cambridge: Cambridge University Press.

European Commission (2005), 'Bulgaria: 2005 comprehensive monitoring report', Brussels, 25 October, COM (2005) 534 final, SEC (2005) 1352.

European Commission (2006a), 'Bulgaria: 2006 comprehensive monitoring report', Brussels, 16 May, COM (2006) 214 final, SEC (2006) 595.

European Commission (2006b), 'Romania: 2006 comprehensive monitoring report', Brussels, 16 May, COM (2006) 214 final, SEC (2006) 596.

European Commission (2006c), 'Accompanying measures in the context of Bulgaria's and Romania's accession', Brussels, 26 September.

Falkner, G. (2006), 'Forms of governance in European Union social policy: continuity and/or change?', *International Social Security Review*, **59** (2), 77–104.

Flonta, V. (1999), 'Valea Jjiului. Un Caz Atipic in Economia Românescă', *Sfera Politicii*, **67**, http://www.dntb.ro/sfera/67/mineriade-4.html (accessed 2 May 2007).

Government of Bulgaria and the European Commission (2005), 'Joint memorandum on social inclusion of Bulgaria, signed by the EC and the Bulgarian government', February, http://ec.europa.eu/employment_social/social_inclusion/docs/jim_bg_en.pdf (accessed 2 May 2007).

Government of Romania and the European Commission (2005), 'Joint memorandum on social inclusion of Romania, signed by the EC and the Romanian government', July, http://ec.europa.eu/employment_social/social_inclusion/docs/jim_ro_en.pdf (accessed 2 May 2007).

Hausner, J. (2001), 'Security through diversity: conditions for successful reform of the pension system in Poland', in J. Kornai, S. Haggard and R.R. Kaufman (eds), *Reforming the State: Fiscal and Welfare Reform in Post-Socialist Countries*, Cambridge: Cambridge University Press, pp. 210–34.

Institution Naţional de Statistică (2004), *Anuarul Statistic al României*, Bucharest: Institution Naţional de Statistică.

Kornai, J., S. Haggard and R.R. Kaufman (eds) (2001), *Reforming the State: Fiscal and Welfare Reform in Post-Socialist Countries*, Cambridge: Cambridge University Press.

Nelson, J. (2001), 'The politics of pension and health-care reform in Hungary and Poland', in J. Kornai, S. Haggard and R.R. Kaufman (eds), *Reforming the State: Fiscal and Welfare Reform in Post-Socialist Countries*, Cambridge: Cambridge University Press, pp. 235–66.

Organisation for Economic Co-operation and Development (OECD) (2005), Taxation database, http://www.oecd.org/document/60/0,2340,en_2649_37427_1942460_1_1_1_37427,00.html, table III.1, III.2, III.3 – social security contribution rates 2000–2005 (accessed 2 May 2007).

Pop, L. (2003), *Imagini Instituţionale ale Tranziţiei*, Iaşi: Polirom.

Pop, L. (2005), 'The dynamics of social security in a partial reform equilibrium society: the Romanian case', *Romanian Journal of Sociology*, 16 (1–2), 45–162.

Pop, L. (2006), 'Access to utilities, consumption patterns and payment capacity of energy bills', paper presented in the workshop on 'Access to Energy and Supportability of Energy Prices', Bucharest, 10 March (organized by USAID, the IRG (International Resources Group) and the Romanian Chamber of Commerce within the Romanian Energy Program, Phase III).

Preda, M., L. Pop and F. Bocioc (2006), *Report on the Gender Dimensions of Social Security Reform in Romania*, Budapest: ILO.

Sotiropoulos, D.A. (2005), 'Poverty and the safety net in Eastern and South-Eastern Europe in the post-communist era', in M. Ferrera (ed.), *Welfare State Reform in Southern Europe: Fighting Poverty and Social Exclusion in Italy, Spain, Portugal and Greece*, London: Routledge, pp. 266–96.

Sotiropoulos, D.A., I. Neamtu and M. Stoyanova (2003), 'The trajectory of post-communist welfare state development: the cases of Bulgaria and Romania', *Social Policy & Administration*, 37 (6), 114–30.

Sotiropoulou, V. and D.A. Sotiropoulos (2007), 'Childcare in post-communist welfare states: the case of Bulgaria', *Journal of Social Policy*, 36 (1), 141–55.

Stanchev, K. (2006), 'Bulgaria in a longer-term perspective: the risk associated with the pension system', in D. Keridis, C.M. Perry and M.R.P. d'Assuncao Carlos (eds), *Bulgaria in Europe: Charting a Path Toward Reform and Integration*, Hendon, VA: Potomac Books, pp. 94–9.

Stubbs, P. (2001), *Rights in Crisis and Transition: Developing a Children's Agenda for South Eastern Europe*, Belgrade: 'Save the Children' and SEECRAN.

Vaughan-Whitehead, D. (2003), *EU Enlargement Versus Social Europe? The Uncertain Future of the European Social Model*, Cheltenham: Edward Elgar.

84   *Social policy and international interventions in South East Europe*

World Bank (2000), *Making Transition Work for Everyone: Poverty and Inequality in Europe and Central Asia*, Washington, DC: World Bank.
World Bank (2005), 'World development indicators database', April, www.web. worldbank.org/WBSITE/EXTERNAL/DATASTATISTICS (accessed 2 May 2007).
World Bank (2006), 'Bulgaria at a glance', www.worldbank.org (accessed 2 May 2007).
Zamfir, C. (1999), 'Politica Socială în Tranziţie', in C. Zamfir (ed.), *Politici Sociale în România*, Bucharest: Expert Publishing House, pp. 41–113.
Zamfir, C. (2002), 'Politica Socială în România în Tranziţie', in L. Pop (ed.), *Dicţionar de Politici Sociale*, Bucharest: Expert Publishing House, pp. 539–59.
Zamfir, C. (2004), *O Analiză Critică a Tranziţiei*, Iaşi: Polirom.

5. Croatia

Paul Stubbs and Siniša Zrinščak

INTRODUCTION

This chapter covers 16 years of turbulence, with independence, war and destruction, mass forced migration and associated demographic change, and semi-authoritarian nationalist populism, followed by a kind of democratic catharsis and a delayed but now rapid Europeanization, in which Croatia has moved from a somewhat isolated and embattled semi-state into being a consolidated democracy. In this time, the ground upon which social policy operates and has effects has become much more fragmented and contradictory. Successive waves of reforms, and the presence and influence of different kinds of international actors always, of course, working in implicit or explicit alliance with national forces, have produced a kind of uneven welfare patchwork.

We explore contemporary Croatian social policy as a complex product of four historical processes/legacies and ideational frameworks/policy spaces which, while analytically separable, do, of course, contain overlaps, continuities and contradictions. The first is the longer-term legacy of a quite specific combination of Austro-Hungarian Bismarckian and Yugoslav Communist social policy which we address in brief. The second is the no less specific combination of independence, war, authoritarian nationalism with a democratic coating, and humanitarianism in a complex political emergency in a developed society in Europe in the first half of the 1990s. The third is the rather delayed and somewhat highly mediated period of attempts at 'structural adjustment' associated with neo-liberal globalization and, in particular, the influence of the World Bank and the International Monetary Fund. The fourth is the even more delayed process of Europeanization, in the context of democratic change, and, in particular, the emerging disciplinary impacts of the EU accession process.

Four aspects of the pre-1991 legacy are important for our purposes here. The first is Croatia's inclusion within a Bismarckian social insurance model and health-care system at the end of the nineteenth century, enjoying benefits on a par with those elsewhere in the Austro-Hungarian Empire (Belicza and Szabo, 2000; Puljiz, 2005). The second, as noted by a number of authors on former Yugoslav states in this collection, is the long-standing legacy, since the 1950s, of professional social work education within the universities and, slightly later, the universal establishment of Centres for Social Work, regulated by law from 1961 and tasked with 'analysing social problems in the municipality, suggesting measures to solve them, undertaking professional guardianship work and solving other social problems' (Šućur, 2003: 8). Third, the advent of socialist self-management introduced a high degree of decentralization and some tokenistic efforts towards participatory democratic control of social welfare. Fourth, in the context of crisis in the 1980s, new kinds of social movements and autonomous actors, notably women's organizations, began to claim a certain space for alternative forms of welfare activism and service delivery. The nature of this legacy differed considerably from the more limited attention to social problems in those states under the Soviet sphere of influence. Indeed, its success over many years is relevant in terms of the perception of a successful, well-developed system rather more than the converse side, which is its deep conservatism and overemphasis on professional power.

SOCIAL WELFARE IN THE CONTEXT OF WAR AND INDEPENDENCE: HUMANITARIANISM AND 'NEW WELFARE PARALLELISM'

Following Croatia's declaration of independence, war broke out in 1991 between a makeshift Croatian defence force, on the one side, and the Yugoslav People's Army, rebel Serbs in a self-declared Independent Republic of Krajina and various paramilitary groupings, on the other. The war, seen most dramatically internationally in the shelling of Dubrovnik and siege of Vukovar in late 1991, affected directly 56 per cent of Croatian territory with, at one time, 26 per cent of the country not under government control, and led to the deaths of 13 583 people. Croatian government figures estimate war damages to be in excess of US$20 billion (Bošnjak et al., 2002: 7). At its height, the crisis of forced migration meant that some 15 per cent of the Croatian population were refugees or displaced persons, with some 10 per cent of GDP devoted to their care (Puljiz, 2005: 81). In March 1992, a UN Protection Force (UNPROFOR), numbering some 14 000 troops, was deployed in three United Nations Protected Areas or 'UNPA zones'. The force's mandate was revised in 1995 but, in effect, it merely served to maintain an unsustainable status quo. Following Croatian military actions in May and August 1995, which re-took occupied territory covering two of the three UNPA zones, some 300 000 ethnic Serbs fled Croatia, only 117 488 of whom had been registered as having returned by 1 July 2005 (OSCE, 2005).

Table 5.1   Real GDP and inflation: Croatia, 1989–1995

Year	Index	Inflation rate	Registered unemployment rate
1989	100.0	n.a.	8.0
1990	92.9	609.5	9.3
1991	73.3	123.0	14.9
1992	64.7	665.5	15.3
1993	59.5	1517.5	14.8
1994	63.1	97.6	14.5
1995	67.3	2.0	14.5

Source: UNICEF (2006).

Some 150 000 ethnic Croats, mainly from Bosnia-Herzegovina and Serbia, have obtained Croatian citizenship since 1991. The third UNPA zone, the Eastern Slavonia region, was reintegrated peacefully into Croatia under the terms of the Erdut agreement, in January 1998, after a two-year UN interim administration. The changed demographic structure of Croatia is shown most clearly by comparing the 1991 and 2001 censuses. In this time, Croatia's population declined by 7.25 per cent from 4 784 265 to 4 437 460, with the ethnic composition also changing considerably, ethnic Serbs in particular declining from 12.16 per cent in 1991 to 4.54 per cent in 2001.[1] The decline in GDP, taking 1989 as the baseline was dramatic, accompanied by high unemployment and endemic inflation before a stabilization programme introduced in 1993 took effect (Table 5.1).

Viewing Croatia in the period from 1991 to 1995 as 'a case study in the problems of aid, familiar in the development studies literature, in a European setting' (Deacon et al., 1997: 178) captures only some of the complexities of the relationship between international actors in the context of rapidly changing modalities of development assistance and the rapidly changing internal political and social landscape of Croatia. The former was, certainly, framed in terms of the difficulties development agencies and their staff faced in understanding and dealing with their encounter with a complex emergency in a country with high levels of human development and a sophisticated and long-standing social welfare infrastructure. The latter was framed in terms of a late and complex transition involving the gaining of independence (state-building), war and lack of governmental control over part of the territory (state-destruction), and a renewed centralization of state functions in the context of a growing political authoritarianism.

Certainly, the first wave of international intervention can be seen as a kind of 'implicit social policy', involving large numbers of international organizations (supranational and non-governmental) focused on emergency relief assistance to war-affected areas and to large numbers of refugees and displaced persons. As a number of commentators remarked at the time, this was a kind of substitution of humanitarianism for political action, in the absence of any clear international consensus on the causes of the conflicts, much less on modes of resolution (cf. Duffield, 2001). To an extent, this was overdetermined by uncertainty regarding the political legitimacy of the Croatian state, only partly and formally overcome by international recognition, and the need to work in those parts of Croatia not under governmental control, combined with a wider concern regarding Croatian involvement in the war in Bosnia-Herzegovina.

Initially, UNHCR as the lead agency seeking to co-ordinate international assistance, tended to respond through its traditional implementing partners, mainly European or North American-based international NGOs specializing in relief, such as Cooperative for Assistance and Relief Everywhere (CARE) International, World Vision, Catholic Relief Services, the Scandinavian Refugee Councils, and so on. In terms of methods, techniques and, indeed, staffing, this was little different from interventions in crisis regions in the developing world. Apocryphal stories of medical kits containing anti-malarial tablets and other unnecessary and unusable medicines, water purification systems, and so on, abounded. The newly formed European Community Humanitarian Office (ECHO) also reacted in terms of a 'typical' humanitarian emergency, although later, in the context of encountering 'war in Europe', it embarked on supporting a programme of psycho-social assistance, targeted to those deemed to be suffering from 'trauma'. In itself not particularly problematic, this tended to be the main focus of intervention rather than more traditional social development concerns (cf. Stubbs, 2004). In addition, ECHO had a very clear policy of not channelling any of its support through governmental bodies, based on a somewhat simplistic notion of 'neutrality'. The UN agencies did have some level of contact with government but, on the whole, also tended to create their own structures and interventions or, at best, used networks of local institutions, including Centres for Social Work, merely as distribution hubs for assistance.

The complexity of the nature of the Croatian state in the early 1990s belies 'normal' distinctions between 'strong' and 'weak', or 'democratic' and 'authoritarian'. We argue that an understanding of the Croatian state as both 'weak' and 'strong', as having democratic legitimacy but with widespread authoritarian tendencies, is central to situating the encounter between the state and international organizations, generally and in terms of social policy. It would be wholly erroneous to describe Croatia as a war state, since significant parts of Croatia were never directly affected by war and other parts existed in a part war, part peace limbo situation. As the Croatian sociologist Josip Županov noted, ethnicized conflict went along-side and, indeed, to a large extent was superseded by, a sharp increase in social solidarity and national homogenization (Županov, 2001: 46–7). In terms of values, processes of re-traditionalization and de-secularization occurred, and had a significant impact, but did not completely erode more 'modern', 'secular' values (Črpić and Zrinščak, 2005). Alongside this, the figure of President Tudjman himself, personalizing the office and the state, symbolized this semi-modernism but, always, had a kind of political legit-imacy through more or less free and fair electoral victories, allied with his frequent changing of 'technocratic' prime ministers charged with steering the economy at a time when privatization clearly rewarded a new elite. Croatia, not unlike earlier transitions in Latin America, and akin to parts of South Eastern Europe and the former Soviet Union, developed a kind of 'crony capitalism' which was 'characterized by the dominance of insider interests, extreme clientelism, non-market based financial sector allocation, and a close link of the state and government with entrepreneurs and the financial sector' (Bićanić, n.d.: 1), leading to 'a large institutional and democratic deficit' (Bićanić and Franičević, 2003: 16).

While these meta-concerns may seem a long way from everyday social policy, they are relevant in terms of the legacy of a kind of 'welfare paral-lelism' throughout the period, particularly in the time of greatest social crisis as a result of war and endemic forced migration. On the one hand, Croatian institutions such as the network of state Centres for Social Work and the Governmental Office for Displaced Persons and Refugees, some-times allied with older Croatian NGOs such as Caritas and the Red Cross, and newer nationally oriented NGOs, sought to provide cash and services in the context of massive resource constraints. On the other hand, UNHCR, a network of INGOs and emerging new, often professionally led, service-oriented local NGOs offered a kind of parallel set of services, ignorant of, or distrustful of, state and pro-state bodies.

In these conditions, any thoughts of long-term social policy planning were put on hold as the government reacted through crisis management. Some social rights were cut back and the widespread use of early retirement as a way to respond to rising unemployment was promoted. This soon created enormous problems in the sustainability of the pension fund and, provided the grounds for the radical change in the pension system which occurred in the late 1990s. The government implemented an economic sta-bilization programme in 1993 which effectively ended a period of high inflation and stabilized the currency, advised by the IMF in particular as well as the World Bank. As one commentator has argued, the effects of this were stagnant growth rates, increasing unemployment and rapid social differentiation (Teodorović, 2003: 213). When this is coupled with a non-transparent, nepotistic, privatization process, later slowed down in the face of public criticisms, then, the possibility of rational social policy reform was, clearly, limited. Beyond this, in any case, humanitarianism essentially substituted for longer-term developmental initiatives.

In this period there were, however, two major policy changes in broad social policy. The first concerns the recognition, albeit highly mediated, of new NGOs as legitimate non-state actors in social policy, themselves regulated within a 'humanitarian' paradigm making no distinction between international and domestic bodies. The second concerns health care, with a major reform as early as 1993 (Hebrang et al., 1993; Zrinščak, 2000). This health reform contained two aspects, centralization and privatization, which did not sit easily together. As in other social policy fields, the state reclaimed the ownership of key institutions which had been the 'property' of local communities under communism. The central state became the owner of clinical hospitals and some other central health institutions, while counties (a new regional tier of government) became owners of general and special hospitals, local health centres, pharmacies and all other health institutions. In some contradiction to this, health-care finance, from contributions and partly from the state budget, became highly centralized inside the newly formed Croatian Institute for Health Insurance, the governing board of which was almost completely controlled by the Croatian government.

At the same time, a process of privatization was initiated, which can be seen in three different dimensions. First, all general practitioners (GPs), previously part of the public system, were forced to become private practitioners. Second, within public hospitals, senior medical professionals gained rights to establish their own private practice, in state premises and with state supplies, after normal working hours. Third, new private health institutions were legalized, although in reality very few emerged. In terms of the consequences, it can be argued that, for the first time, service users obtained rights to choose their GPs or an alternative service. However, in state hospitals, the public–private mix was unregulated, confusing and unfair. In addition, the practice of informal payments to medical professionals for services, already present in the communist system, became more widespread (Mastilica and Božikov, 1999). General practitioners, far from thriving under their new status, became constrained by financial and other regulations issued by the state-run Croatian Institute for Health Insurance. The reformed heath-care system soon became, at least in financial terms, very unstable which contributed eventually to a series of heath-care reform plans drawn up under the tutelage of the IMF and the World Bank.

CONTRADICTORY GLOBALIZATION: NEO-LIBERAL CROATIA IN THE MAKING?

The de facto end of the war and the guarantee of Croatian statehood did not usher in a period of greater international integration but, rather, renewed isolation as the Tudjman regime focused increasingly on 'enemies within'. The issue of the appropriate role and status of non-governmental organizations came to a head when a highly repressive Law on Associations was passed in 1997, at the height of a media-led campaign to paint NGOs as an anti-Croatian conspiracy, and after mass protests in late 1996 at the refusal to grant a new licence to Zagreb's independent Radio 101. Croatia's isolationism was compounded by a European Union decision to suspend Croatia's membership of the PHARE programme, agreed to just a couple of months earlier, in immediate response to the August 1995 military actions.

The field of social policy was marked by a process of 'post-war social claims making' (Puljiz, 2005: 83) or a kind of 'captured social policy' (Stubbs and Zrinščak, 2005). In the context of widespread perceptions of the unfairness of the privatization process and of increasingly visible social differentiation, groups such as war veterans and their families and, to an extent, pensioners, were able to press their demands on a populist regime. At the same time, the opposition parties began to make breakthroughs and hold power in some of the major cities, also offering somewhat populist visions of a new kind of 'welfare parallelism'. From 1998 onwards, cracks in the ruling party widened with a new moderate wing emerging pledged to reforms and, to an extent, committed to European integration. This period saw the establishment of a Governmental Office for Co-operation with NGOs, strongly supported by UNHCR and USAID, and new laws setting the basis of a reformed social protection system.

While the EU remained a rather absent presence, devoid of any real impact, the World Bank and the IMF consolidated their impact, particularly in the field of pension reform and, to an extent, in health-care reform. The most ambitious reform occurred in the Croatian pension system, in which the influence of the World Bank signalled a move towards integration into a neo-liberal global consensus. There is no denying the deep crisis which the system faced in the war years, marked by huge falls in GDP, a sharp rise in unemployment and the government's explicit use of early retirement as a strategy to avoid ever greater social problems caused by the bankruptcy of a large number of firms. Thus, the ratio of insured to retired persons fell from 3:1 in 1990 to 1.81:1 in 1995 and further to 1.38:1 in 1999. Pension expenditures dropped from 11.27 per cent of GDP in 1990 to 7.71 per cent in 1992, but rose further to 13.27 per cent in 1999 (see Table 5.2).

Table 5.2   Main trends in the Croatian pension system

Year	Dependence rate (pensioners/insured)	Ratio (insured/ pensioners)	Expenditures, % of GDP
1980	24.7	4.04	
1985	27.1	3.68	
1990	33.3	3.00	11.27
1995	55.2	1.81	10.84
1999	72.4	1.38	13.27
2000	73.8	1.36	13.30
2001	73.6	1.36	13.90
2002	73.3	1.36	13.20
2003	73.0	1.37	12.80
2004	73.0	1.37	12.60

Sources: Bagarić and Marušić (2004); Vuković (2005).

In the same period, the value of the average pension dropped to about 45 per cent of the average salary, itself falling. The rise in pension expenditures at the beginning of the 1990s was connected with the adjustment formula which adjusted pensions in line with rises in salaries. This was changed by a government decision in 1993 to restrict the rise in pensions, which was a part of the successful government programme to reduce inflation and stabilize the Croatian currency. However, the decision was undertaken without necessary changes in respective laws and subsequently caused a worsening of the economic position of pensioners. It is interesting to note that this decision soon became the hottest public issue, overshadowing all other aspects of reform. The Constitutional Court in 1998, in a sign of growing independence and separation of the judiciary from the state, labelled the government decision unconstitutional and ordered the government to pay back what became known as the 'pensioners' debt'.

The grounds for reform were established in these crisis conditions. Although the first discussions on reforms took place within a small circle of experts and state officials around the pension fund with some proposals for technical changes inside the system, war intervened so that these proposals were never completed nor implemented. The end of the war in 1995 together with the erosion of the pension system's sustainability opened the door for new reform steps. This coincided with the well-known World Bank study *Averting the Old Age Crisis* (World Bank, 1994; cf. also Wodsak, 2006). World Bank plans to transfer the Chilean pension model were welcomed by the political elite, and some experts in Croatia which, at the time, was looking for a fast solution for its endangered pension system.

In November 1995, a conference was organized by the Croatian government and the World Bank on pension reform involving senior bank experts and José Pinera, the Chilean Minister from Pinochet's government responsible for the privatization of the pension system in 1981. The Croatian Prime Minister announced a firm decision to undertake radical reform to solve almost all pension problems. In March 1997, the World Bank released in draft form, its first comprehensive study on Croatia, interestingly entitled: 'Croatia: The Peace Challenge', renamed in the final version published in December 1997 to *Croatia: Beyond Stabilization* (World Bank, 1997). The document emphasized the need to introduce, alongside the public pillar, a second mandatory pillar based on private savings in private pension funds. In February 1998, the government established a Committee for Pension Reform and new laws were passed in 1998 and 1999. The law from 1998, which became effective from January 1999, regulated changes in the existing public system, while several laws passed in 1999, and effective from January 2002, regulated the introduction of the second, mandatory, and third, voluntary, private pension fund pillars.

Analyses by the leading scholar of pension reform in the region suggest the importance of two preconditions: a crisis of the system and a preferred reform model (cf. Müller, 1999; 2001; 2002a; 2002b). Both preconditions were present in Croatia, as in other post-communist countries such as Hungary and Poland (Ferge, 1999; Fultz, 2004; Mácha, 1999; Müller et al., 1999; Schmähl and Horstmann, 2002). As explored above, the crisis of the system was profound, and the stabilization of the system was required as part of the stabilization of state finances. This explains the involvement of the international financial institutions (IFIs), both the IMF and World Bank. A preferred reform model was also in place, not least in the context of the World Bank's influence in terms of the spread of ideas of reform, of which *Averting the Old Age Crisis* was an early, and important, exemplar. In the end, although the Chilean privatization served as a kind of inspiration, pension reform in Croatia, as in much of Eastern Europe, took shape along the lines of the more modest Argentinean model which did not abolish the public system but combined it with new private pillars. In the context of a new dawn of democracy in post-communist Central and Eastern Europe, the political context of the Chilean reform, implemented during a right-wing dictatorship, perhaps proved problematic, although this was not a subject of debate in Croatia at the time.

The World Bank-led reform offered a kind of two-pronged solution for the future. The pension model with a reduced public pillar and more diverse private and occupational pillars is meant to be more robust and react better to demographic ageing. The model stresses the need for savings for the future as well as private responsibility for social security. In addition, since private pension funds were an important new player on capital markets, the reforms were portrayed as stimulating economic growth and building the emerging markets of post-communist Europe.

A number of other factors are important in terms of understanding the reform. The first is the magical faith in proposed market solutions for pension financing problems. In Croatia, few questions were raised and opposition to reform plans was almost non-existent. The European Union, largely inactive in policy debates in Croatia, did not register any interest to become involved or take a position, other than for its macroeconomic division to concur with the IFIs on the need for financial stabilization. Other international actors, particularly the ILO, appeared able to exert an influence only in the absence of a financial crisis, as in the case of the Czech Republic and Slovenia (Müller, 2002b; Stanovnik, 2002). As a result, at the time of pension reform in Croatia, there was no ILO presence and no presentation of possible alternative reform options.

A discursive link between the pension system and its alleged communist character, alongside evident financial problems, contributed to a loss of legitimacy and the impossibility of opposition to reform. As the following quote from one of the leading Croatian advocates of privatization shows, even the Bismarckian legacy could be criticized:

> A pension system with inter-generational solidarity is a recent phenomenon. It was introduced in the late 19th century by the iron chancellor Otto von Bismarck, and was spread later throughout all the countries of the developed world and to those less developed countries which underwent national and social revolutions, *in which both left-wing and right-wing populist movements, obsessed by the idea of national and class solidarity, played a pioneering role.* (Ostović, 2000: 313, emphasis added)

In this construction who could possibly be against pension reform?

In terms of the key actors involved and their positions in debates regarding pension reform in Croatia, we find that the picture resembles that in most other countries in the region, where opposition was weak and advocates of reform strong. In a sense, this was amplified in Croatia, as the opponents were even weaker, and reform did not become a pressing public issue, unlike the pensioners' debt question. The positions of key actors is presented in Table 5.3.

Table 5.3 shows that a critical stance towards the reform was formulated by only a few persons linked to some trades unions and some social policy scholars. These voices, urging restraint, had no influence on the pro-reform movement nor on the social democratic-led opposition. During technical negotiations, they had a limited influence on some aspects of the reform. Specifically in Croatia, the already mentioned so-called 'pensioners' debt'

Table 5.3   Actors and their positions in the Croatian pension reform

Pro-reform voices	Oppositional voices	Neutral/no stated position	Concerned with 'pensioners' debt'
Government – ministers (without any internal conflicts)	Some social policy experts (urging restraint)	Other political parties	All actors (including the Constitutional Court)
IFIs (WB, IMF)	Some trade unions	Pensioners' organizations	
Domestic FIs		Some trade unions	
Experts (neo-liberal and technocratic economists)			

following the 1993 government decision to restrict the rise of pension benefits, overdetermined the public and political debates. This was the issue which opposition political parties and the trades unions found most attractive to mobilize around. In addition, the political authoritarianism of parts of the regime was also relevant. As noted above, the Croatian government had democratic legitimacy, coming to power in relatively free democratic elections, but faced many more problems in democratic development than other neighbouring Central European countries. Political debates were still framed by national security issues, and by issues that lend themselves to populist themes: the unjust privatization of state property; rising inequality and impoverishment; and the pensioners' debt. More sophisticated technical issues about the pros and cons of pension privatization had little realistic chance of reaching the public domain. Instead, the World Bank assured a continued influence on the reform by seconding a Croatian Bank staff member to be adviser to the government on the reforms (cf. Orenstein, 2005: 195). In addition, the ruling party effectively used pension reform as a way of demonstrating its willingness to implement market reform, its ability to stabilize the country's economy and its readiness to engage with international financial institutions. In short, all of the structural, political, institutional and agent-specific 'drivers of change' were working in one direction, in a rare example, in 1990s Croatia, of a converging of the interests of the ruling regime with those of domestic and international financial institutions. Successful implementation, itself no guarantee of a problem-free future, of course, cannot be understood outside the particular, even peculiar, Croatian domestic conditions.

Contrary to the 'success' of the World Bank's involvement in pension reform, the health-care sector proved to be extremely resistant to comprehensive reform, although there were a number of initiatives and projects following on from the 1993 reform. While reforms had the goal of curbing health expenditures, unlike in the field of pensions, there was no overall reform 'package' which the World Bank was seeking to have adopted. The first project funded by the World Bank, which began in 1995, was somewhat low key, seeking to support the earlier health-care reform, and provide financing for computer hardware and software, medical equipment, fellowships, study tours, foreign and local training and expert advisory services, public education materials and incremental recurrent costs. The previously mentioned World Bank study from 1997 which argued for privatization in the pension system, argued that the health-care system would impose a significant burden on public finance unless the reforms of 1993 were continued and extended. The second reform project funded by the World Bank from 1999 to 2005 had the ambitious aim to enhance Croatia's capacity to achieve a more effective, efficient and financially sustainable health system. Very interestingly, one sub-component financed group practice pilots for GPs, ironically along the lines of the primary health-care system in health centres in communist Yugoslavia which had been abolished by the privatization process starting in 1993. A series of World Bank studies and publications followed regarding the health-care system and health-care financing. In April 2004 a special *Croatia: Health Finance Study* (World Bank, 2004) was published. All paint a similar picture of spiralling high costs endangering public finances and a lack of noticeable improvement following reform implementation. In a sense unlike the pension system, then, health care has proved to be a much more difficult issue, in part at least because of vested interests, notably from a politically strong doctors' lobby, in the status quo.

DELAYED EUROPEANIZATION: GOVERNING AND REGULATING SOCIAL CROATIA?

The victory of the Social Democratic Party-led coalition in the January 2000 elections, following the death of President Tudjman, appeared to signal a new dawn of democratic politics coupled with economic growth for Croatia. The Croatian political scene became dominated by the push for EU membership, now part of a new political consensus encompassing the reformed HDZ (Croatian Democratic Union). A Stabilization and Association Agreement was signed in October 2001 and Croatia applied for membership of the European Union on 21 February 2003. Following a positive *avis* (notification) in April 2004, Croatia obtained official candidate status in June 2004. However, at the European Council meeting on 16 March 2005, the start of formal negotiations, due the next day, were postponed, pending full co-operation by Croatia with the International Criminal Tribunal for the Former Yugoslavia in The Hague. Negotiations proper began in October 2005, following a positive report by the Tribunal's Chief Prosecutor. The arrest of fugitive General Gotovina in December 2005 added impetus to the negotiations. Most commentators predict Croatia's EU membership by 2010 or 2011 although external constraints, notably the EU's 'enlargement fatigue' and lack of a new administrative framework may conspire with internal problems, notably failure to tackle judicial reform in the context of more stringent EU monitoring of actual practice as well as laws and commitments, to put the date back.

Notably, the SAA contained hardly any provision concerning social policy, calling merely for general modernization and adaptation of the social security system. Therefore, two general paths can be traced in the period from 2000 to 2003 concerning EU influence on social policy. Contrary to the loose treatment of social policy in the SAA, the new political framework helped address issues that were already 'prepared' by the work of numerous non-profit organizations, mainly in the field of gender equality, family violence and children's rights. At the same time, the World Bank and the IMF remained as key actors dominating the overall policy framework. Indeed, it fell to the new government to complete, and fully implement, the second phase of pension reform, that is, to introduce the fully funded mandatory and voluntary pillars. In addition, under considerable pressure from the IMF and others, a new Labour Law was introduced, based on a critique of inflexible labour markets. The government also cut and restructured some social benefits (child and maternity benefits) in order to comply with conditionalities requiring the lowering of public expenditures.

A comprehensive social welfare reform project was also launched, led by the then Ministry of Labour and Social Welfare. It began in April 2002, with the first phase, lasting a year, financed by the World Bank, the UK's Department for International Development and the government of Japan. As perhaps one of the more dramatic examples of the problems of subcontracting and the role of consultancy companies (cf. de la Porte and Deacon, 2002; Stubbs, 2003), no less than eight consultancy teams or companies were contracted to work on the reforms. In addition to work on the reform of social services, social assistance and labour market policies, one part of the project was devoted to the problem of monitoring poverty and, in particular, strengthening institutional capacities for measuring poverty. Very specific recommendations were developed and, in 2004, the Croatian

Bureau of Statistics for the first time issued data on poverty which included some, although by no means all, of the Laeken indicators utilized by the European Union in the fight against social exclusion.

The elections of November 2003 returned HDZ, the ruling party throughout the 1990s, to power, albeit reliant on the support of the Pensioner's party and the Serbian Democratic Party, an uneasy coalition of 'claims makers' which has, in fact, led to a costly decision to repay pensioners' debts from 1993 and 1994. One of the most important steps taken in terms of social welfare was the shift in responsibility, after the election, from the Ministry of Labour and Social Welfare to the medical-doctor and health-dominated Ministry of Health and Social Welfare and to the Ministry of Economy and Labour. In addition, a number of social policy responsibilities have been moved to the newly created Ministry of Family, Veterans and Inter-Generational Solidarity, such that social policy is now more institutionally fragmented than ever before, between three ministries. Significantly, the much delayed social welfare reform project, with a World Bank loan, was skewed rather more in line with the need for repairs to institutional care facilities and away from a dynamic new welfare mix.

In the context of a large budget deficit, sections of the government, allied with liberal think tanks, and key international organizations, have continued to paint Croatia as a high social spending country. Using Ministry of Finance data, social expenditures as a proportion of GDP actually fell from 26.6 per cent in 2000 to 23.4 per cent in 2004. Nevertheless, the World Bank and IMF seem more concerned with social assistance benefits which have now been placed in a separate project detached from social protection reform, forming part of a Programme Adjustment Loan (PAL). The PAL commits the government to form an inter-ministerial working group and to formulate an agreed social benefit strategy, with the goal of reducing total spending on social benefits from 4.1 per cent of GDP to 3.5 per cent of GDP, while increasing the share of the best-targeted and means-tested social support allowance (World Bank, 2005).

The preparation of Croatia's Joint Inclusion Memorandum prior to EU membership, which began in autumn 2005, signalled a significant change in terms of a more active interest and involvement in social policy by the European Commission (EC). Four broadly positive aspects of the process can be discerned. First, the JIM has led to a greater harmonization of social statistics with EUROSTAT methodology and a clearer awareness of the gaps which remain. Second, there has been a process of stakeholder participation, through a series of conferences and meetings which, while far from perfect, represents an improvement on the previous practice of 'behind closed doors' strategy document preparation. Third, key social policy experts have been involved in the drawing up of the JIM, within a clearer framework, supervised by the European Commission, in which policy measures, indicators and funding possibilities were more aligned than previously. Fourth, substantive comments from the Commission on aspects of social policy, particularly relating to issues around discrimination, active labour market policies and co-ordination of services, have added to the quality of debate. Of course, the JIM process has not significantly raised the profile of social policy within the accession process, nor, even more importantly, has it altered the marginal position of social policy in the government.

The World Bank and, interestingly, UNDP, have both positioned themselves as working with the government on social policy issues in the context of Europeanization. This has manifested itself, most recently, in ongoing work on the regional dimensions of poverty and social exclusion in Croatia, although the World Bank continues to merge quite objective analysis with normative recommendations for the cutting of all but the most clearly 'targeted' social benefits and for a greater emphasis on intra-regional labour market mobility. Crucially, the three key international agency players are all forced to call on the same small pool of social policy 'experts'.

CONCLUSIONS

In the context of a broad understanding of national–international agency interactions in countries in transition, we have noted in this chapter some of the commonalities and specificities of the Croatian situation in the past 16 years. In terms of commonalities, Croatia has seen a coalition of international and domestic actors united in an economistic notion of 'the social' as an unproductive, uneconomic 'burden', in need of radical reforms as part of a structural adjustment package, reducing expenditures, increasing efficiencies, and shifting the balance towards market mechanisms and new non-state actors. The debate has been dominated by the World Bank and IMF with EU influence much later and, to a large extent, sharing many of the macroeconomic assumptions of the IFIs. The fact that reform messages came after the experience of 'shock therapy' in parts of Eastern Europe, and in the context of the institutional legacy of a well-developed, if conservative, system noted above, has meant that, in reality, the impacts of changes have been rather limited and muted.

Crucially, the chapter has pointed to the specific conditions of a mix of war, nation state-building and humanitarian crisis in producing a particular kind of welfare parallelism in Croatia in the first half of the 1990s which still has impacts and effects today. In the absence of clear principles and outcome indicators at national level, a kind of ad hoc decentralization, in terms of the proliferation of parallel, local, welfare settlements has emerged, prone to being captured by particular claim-makers. In addition, there remains an uneven playing field in which state agencies remain highly bureaucratized and reluctant to enter into partnerships with non-state actors existing on short-term, project-specific funding. 'Delayed transition' including 'late Europeanization' have worked together to limit reforms and to privilege a recommodification of welfare playing itself out unevenly in different sectors. Above all, the chapter illustrates the importance of the complex nature of the relationship between 'the international' and 'the domestic' in reform, and the importance of studying structures, institutions and actors in a historical context and frame.

NOTE

1. Census methodology changed in this period: the 2001 census did not count those absent from the country for more than one year as the 1991 census had done. A recalculation of both censuses by leading demographers still suggested a decline of 7.03 per cent in the Croatian population from 4 499 049 in 1991 to 4 203 831 in 2001 (Gelo et al., 2005: 19).

REFERENCES

Bagarić, N. and L. Marušić (2004), 'Access to social rights in Croatia: pension insurance' (Croatian language text), *Revija za socijalnu politiku* (*Croatian Journal of Social Policy*), **11** (1), 39–61.

Belicza, B. and A. Szabo (2000), 'Public health reform and the development of health services in Ðakovo district 1820–1899', *Croatian Medical Journal*, **41** (1), 81–95.

Bićanić, I. (n.d.), 'The economic role of the state in Southeast European economies in transition', http://www.wiiw.ac.at/balkan/files/Bicanic.pdf (accessed 27 December 2006).

Bićanić, I. and V. Franičević (2003), 'Understanding reform: the case of Croatia', *GDN/WIIW Working Paper*, http://www.wiiw.ac.at/balkan/files/GDN_UnderstandingReform_Croatia.pdf (accessed 27 December 2006).

Bošnjak, V., J. Mimica, V. Puljiz, T. Radočaj, P. Stubbs and S. Zrinščak (2002), *Aspects of Social Policy and Social Welfare in Croatia* (Croatian language version), Zagreb: UNICEF. (English version: http://www.ceecis.org/child_protection/PDF/Croa_Socpol.pdf#search=%22Bosnjak%20unicef%20social%20welfare%20Croatia%22 [accessed 28 August 2006).

Črpić, G. and S. Zrinščak (2005), 'Between identity and everyday life: religiosity in Croatian society from the European comparative perspective', in J. Baloban (ed.), *In Search of Identity: A Comparative Study of Values: Croatia and Europe*, Zagreb: Golden Marketing – Tehnička knjiga, pp. 45–83.

De la Porte, C. and B. Deacon (2002), *Contracting Companies and Consultants: The EU and Social Policy of Accession Countries*, GASPP Occasional Paper 9, Helsinki: STAKES.

Deacon, B., with M. Hulse and P. Stubbs (1997), *Global Social Policy: International Organizations and the Future of Welfare*, London: Sage.

Duffield, M. (2001), *Global Governance and the New Wars: The Merging of Development and Security*, London: Zed Books.

Ferge, Z. (1999), 'The politics of the Hungarian pension reform', in K. Müller, A. Ryll and H.-J. Wagener (eds), *Transformation of Social Security: Pensions in Central-Eastern Europe*, Heidelberg and New York: Physica-Verlag, pp. 231–46.

Fultz, E. (2004), 'Pension reform in the EU accession countries: challenges, achievements and pitfalls', *International Social Security Review*, **57** (2), 3–24.

Gelo, J., A. Akrap and I. Čipin (2005), *Temeljne značajke demografskog razroja Hrvatske (Bilanca 20. Stoljeća) (Fundamental Characteristics of Demographic Development in Croatia – the Twentieth Century Balance of Accounts)*, Zagreb: Ministarstvo obitelji, braniteljai međugeneracijske sloidarnosti (Ministry of the Family, Veterans and Intergenerational Solidarity).

Hebrang, A., I. Mrkonjić and J. Njavro (1993), *Comments on Health Care Law and Law on Health Insurance* (Croatian language text), Zagreb: Privredni biro.

Mácha, M. (1999), 'Political actors and reform paradigms in Czech old-age security', in K. Müller, A. Ryll and H.-J. Wagener (eds), *Transformation of Social Security: Pensions in Central-Eastern Europe*, Heidelberg and New York: Physica-Verlag, pp. 247–57.

Mastilica, M. and J. Božikov (1999), 'Out-of-pocket payments for health care in Croatia: implications for equity', *Croatian Medical Journal*, **40** (2), 152–9.

Müller, K. (1999), *The Political Economy of Pension Reform in Central-Eastern Europe*, Cheltenham, UK and Northampton, MA, USA: Edward Elgar.

Müller, K. (2001), 'The political economy of pension reform in Eastern Europe', *International Social Security Review*, **54** (2–3), 57–79.

Müller, K. (2002a), 'From the state to market? Pension reform paths in Central-Eastern Europe and the former Soviet Union', *Social Policy & Administration*, **36** (2), 156–75.

Müller, K. (2002b), 'Privatising old-age security: Latin America and Eastern Europe compared', *Research Report*, Frankfurt Institute for Transformation Studies.

Müller, K., A. Ryll and H.-J. Wagener (eds) (1999), *Transformation of Social Security: Pensions in Central-Eastern Europe*, Heidelberg and New York: Physica-Verlag.

Orenstein, M. (2005), 'The new pension reform as global policy', *Global Social Policy*, **5** (2), 175–202.

Organization for Security and Co-operation in Europe (OSCE) (2005), *Background Report on Refugee Returns to Croatia*, Zagreb: OSCE Croatia, 29 July, http://www.osce.org/documents/mc/2005/07/15886_en.pdf (accessed 28 August 2006).

Ostović, D. (2000), 'Capitalized systems and the question of justice' (Croatian language text), *Financijska teorija i praksa (Croatian Journal of Financial Theory and Practice)*, **24** (3), 311–19.

Puljiz, V. (2005), 'Croatia: searching for a new social model', in S. Kuhnle (ed.), *Social Policy Development in South Eastern Europe: Outside Influences and Domestic Forces*, Bergen: Stein Rokkan Centre for Social Studies, pp. 79–92.

Schmähl, W. and S. Horstmann (eds) (2002), *Transformation of Pension Systems in Central and Eastern Europe*, Cheltenham, UK and Northampton, MA, USA: Edward Elgar.

Stanovnik, T. (2002), 'The political economy of pension reform in Slovenia', in E. Fultz (ed.), *Pension Reform in Central and Eastern Europe*, vol. 2, Budapest: ILO, pp. 19–73.
Stubbs, P. (2003), 'International non-State actors and social development policy', *Global Social Policy*, 3 (3), 319–48.
Stubbs, P. (2004), 'Transforming local and global discourses: reassessing the PTSD movement in Bosnia and Croatia', in D. Ingleby (ed.), *Forced Migration and Mental Health: Rethinking the Care of Refugees and Displaced Persons*, New York: Springer, pp. 53–67.
Stubbs, P. and S. Zrinščak (2005), 'Extended social Europe? Social policy, social inclusion and social dialogue in Croatia and the European Union', in K. Ott (ed.), *Croatian Accession to the European Union. Facing the Challenges of Negotiations*, Zagreb: Institute of Public Finance, Friedrich Ebert Foundation, pp. 161–84.
Šućur, Z. (2003), 'The development of social assistance and social care in Croatia after World War II' (Croatian language text), *Revija za socijalnu politiku* (*Croatian Journal of Social Policy*), 10 (1), 1–22.
Teodorović, I. (2003), 'Transition process and global environment', in M. Mestrović (ed.), *Globalization and its Reflections On (In) Croatia*, New York: Global Scholarly Publications, pp. 205–24.
United Nations Children's Fund (UNICEF) (2006), TransMONEE 2006 database, Florence: ICDC, http://www.unicef-icdc.org/resources/transmonee.html (accessed 28 August 2006).
Vuković, S. (2005), 'The pension system in the Republic of Croatia – basic indicators' (Croatian language text), *Revija za socijalnu politiku* (*Croatian Journal of Social Policy*), 12 (3–4), 377–91.
Wodsak, W. (2006), 'The travel of ideas: origins, diffusion, and reception of the World Bank's approach to old age security', paper presented to RC 19 World Congress of Sociology, Durban, July.
World Bank (1994), *Averting the Old Age Crisis: Policies to Protect the Old and Promote Growth*, New York: Oxford University Press.
World Bank (1997), *Croatia: Beyond Stabilization*, Zagreb: World Bank.
World Bank (2004), *Croatia: Health Finance Study*, Zagreb: World Bank.
World Bank (2005), *Programme Document for a Proposed Pal of 150m Euro. Report no. 30293-HR*, 10 August, Zagreb: World Bank.
Zrinščak, S. (2000), 'The challenges of decentralization in the system of health services' (Croatian language text), *Hrvatska javna uprava* (*Croatian Public Administration*), 2 (2), 223–41.
Županov, J. (2001), 'Theses on social crisis: the case of Croatia', *South East Europe Review*, 1 (2001), 39–50, http://www.boeckler.de/pdf/South-East_Europe_Review-2001-01-p 039.pdf (accessed 23 June 2006).

6. Turkey

Burcu Yakut-Cakar

INTRODUCTION

This chapter aims to shed some light on social policy developments in Turkey within the last two decades with a particular focus on the role of international actors. The analysis will be centred in the post-1980 period which marks the shift from an inward-looking economic regime to the implementation of outward-looking market-oriented policies. While international actors were influential in the pre-1980 period, the period under scrutiny serves to frame the discussion within the contemporary discourses of the actors involved. In particular, this chapter seeks to explore the following issues: (1) the legacy of social policy drawing attention to the development and components of the welfare regime in Turkey and challenges facing that regime; (2) key aspects of the socio-economic and political setting; (3) international actors involved in the transformation; and (4) an overview of the main sectors of policy reforms, that is, pensions, health and social protection.

THE LEGACY AND CONTEMPORARY CHALLENGES

The welfare regime in Turkey can be considered to share similar characteristics with its southern European counterparts (Andreotti et al., 2001; Gough, 1996; Saraceno, 2002). Discussed widely in the comparative welfare regimes literature as a distinct group (Andreotti et al., 2001; Esping-Andersen, 1999; Ferrera, 1996; 2000; 2005; Gough, 1996; Leibfried, 1993; Moreno, 2006; Symeonidou, 1996; Trifiletti, 1999), the following typical characteristics of the Southern European regime cluster, in summary form, also hold true for the Turkish welfare regime:

- Highly protective employment regimes for core sectors gradually serving to segment the labour market into 'insiders' as a hyper-protected, core workforce, 'periphery' in terms of those in between, and 'outsiders' or workers in the informal economy, young people and the long-term unemployed or marginalized workers typically employed in small enterprises without job security (Ferrera, 1996; 2005; Moreno, 2000).

- The co-evolution of social insurance programmes with this segmented labour market based on occupational status with distinct schemes for private employees, civil servants and the self-employed. Such fragmentation is coupled with different regulations in terms of contributions and benefit determination (Ferrera, 1996).
- Heightened protection of the risk of old-age and marginal, sometimes non-existent, family benefits.
- Patchy and ineffective safety nets evolving slowly in a fragmented and categorical fashion with disparate rules and differentiated benefit levels (Ferrera, 2005; Saraceno, 2002).

In line with the above-mentioned characteristics, when analysed in detail, social policy developments in Turkey tend to resemble what Seekings (2004) calls *inegalitarian corporatist* regimes, which mainly refers to the corporatist element where claims are highly dependent on membership of occupationally defined corporate groups with a fundamentally inegalitarian character as regards the exclusion of the poor from formal employment and hence membership of these corporate groups.

Up to the Second World War, under a single party regime, social policies in Turkey were mostly concerned with protecting civil servants as regards to their pension and health service entitlements while at the same time being motivated by traditional paternalistic considerations. As far as the 'statism' as the mode of economic development in the 1930s is concerned, the priority given to industrialization had been realized through expanding state economic enterprises (SEEs) as the dominant mode of production and these considerations were manifested not only in responding to the rural and urban challenges of social disintegration due to long wars and population exchanges, but also in terms of measures aimed at protecting employees within the workplace and creating an attractive social environment around and within SEEs (Boratav and Ozugurlu, 2005).

The elections of 1950 marked a shift towards a multiparty democracy in the political sphere but also a liberal free-market regime in the economic sphere. The aftermath of the Second World War witnessed the establishment of the Ministry of Labour as well as the Workers' Insurance Institution in 1945, renamed the Social Insurance Institution (SSK) in 1965, which aimed at protecting private sector employees and blue-collar public workers in the manufacturing and service sectors against a broad range of risks such as old-age, disability, health, and so on, to be co-funded by employer and employee contributions. Though the history of social insurance or social security for public sector employees can be traced back to the Ottoman period when soldiers, the *ulema* and civil service classes formed *Tekaüd* (Pension Chests) under the treasury (Ozbek, 2002), the system was only institutionalized in the post-Second World War period with the establishment of the Retirement Chest (ES) in 1949 for public sector employees covering both active and retired civil servants.

Prepared immediately after the military takeover of May 1960, the 1961 Constitution marks the specification of the *social* component of the state by emphasizing the granting of constitutional rights for all citizens to have access to education, health and employment – rights which have never been fully achieved, as will be shown in the following sections. The development strategy of this period based on import-substituting industrialization achieved some kind of a class alliance where all employees and employers benefited from high wages, high profits and the expansion of domestic demand and the domestic market. In the early 1970s, the establishment of Bag-Kur (BK) to cover craftsmen, artisans, merchants and other self-employed people has completed the formation of the social security system in Turkey. In 1983, BK and SSK extended their coverage to include agricultural workers and the self employed. Table 6.1 presents a snapshot regarding the coverage of the social security system.

With the shift towards an export-oriented mode of industrialization in the 1980s, such segmentation within the social security system, offering differential protection schemes of pensions or health in terms of eligibility criteria and benefit determination for different occupational groups, was coupled with a segmentation in the labour market in terms of formally and informally employed groups of workers. This can be traced through intensified privatization significantly decreasing the number of previously well-paid, socially secure workers who were employed either in over-staffed SEEs or private companies, and the informalization of production processes where subcontracting relations became the dominant mode for cost-cutting strategies to enhance 'competitiveness' in the global market. It can be argued that the coexistence of this segmented social security system with a peculiar labour market structure where self-employment, unpaid family labour and informal employment have predominantly been evident, hampers the possibility of the system providing an adequate level of protection for all.

The establishment of a minimum pension scheme for the elderly and disabled who lacked social security coverage in 1976 and the establishment of the Fund for the Establishment of Social Assistance and Solidarity (henceforth the Solidarity Fund) in 1986 to provide emergency relief (either in cash or in kind) 'to help citizens in the state of poverty and destitution, or, when necessary, to help non-citizens who are in Turkey legally or otherwise,

Table 6.1   Social security coverage in Turkey

	1998	1999	2000	2001	2002	2003	2004	2005
Number of active members* (thousands)								
SSK	5 551	5 225	5 468	5 945	6 348	6 354	6 734	7 411
ES	2 072	2 118	2 164	2 236	2 373	2 408	2 404	2 402
BK	2 708	2 801	3 058	3 336	3 322	3 383	3 493	3 354
Coverage in total employment (%)								
SSK	26.60	24.40	26.57	30.11	29.73	30.05	30.90	33.62
ES	9.93	9.89	10.52	11.33	11.11	11.39	11.03	10.90
BK	12.97	13.08	14.86	16.90	15.56	16.00	16.03	15.21
Number of dependants** (thousands)								
SSK	24 380	23 536	24 488	23 635	25 166	24 611	26 772	29 448
ES	6 076	6 191	6 305	6 546	6 917	6 830	6 866	6 868
BK	9 207	9 656	10 446	10 601	10 833	11 052	11 266	11 036
Coverage in total population*** (%)								
SSK		47.71	47.74	45.28	47.47	49.53	52.34	57.06
ES		18.77	18.88	19.23	13.02	13.51	13.07	13.12
BK		21.55	22.31	22.25	22.33	22.46	22.61	22.19

Notes:
These figures must be treated carefully as the official records of SSK and BK count those registered but not paying contributions under the 'active' group.
*   Includes active contributors in agricultural as well as non-agricultural sectors.
**   Estimates.
*** Coverage as the sum of active members, pensioners and dependants.

Source: State Planning Organization Annual Programmes (1998–2006).

to take measures that will enforce social justice by ensuring the fair distribution of income, to encourage social support and cooperation' (Article 1, Law No. 3294) can be regarded as the main components of a patchy social assistance framework for those not covered by the corporatist social security system. In terms of financing, the former has been financed from the general state budget and managed by ES while the latter operates through an extra-budgetary public fund.

Inherent in the establishment of the former is the central role attached to the family or kinship ties as an essential pillar of the welfare regime. Article 1 of Law No. 2022 on minimum pensions for the elderly and the disabled states clearly that 'the elderly or disabled who are not covered by any social security institution, do not own any property or any other source of revenue and do not have anyone legally responsible for caring for them [their own family or close relatives]' are entitled. Just as is the case in southern European countries, it is assumed that 'the family' is a proxy for welfare institutions for individuals who fall outside the coverage of formal social security schemes, assuming reliance on either their family, some extended forms of kinship or other social networks such as neighbours (Mingione, 2001; Saraceno, 2002). In other words, social assistance mechanisms are regarded as a residual last resort to cater for those who even lack support from informal safety nets, that is, family. Actually, implicit in the introduction of emergency relief through the Solidarity Fund was the understanding that the family can no longer bear the care burden it had traditionally assumed. However, the formation as well as the functioning of the fund failed to provide rule-based, systematic, transparent and universal social assistance that would counterbalance all the risks which families fail to meet. That is to say, the Fund, acting as a sheltering institution for 931 local foundations managed by various levels of local government, was marked by a certain lack of clarity concerning criteria as regards entitlement, duration, extent, amount and form of benefit. This has tended to limit the anti-poverty function of the fund and has not achieved its aim of 'reinforcing the trust towards the state by making the citizens feel that the *state* is there to support them.'[1]

Another mechanism introduced in 1992 was the establishment of a Green Card scheme for the poor who were not covered by any social security programme either by contributions or being dependent. Financed from the general budget, this scheme grants free in-patient and out-patient health services without any co-payments. Though the scheme has been regarded as 'a transitory mechanism until the establishment of universal health insurance' (Article 1, Law No. 3816), for more than 10 million Green Card holders it turned out to constitute a kind of life-saving mechanism.

To summarize, the inegalitarian corporatist structure of the welfare regime in Turkey resulted in the formation of a patchy social safety net which is far from granting universal, adequate and systematic provision of benefits to all citizens. The regime faces certain contemporary challenges underpinning reform debates and the involvement of international actors. First and foremost, current labour market realities do not match with the corporatist setting of the formal social security system, which was designed at a time when it was possible for the urban population to be formally employed and for the rural population to rely on traditional subsistence production. Processes of de-ruralization and rapid urbanization, which started in the late 1970s and accelerated in the 1980s, marked a transformation in the labour market, increasing the share of informally employed, either in the form of unpaid family workers in rural areas or self-employed in both rural and urban settings and lacking the access to formal social security coverage. It is quite common for the family to act as a social clearing house where one member attached to formal employment can provide access to health services

Table 6.2   Sectoral distribution of employment: gender breakdown in Turkey (percentage)

	Agriculture			Industry*			Services		
	Male	Female	Total	Male	Female	Total	Male	Female	Total
1988	33.78	76.77	46.46	26.79	8.85	22.29	39.42	14.37	31.24
1989	34.20	76.61	47.41	26.13	8.97	21.58	39.66	14.42	31.02
1990	33.89	76.62	46.88	25.11	8.82	20.96	41.00	14.56	32.16
1991	34.78	77.26	47.81	25.48	8.43	20.16	39.74	14.32	32.04
1992	33.28	72.08	44.67	25.98	11.27	21.56	40.75	16.63	33.77
1993	33.29	68.93	42.16	26.38	11.72	22.64	40.33	19.34	35.21
1994	32.83	71.44	43.55	27.38	10.59	22.64	39.79	17.99	33.80
1995	32.88	71.65	43.40	27.03	9.72	22.26	40.09	18.61	34.34
1996	32.12	72.12	42.85	27.70	9.94	22.90	40.17	17.92	33.91
1997	31.81	67.87	40.76	28.33	11.60	24.12	39.87	20.54	35.12
1998	31.30	67.79	40.54	27.92	10.93	23.61	40.78	21.27	35.85
1999	29.57	66.44	41.43	28.02	11.76	22.76	42.40	21.80	35.81
2000	27.00	60.47	34.52	27.95	13.15	24.54	45.04	26.36	40.94
2001	27.70	63.33	32.58	26.74	12.13	24.31	45.55	24.54	43.12
2002	24.84	60.01	34.92	26.73	13.72	23.00	48.43	26.25	42.07
2003	24.37	58.51	33.88	26.35	13.43	22.76	49.28	28.08	43.36
2004	25.59	57.19	33.96	26.24	14.08	23.02	48.16	28.73	43.01
2005	21.72	51.63	29.45	28.13	15.05	24.73	50.15	33.32	45.82

Note: * Industry includes manufacturing as well as mining and quarrying; electricity, gas and water and construction sectors.

Sources: OECD (2006), SIS (various years).

for informally employed members of the family as dependants, a fact supported by high coverage figures.

On the other hand, declining employment and labour force participation rates for both men and women point to the fact that migration from rural to urban areas forces them either to drop out from the labour market or to be unable to find a job, leading to high unemployment in urban settings. As mentioned above, the peculiarity of the post-1980 period lies in the significant decline in formal employment opportunities with the transformation from an inward-looking, protectionist, state-subsidized and public employment strategy into one that is outward-looking and market oriented where deregulation, subcontracting and privatization of SEEs has seriously affected access to stable and formal employment (Şenses, 1994).

The sectoral distribution of employment seen in Table 6.2 demonstrates the significance of the agricultural sector, composed of small peasant

Table 6.3   *Distribution of employment according to status at work in Turkey (percentage of total employment)*

	Employee	Working on own account	Unpaid family worker
1988	40.38	29.42	30.20
1989	38.50	30.17	31.47
1990	38.96	30.93	30.11
1991	37.83	30.50	31.67
1992	39.71	31.16	29.14
1993	42.32	31.21	26.48
1994	41.17	30.87	27.96
1995	41.93	30.45	27.62
1996	43.31	29.23	27.45
1997	45.20	30.16	24.64
1998	45.18	29.80	25.02
1999	44.30	29.16	26.54
2000	49.56	29.83	20.67
2001	50.61	30.78	18.61
2002	49.75	29.38	20.86
2003	50.63	29.80	19.57
2004	50.84	29.41	19.75
2005	54.20	29.80	16.00

Source: OECD (2006).

holdings relying mostly on unpaid family labour (also see Table 6.3 for employment according to status at work). In this setting, migration from rural to urban settlements had previously allowed for the possibility of family support from the rural hinterland (that is, those who remained in the village) in the form of in-kind or sometimes income supplements. However, the withdrawal of state support programmes in the form of input subsidy or output price support as well as the changing characteristic of rural–urban migration from 'pull factors' in the city to 'push factors' due to war conditions throughout 1990s for the case of migrants of eastern and south-eastern origin has weakened the sustainability of informal mechanisms of support.

In summary, the inegalitarian corporatist nature of the Turkish welfare regime, lacking a comprehensive safety net while assuming family support as the traditional informal support mechanism backing the patchy schemes of social assistance and social security, has seriously been challenged in many ways: de-ruralization, rapid urbanization, transformation of the labour market towards informality in a sense of fewer opportunities for formal employment, and the changing nature of rural–urban migrations.

These have all acted to underpin the main pillars of the regime and called for consequent policy reforms.

KEY ASPECTS OF SOCIO-ECONOMIC AND POLITICAL DEVELOPMENTS IN POST-1980 TURKEY

Socio-economic Setting

Within the setting of an inegalitarian corporatist welfare regime, a brief snapshot of the major demographic and socio-economic information helps to frame the discussion regarding contemporary policy reforms. Related to the debates on transformation of the labour market and declining employment opportunities, population figures reveal some important evidence. In Turkey, the rate of growth of population has begun to slow down in the 1980s to reach 1.5 in 2003 (SIS/World Bank, 2005). However, given the nature of past demographic trends, both the share in total population and the rate of growth of working-age people still remain high. The employment opportunities for this group remained highly limited as regards the changes in the structure of employment. Declining share of agricultural employment, not coupled with compensating employment creation in industry and services, failed to absorb the new entrants in the labour market.

In terms of a general overview of poverty, in Turkey the population at risk of poverty, at 26 per cent of total population, is significantly higher than those prevailing in EU countries as well as in Romania and Bulgaria. Related to the transformation in the labour market and relevant for the policy reform debates, the high incidence of working poor deserves attention. Notwithstanding the fact that poverty and unemployment are surely related, the peculiarity of in-work poverty in Turkey lies in the striking feature of informal employment, which is estimated to be around half of total employment and about one-third of urban employment. Twenty-three per cent of those employed are at risk of poverty (EUROSTAT, 2004).

As far as the regional aspects of socio-economic development are concerned, the eastern and south-eastern provinces of Turkey have historically been more disadvantaged than the other regions of the country. The average GNP per capita is about one-third of the country average in this region whose population is 15 per cent of the total population of Turkey, a trend which has deteriorated in the course of 1990s (TESEV, 2006). A comprehensive picture of some aspects of regional disparities can be addressed by reference to the regional data on basic human development indicators of GDP per capita at PPP, life expectancy, adult literacy and combined school enrolment ratios, where the gap between the most developed regions in the West and the least developed regions in the East are indeed very high, as can be seen in Table 6.4. Out of the 20 least developed provinces, 18 are located in eastern and south-eastern Turkey. The 2003 national composite index of development, introduced within the regional development programme of the State Planning Organization, confirms this picture, with eastern and south-eastern provinces ranking at the very end of the list of 81 provinces (TESEV, 2006).

Political Developments in the Post-1980 Era

The highly complex political terrain in Turkey can be viewed throughout the political developments of the post-1980 period where instability, short-lived coalitions pushing for populist policies, and vicious cycles of economic instabilities as a result of fiscal imbalances have long been the norm. The political and economic turmoil of the 1970s led to a military coup in September 1980.

The general elections of November 1983 allowed limited participation by some political parties and the contemporary political alignment did not emerge until a change in the constitution in September 1987, with the power of the ruling centre-right Motherland Party (ANAP) gradually eroded until defeat in 1991 by the True Path Party (DYP) and SHP, a merger of the Populist and Social Democratic parties. The Islamist Welfare Party won key local elections in March 1994 and was part of a short-lived coalition government after general elections in December 1995. They were removed from power in 1997, and the 1999 general elections resulted in the formation of an interesting coalition between the left-of-centre Democratic Left Party (DSP), the right-of-centre ANAP and the ultra nationalist Nationalist Action Party (MHP), united by a political imperative to 'protect' the secular and unitary foundations of the republic and oppose the rise of political Islam. Even though the initial years of the coalition were stable due to the establishment of a standby agreement with the IMF conditional upon the implementation of an extensive public sector reform programme, the country experienced the 'twin crises' of 2000 and 2001, which had devastating impacts on different segments of the population. Subsequently, in the 2002 elections, none of the coalition partners were able to pass the electoral threshold of 10 per cent to be represented in Parliament and were gradually eliminated from the contemporary political scene.

The failings of conventional political parties, with left-of-centre parties failing to protect the poor and underprivileged, and right-of-centre parties suffering from involvement in corruption, the Justice and Development Party (AKP) achieved an extraordinary success in November 2002

Table 6.4   Non-monetary human development indicators: selected Turkish provinces, 2000

	Highest human development			Lowest human development*							
	Kocaeli	Yalova	İstanbul	Gümüşhane	Diyarbakır	Yozgat	Erzurum	Ardahan	Erzincan	Adıyaman	Kars
Human Development Index											
Life expectancy at birth (years)	73.8	72.4	72.4	64.7	68.1	64.7	62.3	60.3	59.9	63.1	60.3
Adult literacy rate (% ages 15 and above)	91.8	92.9	93.2	85.3	67	84.8	82.6	83	86.4	77	81.2
Combined 1st, 2nd gross enrolment ratio (%)	99.2	100.3	100.3	58.8	70.5	64.6	70.1	89.5	65.1	76.9	80.4
GDP per capita (PPP US$)	16 536	10 209	9 664	3 263	3 701	2 736	3 178	2 315	3 348	2 736	2 482
Life expectancy index	0.813	0.789	0.791	0.662	0.718	0.662	0.622	0.588	0.581	0.635	0.588
Education index	0.942	0.954	0.956	0.765	0.682	0.781	0.784	0.852	0.793	0.770	0.809
GDP index	0.853	0.772	0.763	0.582	0.603	0.552	0.577	0.524	0.586	0.552	0.536
HDI value	0.869	0.838	0.837	0.669	0.668	0.665	0.661	0.655	0.653	0.652	0.644
GDP per capita (PPP US$) rank minus HDI rank	0	1	1	−1	−8	5	−3	11	−7	2	4

Gender-Related Development Index

	1	2	3	63	70	65	64	66	67	68	69
GDI rank	1	2	3	63	70	65	64	66	67	68	69
GDI value	0.839	0.812	0.810	0.657	0.640	0.653	0.653	0.652	0.652	0.643	0.640
Life expectancy at birth, female (years)	75.7	74.2	74.2	66	69.3	66	62.5	61.9	61.1	64.3	61.9
Life expectancy at birth, male (years)	70.2	69.0	69.0	61.6	65.1	61.6	60.3	57	57	60	57
Adult literacy rate, female (% ages 15 and above)	85.9	87.9	88.7	75.8	49.7	76.5	71.7	72.3	77.3	65.3	68.5
Adult literacy rate, male (% ages 15 and above)	97.2	97.3	97.7	94.5	84.5	93.4	93.1	92.7	94.1	89.2	93
Combined 1st, 2nd gross enrolment ratio, female (%)	94.6	96.9	98.9	55	59.1	60.5	61.1	83.7	61.3	70.9	72
Combined 1st, 2nd gross enrolment ratio, male (%)	103.6	103.5	101.6	62.3	81.1	68.6	78.3	95	68.7	82.4	88.2
Estimated earned income, female (PPP US$)	14594	9068	10304	2625	3175	2144	2669	1943	2592	2519	2098
Estimated earned income, male (PPP US$)	18339	11236	9044	3882	4210	3323	3658	2656	4010	2951	2836
HDI rank minus GDI rank	0	0	0	−1	−7	−1	1	0	0	0	0

Table 6.4 (continued)

<table>
<tr><th></th><th colspan="12">Lowest human development*</th></tr>
<tr><th></th><th>Batman</th><th>Mardin</th><th>Siirt</th><th>Iğdır</th><th>Şanlıurfa</th><th>Van</th><th>Hakkari</th><th>Bingöl</th><th>Bitlis</th><th>Muş</th><th>Ağrı</th><th>Şırnak</th></tr>
<tr><td colspan="13">Human Development Index</td></tr>
<tr><td>Life expectancy at birth (years)</td><td>63.1</td><td>66.2</td><td>63.5</td><td>60.3</td><td>64</td><td>63.7</td><td>60.7</td><td>59.5</td><td>59.9</td><td>62</td><td>60.4</td><td>57.7</td></tr>
<tr><td>Adult literacy rate (% ages 15 and above)</td><td>67.4</td><td>67.6</td><td>65.8</td><td>73.2</td><td>65.7</td><td>66.6</td><td>67.5</td><td>72.4</td><td>71.8</td><td>67.3</td><td>67.4</td><td>62.3</td></tr>
<tr><td>Combined 1st, 2nd gross enrolment ratio (%)</td><td>77.3</td><td>70.4</td><td>76.5</td><td>83.7</td><td>63.2</td><td>68.2</td><td>75.8</td><td>65.5</td><td>53.1</td><td>58.3</td><td>57.6</td><td>70.6</td></tr>
<tr><td>GDP per capita (PPP US$)</td><td>3410</td><td>2519</td><td>3062</td><td>2556</td><td>2847</td><td>2447</td><td>2445</td><td>2331</td><td>1932</td><td>1587</td><td>1803</td><td>1816</td></tr>
<tr><td>Life expectancy index</td><td>0.634</td><td>0.687</td><td>0.642</td><td>0.588</td><td>0.65</td><td>0.644</td><td>0.596</td><td>0.575</td><td>0.581</td><td>0.617</td><td>0.591</td><td>0.545</td></tr>
<tr><td>Education index</td><td>0.707</td><td>0.685</td><td>0.693</td><td>0.767</td><td>0.649</td><td>0.671</td><td>0.703</td><td>0.701</td><td>0.656</td><td>0.643</td><td>0.642</td><td>0.651</td></tr>
<tr><td>GDP index</td><td>0.589</td><td>0.539</td><td>0.571</td><td>0.541</td><td>0.559</td><td>0.534</td><td>0.534</td><td>0.526</td><td>0.494</td><td>0.461</td><td>0.483</td><td>0.484</td></tr>
<tr><td>HDI value</td><td>0.644</td><td>0.637</td><td>0.636</td><td>0.632</td><td>0.619</td><td>0.616</td><td>0.611</td><td>0.601</td><td>0.577</td><td>0.574</td><td>0.572</td><td>0.560</td></tr>
<tr><td>GDP per capita (PPP US$) rank minus HDI rank</td><td>-11</td><td>1</td><td>-8</td><td>-2</td><td>-6</td><td>0</td><td>-2</td><td>-1</td><td>0</td><td>2</td><td>0</td><td>-2</td></tr>
</table>

Gender-Related Development Index

	71	72	73	61	74	75	77	76	78	80	79	81
GDI rank	71	72	73	61	74	75	77	76	78	80	79	81
GDI value	0.628	0.613	0.608	0.664	0.598	0.596	0.590	0.593	0.568	0.556	0.558	0.543
Life expectancy at birth, female (years)	64.3	67.5	64.5	61.9	65.3	63	62.1	60.5	61.1	63.2	61.3	58.9
Life expectancy at birth, male (years)	60	63.1	60.9	57	61	62.5	58	56.8	57	59.1	57.8	55
Adult literacy rate, female (% ages 15 and above)	50.6	49.5	45.4	80.9	46.8	48.2	43.7	57	55	48.3	48.4	35.8
Adult literacy rate, male (% ages 15 and above)	82.8	85.2	84.5	96.2	83.6	85	85.3	87.1	86.9	85.5	85.7	82.6
Combined 1st, 2nd gross enrolment ratio, female (%)	63.7	58.1	56.6	74.7	51.5	49	60.3	52.7	40.6	44.8	43.8	55.2
Combined 1st, 2nd gross enrolment ratio, male (%)	89.7	81.7	94.4	92.3	73.5	86	89.5	77	63.8	70.1	70.2	84.6
Estimated earned income, female (PPP US$)	3 322	2 286	2 215	2 076	2 337	2 068	1 766	1 873	1 854	1 369	1 626	1 580
Estimated earned income, male (PPP US$)	3 496	2 739	3 837	3 005	3 320	2 810	3 014	2 757	2 002	1 787	1 968	2 012
HDI rank minus GDI rank	-1	-1	-1	12	0	0	-1	1	0	-1	1	0

Note: * 20 provinces with lowest 20 rankings in human development.

Source: UNDP (2005: 64–7).

elections. Notwithstanding its Islamist roots and emphasis on religion and conservatism, the AKP managed to build a broad cross-class coalition to resemble a typical right-of-centre party. The rule of the AKP government since November 2002 marks a certain breaking of the trend, with economic stability largely attributable to the strong commitment not only to the implementation of the IMF programme, but also to the realization of an extensive set of reforms, including those in the realm of social policies.

INTERNATIONAL ACTORS INVOLVED IN SOCIAL POLICIES

The involvement of international actors in social policy reforms in Turkey in the post-1980 period paralleled the rise of market-oriented and market-led policies in the process of financial liberalization. This period has witnessed serious economic crises that have been attributed to the vulnerability of the economy vis-à-vis external and internal fluctuations, and these have overburdened the budget as a result of debt payments accumulated in this period. That is to say, one of the striking features of the Turkish experience with neo-liberalism, initiated in 1980 with the implementation of a structural adjustment programme in the aftermath of severe and successive balance of payment crises of late 1970s, was that the loan burden of gradual liberalization from IFIs in the 1980s has been coupled with the high burden of domestic borrowing accumulated in the 1990s and this has resulted in the prevalence of macroeconomic instability reinforced by large public deficits and persistent high inflation. This vicious cycle of fiscal deficit followed by balance-of-payment crisis has always ended up with an inevitable encounter with the standby agreements of the IMF and the structural adjustment programmes of the World Bank.

In this regard, just as is the case for most developing economies, it is not surprising to see the IMF and the World Bank as most influential. Having established themselves as advisers making recommendations to national governments, they became the dominant powers shaping the policy agendas of national economies. The economy in Turkey has long been under close supervision as a result of standby agreements signed with the IMF while the structural adjustment programmes of the World Bank, which have undergone change in terms of now considering the social dimensions of restructuring, aim for a longer-term transformation of the economy. The peculiarity of the programme initiated in the post-1980 period lies in the fact that it was one of the first involving both short-term stabilization and longer-term structural adjustment as a result of close co-operation between the IMF and the World Bank. Later this was referred to as a new form of

World Bank–IMF cross-conditionality and was applied to other developing economies (Onis and Kirkpatrick, 1991). In the initial stages of the programme in the early 1980s, the IMF's attention was focused on sustaining monetary and fiscal balances as well as maintaining external competitiveness, while the World Bank concentrated on reforming SEEs, promoting exports, liberalizing imports and rationalizing public investment towards infrastructure. Areas of responsibilities were never integrated within an overall framework of macro planning, however.

Within a broad framework of increasing the role of the market in welfare provision in the latter period, the IMF and the World Bank in Turkey have been particularly influential in not only constraining in terms of sustaining budgetary discipline, but also shaping contemporary pension and health reforms as well as loan programmes directed to social assistance, the details of which are discussed below. As of June 2006, 15.95 per cent of the active portfolio of the World Bank in Turkey has been devoted to social protection (World Bank, 2006).

Other key international actors are present in Turkey. As the main UN agency, UNDP in Turkey has worked as an associate for more than 50 years especially assuming a role of helping to build capacities for social development. More specifically, the agenda of UNDP for Turkey has highlighted poverty reduction since the early 1990s, the timing of which is parallel to a global shift in its orientation in terms of the adoption of Sen's 'capability framework' emphasizing the multidimensionality of poverty and consecutive conceptualization of the notion of 'human development'. Working in close partnership with government agencies and operating co-funding arrangements with other international agencies including the European Commission, the UNDP country office aims to support the poverty reduction policies of the government through projects for micro-finance sector development, programmes directed to enhancing the social development of south-eastern Anatolia, and the promotion of co-operation in the area of social assistance, as well as promoting the achievement of the MDGs.

The oldest UN agency, the ILO, has been active in Turkey within the areas of its expertise, mainly labour legislation, social dialogue and labour standards. As one of the 'old member states', Turkey has ratified 56 Conventions since the 1950s. The ILO country office, in close collaboration with the Ministry of Labour and Social Security (MoLSS), has developed technical co-operation programmes covering implementation of the international programme on the elimination of child labour, enhancing social dialogue and combating informal employment (with pilot projects), and training programmes for supply chain textile factories on labour standards (co-funded by the EU). These programmes are being transformed into more comprehensive governmental policy commitments.

As a country having a long association with the European Union, the signing of a Customs Union between the EU and Turkey in 1995, and recognition of Turkey as a candidate country at the Helsinki European Council in 1999, mark the beginnings of a pre-accession strategy aiming to support and stimulate reform processes. Notwithstanding the fact that the preparation of Accession Partnerships in 2001 and 2003 refer to assisting the Turkish authorities to meet the accession criteria, with particular emphasis on the political criteria, the decision to start negotiations in December 2004 accelerated the penetration of the EU within the social policy domain in Turkey. This occurred in two ways. First, it led to the preparation of the Joint Inclusion Memoranda (JIM) and the Joint Assessment Paper for Employment Priorities (JAP) under the auspices of the MoLSS, with the participation and contribution of a wide range of social actors together with the representatives of other state bodies with responsibilities in the field of social policy. The JIM process has stirred consciousness of the need to think about poverty and social exclusion as problems that cannot be solved solely by relying on employment creation through economic growth. The need for both active labour market policies and specific measures to deal with the problems of especially vulnerable groups have come onto the agenda and the multidimensional nature of the problems in question has been recognized.

Second, the MEDA programme, through which Turkey had long been a beneficiary of financial assistance under the Euro-Mediterranean Partnership, was replaced by a pre-accession assistance programme extended to 'provide support for institution building, investment to strengthen the regulatory infrastructure needed to ensure compliance with the *acquis*, investment in economic and social cohesion and the promotion of the civil society dialogue' (EC, Enlargement Pages).[2] From 2007 onwards Turkey will be a beneficiary of the new IPA instrument, the human resources development component of which will mainly support activities addressing social inclusion as well as other issues such as employment and education and training.

Considering the challenges facing the welfare regime, which call for a broad set of reforms in social policy domains in Turkey, the slow pace of progress can be attributed to the emergence of tensions that are inherent in the transformation process itself. Having reviewed the involvement of international actors, one should note the conflicting objectives of sustaining sound finance while aiming at social inclusion through employment creation, improved public services and more universal and comprehensive schemes of social assistance. The fact that the IMF appears as an important actor in the socio-economic policy process makes it very difficult to achieve social consensus in the policy environment since even those reforms necessary for reasons different from simple fiscal restraint are sometimes interpreted as resulting from the compliance of the government to international organizations. It is thus quite difficult for the IMF as well as the World Bank to contribute constructively to social policy debates. The EU, on the other hand, seems to show little interest in counterbalancing the impact of the IMF or the World Bank in particular social policy reforms but, rather, involves itself in broader political and policy domains.

MAIN POLICY REFORMS

Pensions

The reform debate around pension schemes in Turkey has always been controversial. Throughout the 1990s, intensified reform discussions tended to emphasize the imbalances within the pension system where the contributions accumulated were much less than the pension expenditures (TÜSİAD, 1997). However, the need for reform can be attributed to the structural changes taking place since 1980 in the process of liberalizing the economy. Within this period, the first reform was attempted by the Ozal government in 1986, aiming to introduce an additional ceiling and flat rates for the calculation of benefits in the SSK system, and hence to enable high-income groups to pay more premiums in order to receive higher pension benefits (which became publicly known as 'super pensions'). As a pattern followed in later reforms, this reform was designed to cater for the deficits expected to increase in the future. Instead of raising the overall level of premiums or changing the whole rates for benefit calculation, which would be quite likely to fail to overcome the deficits since all pension benefits would rise, only additional rates were introduced. Even though the system seemed to accrue higher levels of premiums, the actuarial balance as well as the intergenerational balance among pensioners of SSK was seriously undermined. This reform attempt also created disparities within the social security system in the sense that the ratio of ceiling pension to the flat rate had been 4.6 in the ES system, while it jumped to between 10 and 11 in the SSK (Constitutional Court, 1990). Referring to the social justice clauses in the Turkish Constitution mentioned above, in 1990 the Constitutional Court annulled the law enacting the reform.

Interestingly, in a populist and myopic fashion, the DYP–SHP coalition government introduced early retirement in 1992, with 20 years of full contributions for women and 25 years for men sufficient in order to retire, regardless of the number of days worked, age and so on. In the more recent reforms of 1999 and 2005, the outcomes of these earlier reforms from 1986 and 1992 have been seen as important in evaluating the design of the reform packages. In fact, the reform in 1992 has been seriously criticized on the grounds that it has accelerated the creation of the deficits (TÜSİAD, 1997; World Bank, 2000).

Even though some attempts to introduce minor changes in the social security system were evident after 1992, the major structural reform occurred in 1999. In fact, though the reform package assumed erosion of the financing of the social security institutions as well as misuse of funds collected through contributions for financing domestic debt, thus the emergence of fiscal imbalances, one can argue that the shrinking size of formal employment, increasing unemployment and migration also challenged the sustainability of the schemes.

To offer remedies to these challenges, a pension reform project supported by the World Bank was designed as a two-stage process, the first of which aims to address short-term measures while the second stage has a longer-term vision with administrative measures and establishment of a new system. The first phase reforms should be viewed as kick-starting the radical reform of the whole system in Turkey. Initiated in August 1999, the first phase of the reform package introduced a minimum retirement age for all new entrants in the ES, BK and SSK schemes, while a transitory period is allowed for current contributors. In order to improve the linkage between contributions and benefits, the reference wage period is expanded to the full contribution period for SSK and BK pensioners, but ES pensioners, that is, civil servants, are still privileged in terms of receiving the amount of benefit that is tied to their salary before retirement. The reform has also replaced discretionary pension indexation, generally tied to wage increases of civil servants, by Consumer Price Index (CPI) indexation which was regarded as 'a more transparent and financially conservative rule' (World Bank, 2000: 33).

All these measures were seen to be inadequate in eliminating the deficits in the short term by the World Bank; a second stage of reforms was to be introduced to support and strengthen the initial changes and to build a sound system in the longer term. This second stage is marked by administrative reform necessitated by the shift in the base of the pension calculation from the final years of a person's working life to the full job history of the contributor. This shift requires reorganization based on information-sharing among the three organizations and a consequent upgrading of management information systems so that the PAYG system will be improved in terms of coverage which, in turn, is said to lead to sustainable fiscal balances of the system by covering the non-covered 40 per cent of the working population (State Institute of Statistics, 1998; World Bank, 2000). The pension fund administration is also proposed to be carried out by a single institution. This proposal is also formalized by the completion of the law drafts by the Ministry of Labour and Social Security at the end of 2004 that established so-called 'Social Security Institution' with the enaction of Law No. 5502 in 2006 responsible for the application of the reform process.

The establishment of voluntarily funded private pensions to complement the existing system by requiring the subscriber to contribute to one of the PAYG schemes mainly serves to appeal to higher-income individuals with savings transferred from other instruments to this new scheme. As earlier experiences with Latin American counterparts show, they often fail either to achieve capital market development or a deepening of the financial sector, or to earn high profits from the savings funds as expected (Mesa-Lago, 1997; 2001; 2002; Huber and Stephens, 2000).

The administrative restructuring stage of the reform began with reform proposals in 2004 covering the whole system mainly focusing on four pillars: the establishment of universal health insurance, the restructuring of social assistance and services, the reform of pensions and the foundation of an institutional structure aiming to harmonize the other three pillars. Actually, the reform package has extensively been discussed in a White Paper published by the Ministry of Labour and Social Security in April 2005. Here, the major challenges facing the pension system are defined as: (1) differences regarding technical issues such as minimum contribution period for eligibility, benefit rules and other aspects between the schemes offered by the three different institutions, (2) actuarial imbalances between benefits and contributions leading to deficits needing to be covered by state transfers, (3) since the group of early retired pensioners distorted the actuarial balance of high contributions–low benefits, the system cannot take advantage of the current favourable demographic trend which, in any case, is projected to disappear in 20–25 years time (MoLSS, 2005). Aiming mainly to establish a single pension system, the reform introduced a gradual increase in the retirement age which will be kept at 58 for women and 60 for men until 2035 and will be raised gradually afterwards until 2075 to reach 68 years of age for both groups parallel to the increase in life expectancy documented by demographic projections. The current benefit calculation rule has been changed from different bases to 2.5 per cent accrual rate for the period 2006–2015 and 2.0 per cent thereafter regardless of the threshold of 25 years of working history. Regarding benefit indexation, the CPI indexation rule introduced by the previous reform has not been changed. It must be noted that the reform protects the vested interests of workers already in the system even though their benefit levels seem to be lowered, but in the longer term envisages harmonizing the level of benefits by restructuring the calculation formulas within a single institution. Considering the premium levels, the new system is mainly based on the current system of SSK taking minimum wage as the flat rate and 6.5 times the minimum wage as the ceiling. Employee and state contributions to unemployment insurance are also kept the same at 3 per cent and 1 per cent respectively (MoLSS, 2005). As presented in the projections in the White Paper, the reform seeks to decrease the current deficits so that the pension system will become financially sustainable in the longer term with the share of deficits in GDP kept to less than 1 per cent.

In general, the reform which was hotly debated in 2005 and enacted in 2006 by Parliament has introduced major changes within the social security system, especially concerning health insurance and administrative harmonization questions. However, regarding pension schemes, the reform package seems to address only the actuarial balance problem in so far as the projections are considered. Although the more fundamental problems, such as the informal sector challenging the welfare regime and the schemes themselves are acknowledged, no significant policy remedy has been prescribed within the pension reform package. Rather, all policy changes affect the formally employed and insured workers who constitute only 57.6 per cent of the working population. This piece of legislation marks a turning point in transforming the inegalitarian corporatist characteristic of the regime by replacing the administration of separate schemes of ES, SSK and BK with the establishment of a Social Security Institution under the auspices of MoLSS responsible for the administration of a single pension scheme. In addition to this, the introduction of state contributions to the pension system at 5 per cent resembles a shift in the mentality from viewing budgetary transfers as covering the so-called 'black holes' of the social security system towards assigning certain financial responsibilities to the state. In other words, by committing to contribute to the system by 5 per cent, the state is beginning to assume responsibility in the financing of the pension system rather than making budgetary transfers to compensate for the deficits of the schemes.

Expected to be effective from 1 January 2007 onwards, the objections of the main opposition party and the President of the Constitutional Court has resulted in the cancellation of some articles that regulate the harmonization procedures for civil servants, thus resulting in maintaining the privileges of this group compared with others. As there is a very short time for the law to become effective and parliamentary approval of necessary revisions has been delayed, the government has postponed implementation until July 2007. It should be noted that, as intervening actors, the IMF and, to an extent, the World Bank in its documents, have long been calling for reforms in the social security system on the basis of financial budgetary constraints rather than the need for a universalistic approach. In this context, the IMF also put some kind of 'informal' conditionality on the release of a considerable part of the loan by its announcement of linking the release with the parliamentary approval of the law. Concerning the recent cancellation of some articles, the IMF representative showed a rather defensive attitude in declaring that IMF finds the implementation of the law essential but has not determined its position in the light of this possible delay (Radikal, 2006).

Health-care Services

Carried out as part of a longer-term reform package as mentioned above, the universalization of health-care systems separately from social insurance schemes has also long been on the agenda of the World Bank in Turkey. As mentioned in the first section, the Green Card scheme was introduced in 1992 as a transitory mechanism to switch to universal coverage. Although previous governments in the post-1980 period expressed their intention to reform the health system by separating it from social security schemes, the agenda of the World Bank coincided with the 'Transformation of Health' project that has been prioritized in the party programme of the AKP government, elected in 2003. Designating the Turkish health-care system as 'one of the most complex . . . in the world' (World Bank, 2002: 1), the World Bank has discovered that access to health care is skewed regionally and on an urban–rural basis as well as among different income groups, resulting in a wide gap between the urban and rural population and between regions of East and West in health indicators (World Bank, 2002). Consequently, the Bank aimed to encourage the government to extend health coverage and finance to the whole population and strengthen the delivery of care services through a private care system in the first phase. Subsequently, further investments towards restructuring would be supported and decentralization of the Ministry of Health (MoH) and hospital autonomy would be realized. Actually, World Bank credits to the MoH have been used for the improvement of infrastructure and equipment. This stands as the first serious attempt to implement an integrated and extensive reform towards a universalistic health-care system.

In line with the proposals in the extensive reports of the World Bank (2002 and 2003), the health reform proposal within the 2004 reform proposal package has set the main objective as the establishment of universal social health insurance initiated by the establishment of an autonomous Health Fund managing health-care activities by altering the flow of funds so as to transfer all health contributions collected and state payments of Green Card for the poor, having regional level branches with a high degree of autonomy over routine functions. The proposal, enacted and becoming law with the Social Security Reform Law in 2006, brings the provision of a minimum package of health services in return for the contributions that those earning above the poverty line are obliged to pay while the poor will be granted means-tested access to the services with their contribution paid by the state. For a country like Turkey where approximately 10–20 per cent of the population is not covered by any of the existing schemes, including the Green Card (WHO, 2006), this schema is unrealistic in terms of granting universal access. On the other hand, for the first time, this piece of legislation aims at granting universal access of all the population to health-care services regardless of employment status. In this regard, one should acknowledge the importance of free universal access to health services granted to those under the age of 18 irrespective of the status of their families as regards contribution payments within the context of child poverty, with some 34 per cent of children under the age of 15 at risk of poverty (EUROSTAT, 2004).

Another issue highly debated by health-care professionals is the trend in reform towards the marketization of services and encouragement for the private sector to collaborate in a public–private mix of service provision, which serves to deepen the persistent inequalities within the system. Coupled with public sector reform aiming to decrease state employment, it is expected that family physicians employed on a contractual basis will provide primary-level services. The introduction of performance criteria, which would affect the amount they will receive from the Health Fund in return for services provided, will lead to a situation where they would try to maximize the number of patients to be examined, while the quality of this service as well as equity concerns would remain highly questionable. As this reform has been enacted in a combined package with the social security reform, its implementation has also been postponed.

Social Assistance

In the late 1990s, the Turkish economy experienced cumulative shocks beginning with a devastating earthquake in August 1999 in the Marmara region, seriously affecting Istanbul and Kocaeli, two of the most densely populated industrial sites along the Marmara coast, and which had a severe impact on output growth as well as employment. In order to provide immediate relief to the victims of the earthquake, with the support of the IMF, the then coalition government launched an exchange rate-based disinflation programme coupled with a series of structural reforms as recommended by the World Bank. During the early part of 2000, the programme stimulated considerable recovery not only in terms of output, led by a recovery in industrial production attributed to the consumption boom driven by the disinflation programme, but also in employment. This positive environment was shaken in November 2000 by financial turmoil in the banking sector caused by the liquidity crisis of a medium-sized bank. With confidence in the pegged exchange rate undermined, political tension in February 2001 ignited a fully fledged currency crisis that destroyed the disinflation programme while the exchange rate peg was abandoned in favour of currency flotation, leading to one of the most severe economic crises of the last two decades, pulling the economy into a deep recession. Among the cumulative social impacts of these consecutive developments, unemployment rose sharply, employment in agriculture and construction sectors where the poor used to be employed fell significantly, while the persistently high rates of inflation severely affected the purchasing power of the poorest segments of society. Within this setting, two World Bank loan programmes carried out through the Solidarity Fund are worth mentioning. The first provided cash benefits immediately after the earthquake to the victims through an Emergency Earthquake Recovery Loan in the form of rental or repair allowances, death and disability benefits. Second, a Social Risk Mitigation Project Loan was introduced to moderate the impact of the crises on poor households through the adjustment portion to provide immediate support to the poorest families via the Solidarity Fund and the investment portion to build up the capacity of the fund, to introduce conditional cash transfers (CCTs) targeted to the poorest families by making social assistance conditional upon the use of basic health and education services and to increase income-generating employment opportunities for the poor.

The former fitted well with the emergency relief tradition of social assistance mechanisms in Turkey. However, the latter deserves attention in two ways: expanding grants for income-generating employment projects (sometimes called local initiatives) can be regarded as typical of a liberal view that attributes conditionality for social assistance on some kind of productive activity so as to refrain from encouraging 'welfare dependency'. On the other hand, the implementation of CCT, which is a time-limited (2004–2006) budget programme granting allowances to pregnant women, pre-school children and children attending compulsory primary school conditional on regular visits to health centres and school attendance, has shown significant progress in raising school attendance, while some administrative discretion at the local level as regards to implementing objective criteria for eligibility overshadows the success of the programme as an effective social assistance mechanism (Erdem, 2006). The system is based on computer-based eligibility determination upon the information provided by the application form. The administrative discretion comes out as a by-product of local administration being not informed about the criteria applied by the central administration. Evidence from fieldwork interviews with officials demonstrates that local officers use discretion by initially implementing some kind of categorical eligibility criteria (such as being a widow, orphan, disabled, and so on), based on application forms received, and then transferring the 'discretionally eligible' application forms to the system for further assessment (TESEV, 2006).

An extension to the duration of this project is under way which should be viewed in the light of the draft proposal for the third pillar of social security reform relating to the restructuring of social assistances and services which had been prepared in 2004 but which has never been discussed by Parliament. This draft was very innovative in the way it introduced a coherent social assistance system with a rights-based approach, specifying benefits for the elderly, children and disabled to be funded from the general budget and administered by a single institution, namely the Social Security Institution under the MoLSS. In this context, it would be more meaningful if CCTs would be considered within the new system (after being revised to eliminate discretionary practices) as a form of child benefit rather than a loan-financed temporary programme. Nevertheless, the delay of legislation on this proposal also supports a conservative-liberal tendency (Buğra and Keyder, 2006) in social policy-making combined with the blueprints of a World Bank ideology which sets the priorities and constraints in the policy domain in terms of reforms.

CONCLUSIONS

The Turkish welfare regime has been undergoing a serious transformation within the past two decades. With the challenges undermining the realities upon which its inegalitarian corporatist structure had been built, calls for reform have been inevitable. In this setting, the involvement of international actors in influencing the path the reforms would take were dominated by the IMF and the World Bank legitimated by structural adjustment programmes and standby agreements to reduce the heavy burden of public debt. Notwithstanding the fact that this domination assumes liberal notions of individualization of risks, privatization, marketization and so on, hints towards granting universalism are to be found between the lines of the reform packages. In terms of outcomes, social policy reforms exhibit a hybrid nature complicating the terms on which efficiency and equity principles should be, or could be, evaluated. The influence of EU candidate status has been quite limited as social policy issues have been prioritized far less than political and economic criteria. Nevertheless, consciousness of the need to promote social inclusion steered by the preparation process of the JIM and JAP documents can be considered as an indirect but important involvement by the EU. As seen from the conclusions of the chapter on 'Social Policy and Employment' of the 2006 Progress Report of Turkey, the

EU prefers to mention 'what should be done' rather than 'how this should be done', which remains the domain par excellence of the World Bank.

NOTES

1. This quotation is the combined version of expressions of two officials in charge of the fund (one local, one central) used in our interviews conducted in 2002 during the field work of the project 'New Poverty and Changing Welfare Regime of Turkey', published by UNDP in 2003, See Buğra and Keyder (2003).
2. See http://ec.europa.eu/enlargement/turkey/eu_turkey_relations_en.htm.

REFERENCES

Andreotti, A., S. Marisol Garcia, A. Gomez, P. Hespanha, Y. Kazepov and E. Mingione (2001), 'Does a Southern European model exist?', *Journal of European Area Studies*, **9** (1), 43–62.

Boratav, K. and M. Ozugurlu (2005), 'Social policies and distributive dynamics in Turkey: 1923–2002', in M. Karshenas and V.M. Moghadam (eds), *Social Policy in the Middle East: Economic, Political and Gender Dynamics*, Hoondmills: Palgrave, pp. 156–89.

Buğra, A. and C. Keyder (2003), *New Poverty and Changing Welfare Regime of Turkey*, Ankara: UNDP.

Buğra, A. and C. Keyder (2006), 'The Turkish welfare regime in transformation', *Journal of European Social Policy*, **16** (3), 211–28.

Constitutional Court (1990), Result of Demand for Cancellation of Law No. 3395, http://www.anayasa.gov.tr/general/Kararbilgibank.asp (accessed 2 July 2005).

Erdem, I. (2006), 'Çok Amaçli Bir Sosyal Politika Araci Olarak Şartli Nakit Transferi' ('Conditional cash transfers as a multi-purpose social policy mechanism'), *Social Policy Forum Newsletter*, **1**, 9–11.

Esping-Andersen, G. (1999), *Social Foundations of Post-Industrial Societies*, Oxford: Oxford University Press.

EUROSTAT (2004), http//epp.eurostat.ec.europa.eu/portal (accessed 15 November 2006).

Ferrera, M. (1996), 'The "southern model" of welfare in social Europe', *Journal of European Social Policy*, **6** (1), 17–37.

Ferrera, M. (2000), 'Reconstructing the welfare state', in S. Kuhnle (ed.), *Survival of the European Welfare State*, London: Routledge, pp. 166–81.

Ferrera, M. (2005), 'Welfare states and social safety nets in Southern Europe: an introduction', in M. Ferrera (ed.), *Welfare State Reform in Southern Europe*, London: Routledge, pp. 1–32.

Gough, I. (1996), 'Social assistance in Southern Europe', *South European Society and Politics*, **1** (1), 1–23.

Government of Turkey (1986), *Law on Encouragement of Social Assistance and Solidarity*, No. 3294, Ankara.

Government of Turkey (1992), *Law on State Provision of Health Care Expenses of Citizens (who cannot afford to pay) by Means of Green Card*, No. 3816, Ankara.

Government of Turkey (2006), *Law on Social Security Institution*, No. 5502, Ankara.
Huber, E. and J.D. Stephens (2000), *The Political Economy of Pension Reform: Latin America in Comparative Perspective* (Occasional Paper 7), Geneva: UNRISD Publications.
Leibfried, S. (1993), 'Towards a European welfare state?', in Z. Ferge and J.E. Kberd (eds), *Social Policy in a Changing Europe*, Boulder, CO: Westview Press, pp. 245–79.
Mesa-Lago, C. (1997), 'Social welfare reform in the context of economic-political liberalization: Latin American cases', *World Development*, **25** (4), 497–517.
Mesa-Lago, C. (2001), 'Structural reform of social security pensions in Latin America', *International Social Security Review*, **54** (4), 67–92.
Mesa-Lago, C. (2002), 'Myth and reality of pension reform: the Latin American experience', *World Development*, **30** (8), 1309–21.
Mingione, E. (2001), 'The Southern European welfare model and the fight against poverty and social exclusion', in M. Tolba (ed.), *Our Fragile World: Challenges and Opportunities for Sustainable Development*, Oxford: EOLSS Publications, pp. 1041–51.
Ministry of Labour and Social Security (MoLSS) (2005), *Sosyal Güvenlik Sisteminde Reform* (*White Paper on Social Security Reform*), Ankara, http://www.csgb.gov.tr/sgk/sosyal_guvenlik_beyaz_kitap_2005.pdf (accessed 10 May 2005).
Moreno, L. (2000), 'The Spanish development of Southern European welfare', in S. Kuhnle (ed.), *Survival of the European Welfare State*, London: Routledge, pp. 146–65.
Moreno, L. (2006), 'The model of social protection in Southern Europe: enduring characteristics', *CSIS Working Papers*, no. 06-07, Madrid.
OECD (2006), *Labour Force Statistics (1985–2005)*, Paris: OECD.
Onis, Z. and C. Kirkpatrick (1991), 'Turkey', in P. Mosley, S. Harrigan and J. Toye (eds), *Aid and Lending: World Bank and Policy Based Lending*, vol. 2, London: Routledge, pp. 9–37.
Ozbek, N. (2002), *Osmanli Imparatorluğu'nda Sosyal Devlet* (*Social State in Ottoman Empire*), Istanbul: Iletişim.
Radikal (2006), 'IMF: Hükümet iptal karariyla tabii ki güç durumda kaldi' ('IMF: government is now of course in a difficult position with these cancellations'), www.radikal.com.tr/haber.php?haberno=207914 (accessed 21 December 2006).
Saraceno, C. (ed.) (2002), *Social Assistance Dynamics in Europe: National and Local Poverty Regimes*, Bristol: Policy Press.
Seekings, J. (2004), 'Prospects for basic income in developing countries: a comparative analysis of welfare regimes in the south', paper presented at the 10th International BIEN Congress, 19–20 September, Barcelona.
State Institute of Statistics (1998), *Labor Statistics*, Ankara: State Institute of Statistics and Ministry of Labor and Social Security.
State Institute of Statistics (SIS)/World Bank (2005), *Turkey: Joint Poverty Assessment Report Volume 1: Main Report* (Report No: 29619-TU), SIS and Human Development Sector Unit, Europe and Central Asia Region of the World Bank, Washington.
Symeonidou, H. (1996), 'Social protection in contemporary Greece', *South European Society and Politics*, **1** (3), 67–86.
Şenses, F. (1994), 'Labour market response to structural adjustment and international pressures: the Turkish case', *METU Studies in Development*, **21**, 405–49.

TESEV (Foundation for Economic and Social Studies in Turkey) (2006), *Doğu ve Güney Doğu Anadolu'da Sosyal ve Ekonomik Öncelikler* (*Social and Economic Priorities in the East and South Eastern Turkey*), Istanbul: TESEV.

Trifiletti, R. (1999), 'Southern European welfare regimes and the worsening position of women', *Journal of European Social Policy*, **9** (1), 49–64.

TÜSİAD (Association for Turkish Businessmen and Industrialists) (1997), *Türk Sosyal Güvenlik Sisteminde Yeniden Yapilanma* (*Restructuring in the Turkish Social Security System*), Istanbul: TÜSİAD.

UNDP (2005), *Human Development Report: Turkey 2004*, Ankara: UNDP.

World Bank (2000), *Turkey: Country Economic Memorandum Structural Reforms for Sustainable Growth*, Report No: 20657-TU, Washington, DC: World Bank.

World Bank (2002), *Turkey: Health Sector Reform Project* (Report No: PID10997), Washington, DC: World Bank.

World Bank (2003), *Turkey Reforming the Health Sector for Improved Access and Efficiency*, Report No. 24358-TU, Washington, DC: World Bank.

World Bank (2006), *Country Brief 2006: Turkey*, http://www.worldbank.org.tr (accessed 13 November 2006).

World Health Organization (WHO) (2006), *Turkey: Country Cooperation Strategy at a Glance*, http://www.who.int/countryfocus/resources/ccsbrief_turkey_tur_06_en.pdf (accessed 13 November 2006).

7. Macedonia

Maja Gerovska Mitev

INTRODUCTION

When mapping the impact of international organizations upon social policy in Macedonia, one can notice an outstanding example of 'coerciveness and conditionality' in the process of developing national social policy goals, contents and instruments. International governmental organizations (IGOs) have had the role of being the main catalysts in inducing changes within crucial domains of social policy, such as employment, pensions and social protection. By doing so, they have succeeded in reorienting the country's social policy from a virtually 'universal' into a 'safety net' model. If the 'global tide is turning' back to universal social provision (Deacon, 2005), the case of Macedonia surely does not prove that. This chapter will try to outline the main factors that have contributed towards global policy 'imposition' and illustrate the main effects in the national social policy arena. The chapter is divided into three chronological parts, according to the level of presence and influence of particular intergovernmental organizations within different time periods in Macedonia.

LOCAL INERTIA VS EMERGENCE OF INTERNATIONAL ACTORS (1991–96)

The direction and dynamic of social policy creation in the first years of Macedonian independence (from 1991) can be defined as static and almost identical to the social policy practice which used to exist in the pre-1991 socialist period. The features of this socialist social policy, which were also shared by other countries that were part of that regime in South East Europe, were a bureaucratized and non transparent welfare state; universal social services but with standards that differed for different clientele; non-involvement of social partners and the civil sector in the planning and/or administration of welfare; and centralism and non-independence of the institutions that were administering the social security system. Still, Macedonia as part of the then Socialist Federal Republic of Yugoslavia

(SFRY), developed quite early (by 1965) a dispersed network of centres of social work (social services), established a School of Social Work (early 1960s), and had a degree of decentralized social protection through the so called self-managed communities of interest, where certain social rights and services were created on a local level. Overall, it can be stated that the socialist legacy in social policy contributed towards the creation of comprehensive welfare legislation and an institutional network, which proved to be important attributes for Macedonia in the first years of its independence. Therefore, it seems overstated when Amitsis classifies the period between 1992 and 1996 as a 'phase of creation of the social welfare policy in Macedonia' (2004: 21). It feels more convenient to describe this period as a phase of redefinition of previous legislative norms, although as already mentioned nothing vital changed.

Another important set of factors must be mentioned, which presented an immediate challenge to the universality of the welfare delivery that existed in the past. Unfavourable economic, political and social conditions in the beginning of the 1990s came mainly from the:

(1) loss of Yugoslav markets, frozen Yugoslav bank accounts and the forced closure of many of the largest unproductive enterprises, which had been located in Macedonia in an attempt to counter its underdeveloped status within Yugoslavia; (2) economic sanctions against Serbia also disproportionately affected Macedonia; (3) economic blockage imposed by Greece in protest against the use of the name 'Macedonia' deprived the republic of any southern trade; and (4) existence of an Albanian minority which also contributed to the instability. (Deacon et al., 1997: 188)

All these have contributed towards a permanent increase in the unemployment rates, from 23 per cent in 1990 to 38.8 per cent in 1996, accompanied by a rise in the number of social welfare (in cash) recipients, from 13 937 in 1991 to 28 407 in 1996. These new circumstances distorted an already unfavourable social position that existed in Macedonia. Owing to the rural and urban overpopulation a century ago, the trends of working abroad, emigration and unemployment were already prominent. Efforts to resolve these problems after the Second World War and until 1990 included forced industrialization and over-employment in the existing and new enterprises. But they did not prove efficient. Hence, Macedonia entered independence with a level of registered unemployment that was among the highest in the ex-Yugoslav republics (MANU, 1997).

Rising social problems prompted an increase in social welfare expenditure (Table 7.1), with ascending transfers for the unemployed: pensions and social assistance, on the one hand, and plummeting education, health and family transfers, on the other.

Table 7.1   Social expenditures as percentage of budget in Macedonia comparing 1991 with 1996

Social expenditures	1991	1996
Pensions	36	44
Health	36	22
Education	21	21
Family supplement	4	1
Social assistance (cash)	2	4
Unemployment (cash transfers)	1	8

Source: World Bank (1999).

It can be interpreted that the initial governmental reaction to rising unemployment and other social problems targeted early retirement, unemployment and social assistance cash benefits. Investment in education or training and retraining (as active measures) were not seen as possible solutions. This came back as a boomerang in the later years, with masses of people dependent on public transfers on the one hand and shrinking public money on the other.

Legislative changes that were initiated in this period did not follow either the dynamic or the priority of the social problems that were increasing. New regulative solutions involved: minimal renewal of the existing acts (Labour Law, Employment Law, Family Law); introduction of the new programme for the socially deprived population (which set the compensation for those living below an existence level); and restrictions within the Pension Act (an increase in the age of pensioners, lowering of the replacement rate and elimination of early retirement). This lethargic attitude towards more profound reforms contributed towards the increase in social costs of the transition. The absence of more energetic reforms in the first years of Macedonian independence may be interpreted as a result of the decrease in the economic growth of the country, the lack of a clear ideological orientation of the government, as well the shortage of (local) expertise in tackling new social problems. This trend of sporadic, inert and non-transparent creation of social policy became a fertile ground for international organizations, whose increased presence in Macedonia (Table 7.2) slowly became reflected in the intensity and path of national social policy reform.

Among the first international organizations that initiated a much needed in-depth analysis of the social policy field was the UN Preventive Deployment Mission (UNPREDEP). Although primarily focused on peacekeeping and securing ethnic stability in the country, this mission was

*Table 7.2   International governmental organizations in Macedonia,
1991–96*

	IMF	WB	UN	WHO	ILO	EBRD	COE	EU (mission/ programme)
Membership date	1992	1993	1993	1993	1993	1995	1995	1993 (ECHO) 1996 (PHARE)

also characterized by a very energetic social element. Consultants and experts who were contracted by the mission offered the first really systematic analysis of the social welfare system in the country, accompanied by a proposed social action programme, involving pilot projects for reforms in several social policy sectors (Deacon et al., 1996). However, despite initial acceptance of these project plans by the relevant Ministry of Labour and Social Policy, they were forgotten and abandoned after the UNPREDEP Mission left the country.

Although many other international governmental organizations established their missions and offices in the country in this period, their influence was not yet visible. Many projects were initiated, but their full realization and impact become evident in the period after 1996.

LOCAL DEPENDENCY AND PATERNALISM OF THE INTERNATIONAL FINANCIAL ORGANIZATIONS (1996–2003)

The phase in which international governmental organizations had a major impact in orienting the country's social policy path was the period between 1996 and 2003. Some of the reasons for the increased international presence in this period include: (1) NATO bombardment of Yugoslavia in 1999, which caused a stability crisis both in the region and in the country; (2) the refugee crisis from Kosovo, which brought around 360 000 refugees into the country (around 17 per cent of the total population of Macedonia) and which overburdened the country's economic and welfare resources; and particularly (3) the internal ethnic conflict (between the Albanians and Macedonians) in 2001, which distorted the planned socio-economic development. The armed conflict took more than 200 lives and displaced, at one time or another, more than 100 000 people.

At the same time, internal social trends also continued to remain negative, through an increased rise in the unemployment rate (according to the

Labour Force Survey it increased from 31.9 per cent in 1996 to 37.7 per cent in 2004), an escalating grey economy and a rising poverty rate (relative household poverty rose from 19 per cent in 1997 to 22.6 per cent in 2000), all of which prompted even greater demand for and use of social transfers (in 2003 around 64 453 households were using social assistance benefits and 45 867 people were using unemployment cash benefits in 2004).

Stifled economic growth and escalating social problems, accompanied by the lack of national independent solutions, created a particular space for international financial organizations, who offered their assistance in the form of targeted funds, prearranged reforms and 'safari' experts. The World Bank and the International Monetary Fund (with the emphasis on the former) became main leaders of national social policy orientation, both in an ideological and in a practical sense. Their influence can be tracked particularly in the fields of employment, social protection, poverty reduction and pensions.

Employment

As already mentioned, the employment sector in Macedonia, since its independence, was continuously decreasing. Employment in the formal sector was declining, at the expense of the widespread informal sector. According to Janevska, the grey sector 'served as a "security valve" in calming the social tensions' (2002: 109). A shrinking employment sector and rising unemployment rate made different governments prioritize this sector, and undertake different policy measures. Some of the main governmental activities were targeted towards:

- legislative changes – creation of the Law on Employment and Unemployment Insurance (1997) and the Law on the Promotion of Employment (1997 and 2003);
- institutional adaptation – redefinition of the services offered by the Employment Bureau (later Agency); and
- creation of new jobs – giving agricultural land for use to the social assistance beneficiaries (2003), and so on.

The main financial and expert contributor to employment policy reform was the World Bank, and to some extent the IMF. The Breton Wood's funds and arrangements had an impact on shifting the employment policy direction from mainly passive to active measures, and prompted the increased targeting of unemployment compensation and reductions in the amount and length of unemployment benefits. This was accompanied by measures for the institutional capacity-building of the Employment Bureau, thus making it more reflexive towards new trends by offering tailor-made employment services.

However, the 'activation' policy had a few negative features in the local context, which were manifested through mistreatment of the legal provisions and mismatched targeting, as well as absence of public support. As such, governmental employment measures proved quite ineffective and consequently impaired positive employment growth. All in all, governmental employment policy could be described as 'bland, passive and clichéd', and in desperate need of more original, proactive and customized reforms.

The European Union, as an international factor, did not contribute significantly towards employment policy in this period. Although some of its programmes, such as CONSENSUS, had some connection with the revision of the labour legislation to ensure compatibility with that of the EU, their intervention was far from steering the social policy course or offering any financial or technical support towards the main employment initiatives. However, the EU as part of the international community and together with other players (such as the US administrators) had a role in facilitating the creation and signing of the Ohrid Framework Agreement (2001), which was signed by all political parties in Macedonia, and which instituted 'more' rights for the (mainly) Albanian ethnic community in Macedonia. The Ohrid Framework Agreement impacted upon the employment sector through the introduction of specialized courses for training and employment of public administrative workers for minorities in Macedonia. In this way, almost 600 course participants were involved, out of which 530 belonged to the Albanian minority. This contributed towards dissatisfaction among other ethnic groups in Macedonia (Turks, Roma, Vlachs) who felt that the Ohrid Framework Agreement was an exclusionary project (Working Group on Minority Issues, 2004: 21).

Social Protection

Another important domain which was the object of systematic reforms was social protection. Within this field, new legislation was prepared in 1997,[1] introducing comprehensive and innovative forms of welfare services. This law introduced for the first time the possibility of offering welfare services via the private sector, and also placed an accent on provision of non-residential forms of protection. However, the terms of reference for these services were not specified in the law, which inhibited the immediate practical realization of the new Acts. Additional amendments that followed in the next period[2] focused on issues such as decentralization, de-institutionalization, pluralization and social inclusion.

In parallel with the introduction of the Law on Social Welfare, a new directive on the conditions of use for social assistance was passed. A new decree on conditions, criteria, amounts and the procedure for determining the right to social assistance from 1998 (and later amendments) brought increased rigidity of payments, through reductions in length of period of entitlement as well as through the introduction of more strict criteria for social assistance use. Hence, the amount of social assistance was created on the basis of the relative poverty line, which on the annual level for Macedonia was fixed at 36.000 Macedonian denars (MKD)/585 euros (until 2005), or 3.000 MKD per month/49 euros. For one-person households the amount of social assistance was calculated as 57 per cent from the determined relative poverty line, which works out as 1700 MKD/28 euros. The length of using social assistance benefits was also a subject of permanent reductions, which resulted in paying the total sum for the first two years, then 70 per cent for a period of between three to five years, and then 50 per cent for using social assistance for more than six years.

Along with these changes which were aimed at improving the working motivation of social assistance users, other more strict measures of activation were introduced. The rigid form of workfare resulted in the transformation of social assistance from unilateral transfer to bilateral transfer, that is, the right to assistance was conditioned by an obligatory 'contra service'. In this way, social assistance users capable of work were obliged to accept public work in their local community when it was required, otherwise the right to social assistance was terminated. This rigid activation of social assistance users contributed towards a reduction of the previously existing minimum social standards, and diminished the prevalence of universality and solidarity, as the main principles in the social protection system. Through this, the social policy was reoriented from almost a universal model towards a 'safety net' model, where only a few are guaranteed their social assistance right.

Later legislative changes which supported the welfare mix in social provision were supported by the EU project for the institutional capacity-building and development of the social protection sector (2000–2002). According to Ministry employee Vesna Petkovic, changes that were introduced with this project resulted from the 'positive effects from 11 pilot projects, which focused on co-operation between Social Work Centres, the central government, non governmental organizations and the local community'.[3]

The empowerment of the local communities has been indirectly supported through the adoption of the Ohrid Framework Agreement, which put an end to the armed inter-ethnic conflict in the country in 2001. This agreement stipulates that the development of decentralized governance is one of the key priorities with respect to reforming the political system. Therefore, some of the constitutional provisions regarding local self-government were modified with the constitutional amendments passed in 2001 and more responsibilities returned to the municipalities.

The practical realization of decentralization matters was not initiated until the beginning of 2005, but the transfer of responsibilities to the local governments in the field of social welfare in Macedonia, was stipulated through:

1. the organization and construction of facilities for social and child care, including nurseries and elderly care facilities (ownership, financing, investments and maintenance); provision of social care for disabled people, children without parents and parental care, children with special educational and social needs, children from single parent families, homeless children, individuals exposed to social risks, and drug or alcohol abusers; raising the awareness of the general public; housing for people at social risk; realization of rights related to raising pre-school children;
2. the organization and improvement of education, involving the establishment, financing and administration of primary and secondary schools in conjunction with the central government and in accordance with the law, and the organization of transportation of students and their accommodation in student boarding facilities; and
3. the organization, construction and management of the network of primary healthcare organizations and facilities. This was to be achieved by: management of the network of public primary health care organizations and facilities (which were required to involve the local self-government in all the boards of all publicly owned health-care providers, health education and promotion); preventive activities, health care for workers and occupational health; environmental health monitoring; monitoring of communicable diseases; care for special needs patients (for example, mental health, child abuse, and so on) and other areas specified by the law (Law on Territorial Division of the Republic of Macedonia and Determination of the Local Government Unit Regions).

Finally, if one tries to apply the ethnic lens to perceive the social protection situation in Macedonia, a picture emerges that is not so rosy. Although many legal acts (including the Constitution of the Republic of Macedonia, 1991; the Framework Agreement, 2001; and the Council of Europe's Framework Convention for Protection of National Minorities, 1996/1997) were adopted and ratified in Macedonia in order to guarantee the equal rights and access to services regardless of gender, ethnic, religious, political or social affiliation, there were still indirect legal, institutional and other impediments that prevented the practical realization of these objectives. For example, the attainment of citizenship status (which is among the basic requirements for acquiring social welfare service/benefit) was being hindered due to the legal precondition of having a 'permanent source of income'. Having in mind the huge rate of unemployment in Macedonia, which for the ethnic minorities is even greater (78.5 per cent among Roma, 61.2 per cent among Albanians according to the 2002 Census), this requirement prevented many Roma and Albanians from establishing their basic social rights. According to the Erduan Iseini (mayor of the Roma local community, Shuto Orizari, in 2004) in 1997 there were 4356 Roma without citizenship and 7407 Roma with unidentified citizenship. Another particular aspect of concern with regard to ethnic social welfare rights, was their unemployment/ inactivity rates. The huge level of unemployment among minorities, accompanied with the similarly high rate of their economic inactivity (52.4 per cent among Roma, 70.7 per cent among Albanians) made them particularly dependent upon the social welfare system. However, it must be emphasized that the actual rate of unemployment and economic activity might be lower, having in mind some of the particularities characteristic for these ethnic groups. Both Roma and Albanians tend to have jobs that are not formally registered, or are part of the grey economy. Also, among Albanians this is accompanied by high migration trends, which contribute towards their additional (unregistered) sources of income. Although this informal type of support largely improves their financial stability, it also significantly impacts their labour mobilization and their 'passivity' with regard to the formal labour market. Some of the other more general problems associated with the unequal access of minorities to labour/social welfare rights might be attributed to reasons such as the concentration of the main employment capacities in the bigger cities where minorities (with the exception of Romas in Skopje) are less settled, investments and employments related to ethnic preferences, and the lack of training and retraining customized to the language and needs of particular ethnic groups.

Poverty

Poverty issues, which were neither tackled strategically nor statistically during the first years of transition, became an object of intensified interest after 1996. The poverty level was determined by co-ordinated activities between the State Statistical Office, the Ministry of Labour and unavoidably with the World Bank within the framework of the project for social reforms and its subcomponent for social assistance. The national standard for the calculation of the poverty level is the relative method. For the period 1994–96, the poverty rate, according to experimental calculations, was determined as 60 per cent of the average equivalent expenditure of households (Government of the Republic of Macedonia, 2002). However, since then (1997 onwards) the poverty rate is determined as 70 per cent of the average equivalent expenditure of households. Experimental calculations proved that if 60 per cent of the median expenditure is used as a threshold, the level of poverty would be at least 10 per cent higher, which would indirectly put greater pressure on the public budget. As mentioned earlier, the financing of social assistance in Macedonia is based on the poverty line threshold, hence if this threshold was raised, the number of claimants and recipients would increase considerably.

Basic data sources for the calculation of the poverty line are the Household Expenditure Survey, the national Census, different socio-economic studies of households as well as other sources, such as Labour Force Surveys and administrative sources.

The first and only strategic document aimed at combating poverty was the National Strategy for Poverty Reduction, prepared in 2000–2001 (interim version), and published in 2002 (final version, Government of the Republic of Macedonia, 2002). This document, which was mainly created for the purposes of the Poverty Reduction and Growth Facility arrangement with the International Monetary Fund and the World Bank, represented the first multi-sector and multi-discipline analysis of the poverty problem. The goals of the strategy were to be achieved in the period 2002–2005. However, despite some of its shortcomings, such as lack of quantitative and measurable goals, which prohibited its implementation and efficacy, the Poverty Reduction Strategy Paper (PRSP) in Macedonia proved less significant because of other domestic factors. The timing of the PRSP creation coincided with the 2001 ethnic crisis in Macedonia. This contributed towards a major change and reorientation of the political priorities and funds from economic to national stability measures, hence knocking poverty issues off the current agenda. Another factor that also made the PRSP process marginal was the political change that occurred which disrupted the assigned responsibilities, actors and plans.

Other activities in this field were also prompted by the World Bank, through its expert and technical support within the Social Support Project from 2000 until 2002 and its subcomponent Poverty Monitoring; and also through the Poverty Assessment from 2004 until 2006. Their main goals were to advance the capacities for poverty calculation, to improve analysis for mapping and determining poverty characteristics and to develop analysis for poverty profiles.

Pensions

This domain of social security was subjected to the most profound changes, through the introduction of paradigmatic reform (Holzmann et al., 2003: 8). The leading agent of this reform was again the World Bank, through its

Pension Reform Technical Assistance project (1998–2002). Their pension reform design was no different than that offered to other post-socialist countries: a model, which beside slight parametric reforms, was mainly based on reducing the role of the pay-as-you-go financing based on inter-generational solidarity and the introduction of fully funded pensions. With the exception of Slovenia and the Czech Republic, most other transition countries in South East Europe have accepted the mandatory fully funded pension model. Hence, in Macedonia in April 2002 a new Law on Mandatory Fully Funded Pension Insurance introduced the following pension scheme:

- first pillar, managed by the state and comprising of mandatory pension and invalidity insurance based on PAYG;
- second pillar, privately managed and comprising of mandatory capitalized pension insurance; and
- third pillar, comprising of voluntary and privately managed savings accounts.

Although the contribution rate of 21.2 per cent had not changed (increased) with the reform, now it was being divided between the two mandatory pillars, where the first pillar was financed with a contribution rate of 13.78 per cent, and the remaining 7.42 per cent was channelled into the second pillar, which was financed on a capitalized basis. The first pillar delivered a replacement rate of approximately 30 per cent for a person with a full career. This pension scheme was obligatory for all new employees since January 2003, while others had the option of choosing whether or not to join the multi-pillar system. The practical implementation of this law began in 2006, and since then around 110 000 employees have joined the multi-pillar system (out of 559 702 employed people).

The introduction of the multi-pillar pension system in Macedonia also brought institutional changes, mainly through the creation of the new Agency for Supervision of the Fully Funded Pension Insurance – MAPAS – but also other institutional novelties were seen in the shape of the pension companies governing the pension funds and the custodian of pension funds' assets (the National Bank of the Republic of Macedonia).

Although the new pension system included an energetic public campaign, still very little was said about the downside or the potential pitfalls of this reform. There was a lack of national critical expertise towards the proposed pension model, which left the biggest systematic risks unexplained. Among the few who challenged this reform were the trade unions, but their impact can be described as 'too little, too late'. According to a representative of the Union of Trade Unions in Macedonia 'the characteristics on the new pension system in Macedonia are the worst in comparison to other neighbouring countries'.[4] She named the following problems, which the trade unions considered as worrying:

(1) lack of economic pre-conditions for successful and effective operation of the second pillar (as the low number of new employees is accompanied by a low level of salaries – 60 per cent of the workers have a salary less than 60 euros); (2) high administrative cost of 8.5 per cent (and according to some experts it should not exceed 3 per cent); (3) the small investment market in Macedonia.

Because of this, she noted that the trade unions were in favour of a voluntary rather than mandatory second pillar.

Despite trade union efforts to point out these problems by organizing a general strike in 2000, their activities didn't impact on political will and decisions. As Jankulovska noted: 'the government openly told us that the pension reform is an obligation that they have to fulfil because of IMF and WB arrangements'.[5]

Health

After the initial legislative and institutional changes introduced within the field of health protection and health insurance in 1991, 1993 and 1995, no greater alterations were seen until 1996. The main changes, directed at the introduction of private health services and pharmacies, 'did little to streamline the public health system, create incentives for increasing efficiency, or define legal and regulatory environment for the private providers' (Donev, 1995; Mishovski, 1995). Also the instigation of co-payments for health care in 1993 was not effective and did not improve the revenues of the health institutions. Institutionally, the main reform involved the discontinuation of the previous decentralized system of financing and health provision with the introduction of the Health Insurance Fund. However, this fund was situated within the framework of the Ministry of Health, which prevented its greater autonomy and flexibility.

The period from 1996 brought about comprehensive health-care reform. This was enabled through the World Bank loan of US$16.9 million, which was operationalized through the Health Sector Transition Project (1996–2002). The legislative changes included a new Law on Health Insurance (2000), which contributed towards the separation of the Health Insurance Fund from the ministry framework and its formation as a separate independent institution with the authority to administer the compulsory health insurance. Within the field of primary health care, the positive effects involved increasing patient choice through patient enrolment and capitation-based payment to private family medicine practice. As part of the maternal and child-care endeavours, a dramatic reduction in the rate of perinatal mortality was achieved: the number of foetal and early neo-natal deaths per 1000 births has been reduced by over 20 per cent, thus contributing towards the accomplishment of one of the Millennium Development Goals regarding child mortality.

Throughout the realization of this project, many challenges and problems were signalled, which can also be seen as main obstacles for health reforms in the future. They included: (1) the absence of sustainable polit-ical consensus on the main objectives in the project and frequent changes of ministers and directors; (2) weak capacities in the Ministry of Health and Health Insurance Fund with frequent changes in staff and weak inter-institutional collaboration and support; (3) initial resistance from the doctors and professional associations; and (4) insufficient conditions and possibilities for the trained staff to implement their acquired knowledge (European Observatory on Health Care Systems, 2004).

From this review of social policy changes occurring in the period from 1996 to 2004 it can be said that the previous minimalist approach towards legislative and institutional changes was replaced by a trend of continuous and paradigmatic reforms, which gave a new shape and size to national social policy. The changed social policy model is based on the introduction of elements including: (1) a policy of activation, which manifests itself in the domains of employment and in the delivery of social transfers; (2) the introduction of pluralization, which signalled the abolishment of the trad-itional provider role of the state thus creating a space for private and non-governmental organizations as service providers; (3) a diminished principle of solidarity within the overall social protection system; and (4) the increased selectivity and targeting of social service users. Although these characteristics may be similar to those ongoing in the other countries in the region, it is important to note that these changes were not based on the pre-vious experiences and practices in Macedonia, nor were they realistically linked to the true capabilities of the newly promoted service providers. Also, the current demand for social protection was on a constant rise which did not correspond with the social policy model based on increased target-ing and selectivity. Overall, the model of social policy which was installed in this phase was completely contrary to the needs and capacities of Macedonian economic and social conditions.

EUROPEANIZATION VS AMERICANIZATION (2000 ONWARDS)

The latest phase in social policy development in Macedonia is connected with efforts for greater co-ordination with EU priorities and legislation.

The application for EU membership (22 March 2004), entering into the Stabilization and Association Agreement (1 April 2004) and being given candidate status (17 December 2005) were all important milestones, which necessitated the need to harmonize national public interventions and policies towards the EU standards. These actions also mean that the EU, as an international player, is slowly taking over the leading position in influencing and directing national social policy.

The first concrete EU contribution within the social policy sphere was advocated through the Community Assistance for Reconstruction, Development and Stabilization (CARDS) programme, with the project entitled 'Technical assistance for institutional building as a support to the employment policy in Macedonia'. As a result of the financial and expert assistance given within this project, the government of Macedonia has adopted the first National Action Plan for employment (NAP) for the period of 2004–05 (Ministry of Labour and Social Policy, 2003). The NAP represents a new systematic operationalized programme, which follows the European recommendations on the labour market according to the three priorities (increasing employment, improving quality and productivity of work as well as the strengthening of social cohesion and inclusion) and the ten employment guidelines of the European Employment Strategy, adopted by the European Council in July 2003. Another important component is that this project contributed towards the new organizational setup of the Bureau of Employment (now the Agency for Employment) through the reorganization of the regional units of this bureau (now Centres of Employment), and by providing them with new computers, software applications and staff training. All these have contributed towards the goal of improving the process of supporting clients in their active pursuit of work.

An interesting insight into the European route towards social policy reforms in the country could be seen through the National Strategy for Integration in the EU (September 2004). In the section which elaborates on adequate provision and targeted social protection in order to eliminate negative social consequences from the transition, the document, in a quite contradictory way notes that: 'the system of social protection which is robust and egalitarian and that offers a relatively high degree of protection, needs to be transformed to prevent endangering the balance of the public finances, as well as companies' competitiveness' (Government of the Republic of Macedonia, 2004: 133).Yet, it acknowledges the difficult economic conditions which necessitate the need for more inclusive social protection, so in the continuation it argues that 'the system must be transformed quickly, without damaging the social inclusion in the society and without causing greater social tensions' (ibid.: 134). However, it is difficult to imagine that these two, mutually exclusive goals (reduction of the egalitarian approach without damaging social inclusion) can be achieved quickly, and without social tensions. What is also interesting is that this strategy suggests social reforms based on individual responsibility, reduction of social transfers in line with budgetary capabilities, and enabling the social sector to perform its tasks in the context of the needs of the market economy (ibid.). The proposed reform agenda reads as if it is written by a former World Bank consultant who forgot the EU goals and priorities concerning social cohesion, sustaining adequate social transfers and maintaining market competitiveness through universal social security and protection.

Within the framework of other legislative novelties in this period, a trend of creating and publicly announcing national programmes in different social policy fields was initiated. Hence, the National Programme for Social Protection and the National Programme for Child Protection were adopted in 2006. Both of these programmes comprise activities according to the goals of decentralization, pluralization, deinstitutionalization and social inclusion. The National Programme for Social Protection is based on, and envisaged to be implemented, according to international conventions and recommendations including: the Social Cohesion Strategy of the European committee for social cohesion; the Joint Memoranda for Social Inclusion; the UN Millennium Development Goals in terms of poverty reduction; as well as other documents, all of which are planned to contribute to a greater co-ordination with EU laws.

This period also coincides with the practical initiation of the decentralization of social welfare in Macedonia. This process is starting only incrementally, through modest activities seen via the transfer of kindergartens and homes for the elderly to a local level. The local communities also now develop action plans which they submit to the Ministry of Labour and Social Policy, where the number of planned activities in the field of social welfare, as well as the resources and partners engaged for each planned activity, are being outlined.

A particular interesting aspect, originating from the World Bank, is the newly proposed social assistance model, which is currently being negotiated with the government. This involves the introduction of so-called conditional social transfers. This envisages giving social assistance benefits to families who will accept the conditions, such as receiving the benefits only if their children are enrolled and attending school, or if they are given access to regular health check-ups and so on. This idea seems to be another model exported from Latin America (as with the pension reform model), where the Human Development Index is much lower than in Macedonia. Hence, again we witness IGO proposals being made without any concrete connection with the priorities, particularities or needs of a national social welfare system.

Other international actors, such as bilateral donors or agencies, are present, but are not that influential in the overall social policy trajectory in Macedonia. They involve the Council of Europe, the United States Agency for International Development, United Nations Development Programme, the World Health Organization, the United Nations Children Fund, and so on. Among interesting epi-phenomenona is the Social Institutions Support Programme with an office in Skopje. This programme is a joint CARDS project, mainly funded by the European Commission, and co-funded and managed by the Council of Europe's Directorate General of Social Cohesion (DG III). The programme is a spin-off of a previous activity, carried out within the Initiative for Social Cohesion of the Stability Pact for South East Europe, which contributed to the creation of a network of social security professionals and set the basis for regional co-operation in the field of social security co-ordination. Their activities are by and large of academic or/and networking character, thus having no (or at least very negligible) general impact.

It seems that current social policy is striving to adhere to the EU policy co-ordination on one hand, and endeavouring to sustain policy reforms, already undertaken under the initiative of the financial IGOs, on the other. The orientation or prevalence towards the EU- or the US-led reforms in Macedonia will probably depend on the country's economic growth, where a potential boost might contribute to less economic dependency on international financial institutions, thus creating room for more individual and more inclusive social policy solutions. Yet, this is not the only factor. The international governmental organizations will still play a role, but not only because of their conditionality policy. As Arandarenko rightly notes, their dominance in advice-giving also arises from the potential of 'articulated, elaborated and workable action programmes' in which the World Bank's agenda is superior to others (2004: 49).

CONCLUSION

From the above it is clear that international advice, mainly coming from international financial institutions, was the most prominent agent of national social policy reform. Although this might be the same in other post-socialist South East European countries, the case of Macedonia is special for several reasons. First, the policy of excessive use of external financial and technical support prohibited customized and country specific reforms and agendas. Instead of achieving sustainability within a short period of time, the country engaged in prolonged borrowing, which became a standard pattern for policy creation and made the international financial institutions become embedded in national social policy governance. In the absence of alternative policy options, the IGOs in Macedonia remain 'the Trojan horses of the new millennium' (Mehrotra, 2004). Second, such IGO policy imposition was also enabled through the lack of influence and impact of independent actors, such as trade unions, non-governmental organizations, academia, and so on in preserving previously existing social standards. Although all the above did make efforts to point out the problems, none of them came forward with different and viable policy suggestions. The trade unions themselves were (and still are) in the process of restructuring, which left them under strength and impaired in terms of influencing social policy reforms. The non-governmental organizations in this period were in the process of formation, so there were very few to offer any visible opposition. The academia or independent academic experts were also an interesting part of the story. Some of these experts were in leading positions in the government, which meant that they could not contradict the general political orientation, while the others were working as local experts for the international financial organizations. This introduced a situation where a local critical mass was absent as a source of alternative policy advice. Third, there is an absence of national consensus about a preferred social policy model in the context of the new market economy. The new economic model based on market ideology was not (at least publicly) accompanied by an ideological change of the social policy model. All this explains why there were many ad hoc reforms and why the neo-liberal agenda very easily became implanted in this previously predominantly universal and solidaristic society. To all these internal factors, an additional external factor might be added, which is not country specific but which also contributed to the ideological hegemony of the Breton Woods institutions: the minimal intervention by the European Union, in the period until 2004, towards steering the country's social policy direction close to the 'European social model', and the absence of any concrete EU social policy prescription, created an additional gap, which together enabled the current neo-liberal social policy orientation in Macedonia to take hold.

Finally, it would be interesting to see whether the IGOs' dominance in countries such as Macedonia has distanced them from the European Union and, as noted by Vaughan-Whitehead (2003), has even risked the future of Social Europe in the newly enlarged European Union, or contrarily whether this presented an alternative way for the post-socialist transition countries to achieve EU standards. Judging from the current EU preoccupation with becoming 'the world's most dynamic and competitive economic area', the latter might be more realistic.

NOTES

1. Law on Social Welfare, Official Gazette of R. Macedonia, no. 50/97.
2. Law on changes and amendments of the Social Protection Law, Official Gazette of R. Macedonia, no. 65/04.
3. Interview with Ms Vesna Petkovic, Head of the Sector for international co-operation within the Ministry of Labour and Social Policy, dated 9 February 2005.
4. Interview with Ms Liljana Jankulovska, representative of the Union of Trade Unions in Macedonia, dated 25 January 2005.
5. Ibid.

REFERENCES

Amitsis, G. (2004), *System of Social Protection in the R.M.*, Skopje: Ministry of Labour and Social Policy.
Arandarenko, M. (2004), 'International advice and labour market institutions in South-East Europe', *Global Social Policy*, **4** (1), 27–53.
Deacon, B. (2005), 'From "safety nets" back to "universal social provision": is the global tide turning?', *Global Social Policy*, **5** (1), 19–28.
Deacon, B., M. Hulse and P. Stubbs (1997), *Global Social Policy: International Organizations and the Future of Welfare*, London: Sage.
Deacon, B., M. Heikkila, R. Kraan, P. Stubbs and V. Taipale (1996), *Action for Social Change: A New Facet of Preventative Peace Keeping – the Case of UNPRE-DEP*, Helsinki: STAKES.
Donev, D. (1995), 'Privatization as a part of the health care reform in Macedonia', paper presented at the Hubert H. Humphrey Alumni Regional Conference on Approaches to Privatization: Reality, Dream or Nightmare, 13–16 March, Cairo.
European Observatory on Health Care Systems (2004), *Health Systems in Transition Profile, The Former Yugoslav Republic of Macedonia*, mimeo.
Government of the Republic of Macedonia (2004), *National Strategy for Integration of R. Macedonia in the European Union*, Skopje: Government of the R.M.
Government of the Republic of Macedonia, Ministry of Finance (2002), *National Strategy for Poverty Reduction in the Republic of Macedonia*, Skopje: Government of the R.M.
Holzmann, R., M. Orenstein and M. Rutkowski (2003), *Pension Reform in Europe: Process and Progress*, Washington, DC: The World Bank.
Janevska, V. (2002), 'Macedonia', in *Employment and Labor-Market Policy in South Eastern Europe*, Belgrade: Friedrich Ebert Stiftung.
Law on changes and amendments of the Social Protection Law, *Official Gazette of R. Macedonia*, no. 65/04.
Law on Health Insurance (2000), *Official Gazette of R. Macedonia*, No. 25/2000, 34/2000 and 96/2000.
Law on Social Welfare, *Official Gazette of R. Macedonia*, no. 50/97.
Law on Territorial Division of the Republic of Macedonia and Determination of the Local Government Unit Regions, *Official Gazette of the RM*, Skopje, no. 5/2002.
MANU (Macedonian Academy for Science and Arts) (1997), *National Strategy for Economic Development of the Republic of Macedonia: Development and Modernization*, Skopje: MANU [in Macedonian].

Mehrotra, S. (2004), 'Global institutions in local decision-making: the Trojan horses of the new millennium?', *Global Social Policy*, **4** (3), 283–7.

Ministry of Labour and Social Policy (2003), *National Action Plan for Employment 2004–05*, Skopje: MLSP.

Mishovski, J. (1995), *Health Protection, Comments to the Health Protection Law with its Additional Legal Directives* [in Macedonian], Skopje: Infoprom.

Vaughan-Whitehead, D. (2003), *EU Enlargement versus Social Europe: The Uncertain Future of the European Social Model*, Cheltenham: Edward Edgar.

Working Group on Minority Issues (2004), *Alternative Report on Minority Situation in Macedonia*, Skopje: Minority Rights Group International and European Centre for Minority Issues.

World Bank (1999), *FYROM-Focusing on the Poor*, Volume 1 – Main Report, Report No: 19411-MK, Human Development Sector Unit, Washington DC, p. 36.

8. Bosnia and Herzegovina

**Reima Ana Maglajlić Holiček and
Ešref Kenan Rašidagić**

INTRODUCTION: INDEPENDENCE, WAR AND CONTESTED HISTORY

The war in Bosnia and Herzegovina (BiH), its history and its people, have often been oversimplified or misconstrued by commentators and analysts both within and outside the country. This status of BiH which, in some ways, remains the same to the present day, leads to contested results, in the context of a kind of internationally imposed transformation with often unintended consequences. In this chapter we describe aspects of the country's current social, economic and political situation and its impact on social policy, and reflect critically on the interactions between international and local actors. The chapter is based, first and foremost, on our own experiences of working in the NGO sector in BiH from 1993 onwards. It represents our first attempt to critically reflect on our experiences without the pressure of promoting so-called 'successes' and/or supporting social policy changes which have little chance of being implemented.

In the process of the disintegration of Yugoslavia, after the multi-party elections in 1990, and a referendum conducted between 28 February and 1 March 1992, the citizens of Bosnia-Herzegovina voted to become an independent and sovereign country within its historical borders. On 20 May 1992, through Resolution 755 of the United Nations Security Council, Bosnia-Herzegovina was internationally recognized as an independent state, although by this time war had already begun. Almost 15 years later, it is still difficult to produce a critical analysis of recent BiH history in the context of its effect on life today. The figures available on war damage are varied, hard to properly reference and often tailored to various political purposes. Many figures do not refer to their sources but, rather, rely on figures quoted in international community surveys. The citizens of BiH were affected by the war through mass killing, mass destruction of property, torture inflicted in concentration camps on civilians and combatants, systematic sexual assaults on women, and ethnic cleansing resulting in massive population displacement. Estimates of the number killed range from a conservative 100 000 to as high as 300 000. More than 10 000 people were killed in the capital, Sarajevo, alone and one-sixth of the city's population was injured during the three-year siege from 1992 to 1995. At least 16 000 children were killed and some 35 000 children were injured.

The pre-war population of BiH was approximately 4.4 million. Of this population, over 1 million people fled the country during the war, some 650 000 of whom were children. Since the signing of the General Framework Agreement for Peace in Bosnia and Herzegovina (GFAP, popularly known as the Dayton Peace Agreement) in December 1995, more than 1 million civilians returned, mainly to areas where they are now ethnic minorities (Wilkinson, 2005), in the context of the creation of two or, de facto, three ethnicized entities. According to United Nations High Commission for Refugees data (UNHCR, 2006), at the end of 2005, 182 700 people remained internally displaced. Accurate figures on the current population of BiH are unavailable in the absence of a post-war census.

Economic, social and other infrastructural capacities were destroyed, including businesses, industry, schools, hospitals, and social care institutions, but the main physical capacity affected was housing. In the Federation of BiH (one of the two post-GFAP entities), over 70 per cent of the housing stock was heavily damaged or destroyed (Kljajić, 1999). Periodic violence still occurs in BiH, primarily directed against those attempting to return to their pre-war communities, through the destruction of rebuilt homes and assaults and even murders of returnees. Nowadays, the violence usually takes less apparent forms. Notwithstanding isolated civil initiatives on 'dealing with the past', attempts are often made to stifle any public debate about the violence that happened during the war,[1] as the only way to 'move forward'.

The Dayton Peace Agreement also outlined a new map of Bosnia and Herzegovina in terms of constituent peoples and entities. The country is both 'divided and joined' into the Federation of BiH (of Bosniaks/Bosnian Muslims and Croats) and Republika Srpska (the Serbian Republic or RS), as detailed on the map in Figure 8.1. Many feel that this division of the country legitimizes ethnic cleansing, since it reinforces the 'ethnic supremacy' of certain ethnic groups in certain parts of the country. Indeed, the divisions remain much stronger than any unity even in the context of international attempts to build a central state and to promote a path to eventual EU membership. Recently, leading politicians in RS raised the stakes by suggesting, in the aftermath of Montenegro's independence and talks on the final status of Kosovo, that RS should have the right to have a referendum on secession from BiH.

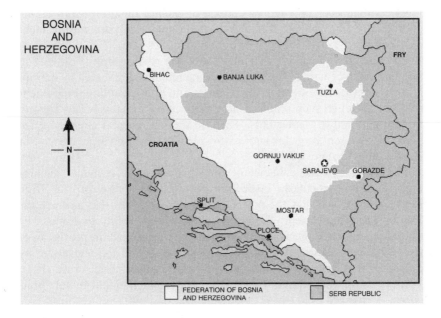

Figure 8.1   Map of BiH, outlining the two entities

THE CONTEMPORARY POLITICAL, ECONOMIC AND SOCIAL SITUATION

Bosnia and Herzegovina has multiple layers of government. At the national level, a weak central government is composed of representatives of all three major 'ethnic' groups (Bosniaks, Serbs and Croats). Each entity also has an elected prime minister and entity-level legislatures that have important responsibilities with respect to social policy, education and health care. The Federation of Bosnia and Herzegovina (FBiH) is further divided into ten administrative units called cantons. Each of these cantons has its own legislature and ministries, including those responsible for social protection services. In Republika Srpska, no such intermediate layer of government exists, with the entity having a centralized government structure with a comparable municipal layer of government. There is also a District of Brčko, a small town about which agreement could not be reached at Dayton which, along the US model, also has its own governmental bodies. Hence, country-level social policy reform requires engagement with 13 ministries responsible for decision-making and legislation.

At national level, only representatives of each of the three major ethnic groups can occupy public office. For example, one cannot become president of the tripartite BiH Presidency if one identifies oneself as a citizen of Bosnia and Herzegovina or as a member of any ethnic minority other than Bosniak, Serb or Croat. The political scene remains dominated by nationalist parties that tend to integrate ethnicity and politics, and to some extent religion, although such practices are criticized by a relatively small group of anti-nationalist intellectuals. There is little or no real alternative for political representation for those who identify themselves as citizens of Bosnia and Herzegovina.

The power and the influence of the international community remains high, and is particularly evidenced through the Office of the High Representative, who has the powers to impose decisions that advance the Dayton Peace Agreement. These powers include the ability to dismiss any elected or appointed officials deemed to be working against the provisions of the GFAP, restructure major institutions, and pass laws and regulations by decree, so that Bosnia still resembles an 'international protectorate' (ICG, 1998: 7). Bosnia and Herzegovina still has a large international military presence now changed from a NATO-led Stabilization Force (SFOR), to an EU-led force, numbering some 7000 troops. In addition, it has been estimated that, in the late 1990s, some 10000 civilian ex-patriots lived in the country, employed by the international governmental and non-governmental organizations from all over the world.

Poverty in BiH remains pervasive with more than half the population lacking the resources to secure even basic necessities. The *Living in BiH: Wave 4* report (FOS, BHAS and RSIS, 2005) established that 35.7 per cent of households in BiH were in poverty defined as two-thirds of median income or a poverty threshold of KM 250 per month (approximately EUR125). Age, employment status, marital status, number of children and level of education were all found to be associated with levels of poverty over the four years. At the time of the survey, 30 per cent of working-age households in BiH had no one in paid employment. Households in the Federation of Bosnia and Herzegovina (FBiH) continue to be generally better off in terms of mean household income from all sources, mainly due to higher levels of employment-based income in FBiH compared to RS.

The depressed economy in BiH is only partly offset by the presence of a large ex-patriot community, chiefly in large urban centres, such as Sarajevo. This huge presence created an artificial economy, with tens of thousands of BiH citizens employed by international organizations, and with thousands of businesses created to provide goods and services to the international community, particularly in Sarajevo.

On the macroeconomic level, BiH is under intense pressure from international financial institutions and donors to undergo an economic transition similar to that implemented in the other post-communist communities. Although there is still much country-level resistance to this process, it is clear that the country has little choice but to adopt the majority of the proposed economic reforms. In December 1998, the Peace Implementation Council met in Madrid to discuss the peace process in BiH. The council made recommendations with respect to the rule of law, democratization, security issues and refugee returns, among other matters, also calling for 'strict conditionality' in the allocation of donors' funds, as deemed appropriate by the Economic Task Force to the OHR.[2]

To its credit, the council also emphasized the need for adequate social protection and a strategy to fight poverty in BiH. Nevertheless, in the same breath, it also urged the privatization of health-care systems, and advocated the transfer of public services to private enterprises.

THE ADMINISTRATION OF SOCIAL WELFARE IN POST-DAYTON BiH

Since its main goal was to secure a permanent ceasefire in Bosnia and Herzegovina, it is unsurprising that the Dayton Peace Agreement paid little attention to social policy (Stubbs, 2001). According to the BiH Constitution (which is part of the Dayton Peace Agreement), none of the social policy responsibilities were afforded to the country-level institutions (Stubbs, 2001). For example, Article III/3 of the Constitution states that 'all governmental functions and responsibilities that are not explicitly afforded to the BiH institutions are considered to be the functions and the responsibilities of the entity-level governments'. Hence, the Peace Agreement allows for two separate social policies and welfare state regimes to exist in BiH (ibid.).

Nowadays, virtually all social functions of the state are split into two politically denominated para-state systems. On the one side, Republika Srpska is a centralized state within a state, possessing only two layers of government: central and municipal. Given also the largely ethnically homogeneous population (as a result of ethnic cleansing during the war), the decision-making and funding process is much easier to accomplish in this entity. On the other hand, the Federation of Bosnia and Herzegovina was created as a composite entity, composed of ten cantons, with either Bosniak or Croat majority, including two ethnically mixed cantons with 'special regimes'. Again, for political reasons, responsibility for most areas of governance was devolved to the lower levels, including cantons.

Ministries on the federal level mostly serve as co-ordination or oversight bodies. The Federal parliament legislates so-called 'umbrella' laws, which outline general principles and frameworks within which the cantonal assemblies are supposed to pass their own specific laws and regulations. As funds for social welfare come from cantonal budgets, realization of social welfare mostly depends on the economic strength of individual cantons. In practice this means that the federal bodies lack effective means for co-ordination and supervision of social welfare efforts.

In the case of the pension system, there is no cantonal provision of pensions and related benefits. Instead, there are two entity pension and disability funds (PIO/MIO funds). Owing to the relatively stronger economic performance of the Federation of BiH, pensions and disability benefits in this entity are larger compared to the RS. Pensions are paid based on the retirees' place of residence, not on the location of the company where they have earned their pension. This has led to a peculiar situation where the majority of Bosniak returnees to RS remain formally registered residents of the federation in order to claim higher benefits. On the other side, pensioners in RS who have earned their pensions in companies located within the present territory of the federation have initiated several class lawsuits to have their pensions paid by the Federal Pension Fund. If realized, these claims would lead to significant overall reduction in Federation pensions.

The pension system in both entities is largely retained from the former Yugoslavia, based on the pay-as-you-go scheme. The inherent instability of funding in such a scheme was offset in the former republic funds through large-scale investment into real estate, notably hotels and old people's homes, which provided both additional income for the funds and a savings opportunity through the placement of old people without family care into long-stay institutions owned by the fund in exchange for their pension monies. However, physical destruction and criminal 'privatization' of these establishments, together with the collapse of the economy and the currency, meant that both pension funds at the end of the war started with empty budgets. Their current performance is dependent exclusively on the monthly realization of benefits through mandatory deductions from tax-payers' salaries. All attempts at reforming the pension system by introducing, for example, a three-tier system, as in neighbouring Croatia, have failed, due to political blockages and worries that the introduction of even partly voluntary schemes would lead to the collapse of the PIO/MIO budgets.

Formal social welfare provision is still primarily implemented through local Centres for Social Work (CSWs) and traditional long-stay institutions for children and adults, following the former Yugoslav tradition. Centres for Social Work cover large geographical areas, sometimes up to 50 000 people, as well as diverse practice – from social security provision to counselling services. The latter were rather neglected in the light of pressing demands for cash payments due to the decrease in living standards.

Data for 2005 indicate that social and child welfare in BiH is implemented through: 101 CSWs, 40 Social and Child Welfare Offices, two cantonal CSWs and a Sub-Department for Social Welfare of the Brčko District (Save the Children UK, 2005). These services employ 534 professional and 622 administrative and other staff (a total of 1156 employed). Over half of the CSWs (62 per cent) do not employ the number of staff proposed in the legislative framework for their operation (Hadžibegić, 1999). It is relevant to note that, in FBiH, an additional 74 staff were employed over a period of two years (2002–2004). However, these were mainly administrative, rather than professional staff.

The BiH Council of Ministers identified various difficulties in the implementation of the reform of social welfare (BiH Council of Ministers, 2004: 145–6). Primarily, there is an increase in the needs of the population, paralleled with the creation of new service-user categories (due to the post-war socio-economic problems). There is also a lack of up-to-date and complete databases on service users. Secondly, there is a lack of resources (from trained staff to adequate work space) and monitoring instruments for social welfare implementation. Thirdly, resource constraints are further exacerbated by normative and accountability difficulties.

THE NGO SECTOR AND SOCIAL WELFARE IN BiH: A PERIODIZATION

The War Period (1991–95)

The first humanitarian mission in BiH began on 7 July 1992. It was entitled 'World to Sarajevo' (Kljajić, 1999). From that point on, various aspects of support for the BiH population were both left to and taken over by foreign non-governmental organizations. In the context marked by the emergency nature of international intervention, remnants of the social sector in the country at the time were bypassed or ignored by the international community with linguistic and cultural barriers operating alongside dominant modes of operation of these organizations. One effect of this circumvention of the public sector in Bosnia and Herzegovina, was the consequential stimulation of a civil sector there. However, rather than being a true civil society, what emerged was almost akin to a parallel private business sector with NGO status as new organizations were established to absorb donor funds.

Bosnian social-sector professionals found themselves both unable to communicate with international aid agencies and incapable of adopting the style of work these organizations brought with them. Consequently, many of these organizations had to recruit and rely upon the service of local staff, whose only qualification frequently appeared to be their fluency in English or other relevant languages. Such freshly minted welfare 'professionals' were certainly ignorant of the profession, but their elevated status as moneyed and influential workers for foreigners made them unwilling to seek advice from those who did know about social welfare but who did not speak the new jargon of international social development. As one commentator noted:

> The best and the brightest Bosnians, especially those who know English, are now working for International Organizations and INGOs as staff, drivers, interpreters, rather than in the BiH society itself or for local NGOs, most of whom cannot afford to pay the very high salaries that their international counterparts pay. Another impact is generational: older, more experienced and educated Bosnians who don't know English are left out, creating not only a knowledge gap for INGOs, but also resentment. (Gagnon, 2002: 223)

Lendvai and Stubbs (forthcoming) note that transnational policies can be seen as translation rather than transfer. The two-way learning, which would help the transfer process, was inhibited by the fact that the majority of INGOs and their consultants often lacked contextualization, or an understanding of BiH society and the history of political and power structures (Gagnon, 2002). It could be said, therefore, that the social sector in BiH was hijacked during the war by an army of translators. There remain huge problems in defining and translating terms that describe these imported policies and practices, such as 'policy', 'care management', 'care planning', 'assessment', 'stakeholders', 'service users'. In many documents, newly coined terms consist of clumsy and descriptive translations, or these terms are left in their original form (mainly in English).[3] What lies beneath these terms – particularly from the standpoint of service users – rarely indicates a shift in actual practical experiences.

Those few social-service professionals who found employment with international aid agencies, failed to lobby for an aid effort which would actually take into consideration the pre-existing tradition, experience and knowledge accumulated in the previous decades by the public social sector in Bosnia and Herzegovina. All this contributed to the fact that the humanitarian relief effort was implemented through a parallel ad hoc social-service network run by international organizations with the support of locally recruited personnel, most of whom not only lacked adequate expertise, but were plagued by their overriding dependence on the agenda and the will of their international employers.

The Immediate Post-war Period (1995–98)

Immediately after the war, governmental bodies were reluctant to commit their scarce resources for welfare. At the time, most of the (meagre) entity budgets were spent on the funding of the respective armies and the payment of benefits to war veterans. The number of foreign organizations increased and donor agendas multiplied and became more complex. At times, especially in the period immediately after the war ended, it seemed like the intervention was driven by the same laws which govern the fashion industry. First, the topics and themes of interventions were based on topics which were at times perceived as 'trendy' – from psychosocial support in the mid-1990s, through prostitution and trafficking in the late 1990s, to Roma issues later. This is due to the fact that INGOs depend for funding on institutions and organizations that themselves have specific interests and perceptions, unrelated to the needs of BiH citizens (Gagnon, 2002).

> The negative effect that occurs when donors drive the process was most clearly expressed by a USAID officer in charge of NGO relations. While he praised the humanitarian international NGOs such as Catholic Relief, the International Rescue Committee and Mercy Corps for their work during the war and for providing invaluable information during the immediate post-war period, he declared that their time was now over. USAID would be shifting its funding, he said, to international NGOs that have experience elsewhere in Central and Eastern Europe and that work specifically on 'democracy assistance'. (Ibid.: 224)

Secondly, major supranational and non-governmental actors were more concerned with branding their investments than co-ordinating them with other existing stakeholders. Last, but not least, each of these trends was present for only a season or two, making it difficult to demonstrate impact on communities on the ground.

As an example, in August 1996, the World Bank launched the War Victims Rehabilitation Project to address 'the most urgent needs in physical and psychosocial rehabilitation' (HealthNet International and SweBiH, 2000). One component of the project foresaw the establishment of 38 new Community Based Rehabilitation Centres in the Federation of BiH. This was actually a fairly good initiative, since the idea was to promote community-based mental health care and family medicine as an alternative to rebuilding classic psychiatric facilities. At the same time, the World Health Organization published their strategy papers, developed in close co-operation with the health authorities in both entities (ibid.). The European Community Humanitarian Office offered financial and technical support for the establishment of some Community Mental Health Centres and financed an INGO, HealthNet International (HNI) to support the reform efforts through training of practitioners to work in these Centres. This built on the prior support of Médecins Sans Frontières (a sister organization of the HNI). There were also other NGO initiatives in the same field, from Queens University (Canada), SweBiH (Swedish Psychiatric, Social and Rehabilitation Project for Bosnia-Herzegovina – a Swedish psychosocial rehabilitation initiative), an EC-funded postgraduate course, activities carried out by the Harvard Trauma Centre in the central Bosnian Canton, just to name a few. Co-operation between these INGOs and the BiH government was unusually good, with joint planning for all of the initiatives, despite the need of each INGO to 'brand' their 'portion' of the investment. However, in early 2002, the funding for further initiatives to support mental health reforms ended. From 2002, the new Community Health Centres received little or no support from INGOs and donor agencies. HealthNet International became a kind of a local NGO, but with no institutional memory of the commitment to support the development of grassroots, community-based services. By 2003, the organization was implementing a project that aimed to support and build the skills of staff working in residential social welfare services for children, since this was the theme which was receiving funding attention at the time.

The Emphasis on Strategies: (I)NGO-initiated Social Policy Reforms (1999–Onwards)

The late 1990s/early 2000s were marked by a sea-change in the world of international intervention in BiH. Half a decade after the war was over, donor money started to dry up due to donor fatigue and the feeling that there were other, more pressing, crises in the world. Figures from the Office for South East Europe of the European Commission and the World Bank (2005) indicate that in the period between 2003 and 2005 grants by various supranational and international organizations decreased from EUR261.6 million in 2003 to EUR170.74 million in 2005. In the same period, loans extended to BiH went up from EUR75.89 million in 2003 to EUR180.17 million in 2005. This resulted in the scaling down of the majority of internationally run operations in the country, with the large international aid organizations gradually pulling out of the country. These organizations have high running costs, due to their high salaries and other overhead costs associated with aid operations. Since their original mandates remained largely unfulfilled, many of these organizations resorted to face-saving exercises – transfers of at least part of their mandates and the majority of their activities to locally registered NGOs. This at least had a cost-saving effect, since the local staff of these NGOs were frequently competent enough and willing to carry out the same amount of activities at a fraction of costs required by their international counterparts.

That said, these local NGOs were practically in the same shape as they were at the inception phase during the war or its immediate aftermath. They were still largely staffed by the same people whose original expertise sometimes consisted solely of the ability to speak English, and which still, after all those years, nurtured the same amount of suspicion and distrust when it came to local authorities and public social-sector professionals in the country.

It was a common belief at the time among public social-sector professionals that internationals intended to abolish the existing public sector and build a new welfare system from scratch. This was mainly due to the Western attitudes towards the contexts they encountered; these can best be described as colonialist, due to the overall lack of knowledge of histories and cultures of BiH. Zaviršek and Flaker describe the renewed 'western imperialisation, which supports the conviction that it is necessary to demolish everything that existed, build it anew and then, somehow from within the previous unsatisfactory and unprofessional situation, to produce something suitable' (quoted in Stubbs, 1997: 19–28). Having barely survived the wartime invasion of the army of translators, one cannot blame local public sector professionals for being apprehensive about the impending changes. The following quote from a Romanian scholar could just as easily have been from BiH: 'Throughout history, for Romanians it was a survival strategy to agree officially with the authorities and unofficially develop one's own agenda.' (Dümling, 2004: 275).

'The authorities' in this case were the donor agencies and other supranational and international bodies. Some NGOs that did manage to accumulate experience in different policies and practices attempted to bridge the gap between the international and local public sector spheres, by applying for and implementing foreign-funded restructuring reform programmes. In social welfare, the Independent Bureau of Humanitarian Issues (IBHI) implemented two major projects of this kind. The first was initiated and funded in 1999, by the Finnish Ministry of Foreign Affairs and was called the Support to Social Sector Project (SSSP). Building on the accumulated experiences of this project, a second phase began in 2001. Almost simultaneously (2002–2005), the UK government's DFID supported a very similar project, also implemented by IBHI, but with considerable involvement of the UK consultancy company, Birks Sinclair & Associates. The similarity is largely due to the fact that the project documents for both projects were written by the same (international) consultant. The goal of the programme was to 'strengthen the social policy regime in BiH at the central and local levels' and to 'promote an effective and efficient social policy at all levels, which is fiscally sustainable, demonstrates social innovation and contributes to the reduction of poverty, inequality and social exclusion' through:

- the strengthening of the municipal and cantonal social policy management and social service delivery; and
- the fostering and enablement of Community-Level Partnerships and Community Action Projects between the civil society actors in four pilot areas. (Birks Sinclair et al., unpublished)

These, as well as many other reform projects, were implemented in so-called 'pilot' municipalities – a selection of three to five municipalities in different parts of BiH. It transpires that the main idea behind the creation of these projects was the so called bottom-up approach of using the accumulated knowledge (not necessarily from the project only) in implementation of pilot approaches in local communities to prepare a set of recommendations, and later policies, which could be fed through to competent authorities in both entities in BiH. Different means of transferring these experiences upward were devised, most of which were constituted in the form of ad hoc bodies with mixed membership, including representatives of municipalities where the project was being implemented, as well as from competent cantonal, entity and state bodies. The projects were grandly conceived with the ultimate objective being the restructuring of welfare regimes in BiH along the lines of modern welfare theory.

The so-called mixed model of social welfare became a kind of mantra to be repeated endlessly by the persons represented in the meetings sponsored by these projects. For those involved in the implementation of the projects, the participation in project activities carried with it a handsome reward. At the local level, grant schemes were devised, whereby local partners would implement small-scale projects in accordance with the established priorities and the principles set forth in the project document. At higher levels, different entity and state officials were involved in writing, or at least signing, different studies, recommendations, policy papers and so on. The carrot-and-stick approach which determined the structure of these two projects promised to make a significant impact in the area of the social sector reform in BiH. Continuing funding by the international donor was made conditional on the achievement of a set of objectives. With all the participants in the process being more than handsomely rewarded for their support and involvement in the project effort, one could justifiably expect that piloting of new structures in the social sector in BiH would ultimately lead to the initiation and successful completion of locally owned welfare system reform.

The experiences accumulated during the implementation, as well as the evaluation of these and similar projects, however, highlight the following concerns:

● The use of the term 'pilot' when referring to the sites where these and other projects were initiated indicates a commitment to roll out the programme once a project is successfully piloted. In this, as well as many other cases, the roll out did not happen (Vesna Bošnjak, personal communication). Even in Western countries the use of pilots to promote policy change does not guarantee that best practices will be promoted widely. In a review of governmental pilots carried out by the UK Cabinet Office (2003), the author notes that, in the US: 'As always, it is difficult to quantify the overall extent to which these sorts of policy trials have influenced the US social policy over the years, whether at the state or federal level. Certainly, the persistence with which randomised policy trials continue to be embraced suggests that they are a highly valued and well-integrated policy aid.'

● Reform through projects is difficult to implement due to the short life of project cycles. On average, a project cycle in BiH lasts only a year (FOS, BHAS and RSIS, 2005; ICVA, 2002).

● The state per se was never made a part of the whole pilot reform exercise. The donor governments and their local implementing partners, after signing formal agreements with the state authorities, recruited representatives of key government ministries and institutions in an individual capacity, through their participation in informal, ad hoc, project bodies. Here they paid lip service to the implementation of project goals, while continuing their everyday work in the government. Project activities brought handsome rewards, but did not create obligations for state agencies or these individuals.

Evaluations of these projects frequently mention that their results were clear, appropriate for the BIH contest, and worthy of follow up, but were inevitably very vague when it came to noting the practical achievements of the project. The evaluation of the Finnish government aid effort in postwar Bosnia lists their social sector restructuring projects as weakest in terms of the actual impact on the welfare regime they were supposed to reform (SIPU International, 2004). Similarly, the evaluation of the DFID-sponsored project relied on a self-evaluation by the projects' British implementers (Birks Sinclair). Hence, it failed to note the practical results and left actual evaluation to an impact assessment at a later date which had limited scope to offer critique.

THE MEDIUM-TERM DEVELOPMENT STRATEGY FOR BiH

The main effect of social policy reform projects in BiH, besides their genuine influence on reforming the mindsets and, to some extent, structures at the local community level, seems to be that a number of lessons learned found their way into measures and recommendations drafted into the Medium-Term Development Strategy (MTDS) for Bosnia and Herzegovina, 2004–2007. This MTDS was adopted by the BiH Council of Ministers together with the entity governments in February 2004, initially as the Poverty Reduction Strategy Paper or PRSP. In accordance with the BiH Constitution, its implementation was accepted by the Parliamentary Assembly of BiH in March of the same year (EPPU, 2004: 2), but also by the respective entity parliaments. In the MTDS, social welfare is recognized as 'a growing function and form of social policy in transitional conditions' (BiH Council of Ministers, 2004: 145). The so-called 'social sector' is one of 12 priority sectors identified within the strategy (ibid.).[4]

The MTDS aims to implement market principles in social welfare and to promote the development of alternative forms of social care (BiH Council of Ministers, 2004: 147). The document does not include a clear elaboration of these declarative concepts, although it indicates a significant transformation of the funding, organization, provision and auditing in BiH social welfare. A brief elaboration includes a readiness to promote co-operation with the non-governmental sector, promotion of voluntary work, initiation of a legal framework that will enable governmental and non-governmental organizations to become equal partners in the social welfare system, as well as the initiation of tax benefits to promote corporate social responsibility (ibid.).

The Action Plan, which represented the key component of the MTDS, spelt out which ministry was in charge of preparation and implementation of each policy, but did not elaborate further. Within these ministries, no clear idea existed on how the task was to be implemented, nor were any instructions prepared by the government(s) on how to proceed with it. Even a brief critical review of the Action Plan indicates a strong pattern of thinking typical of the supranational organizations that were to fund the reform (the World Bank, for instance), as well as a lack of actual understanding by the involved representatives of the governmental and non-governmental organizations about exactly what measures are necessary to initiate and implement the reform. For example, within a proposed measure to transform the financial and operational structure of Centres for Social Work towards a project-based funding framework, a time frame of only half a year was proposed, with responsibility outlined only as belonging to the relevant entity ministries in charge of social welfare.

Having criticized the international community throughout this text, it must eventually be recognized that, in spite of all misgivings, BiH has, through the support of the international community, incrementally developed a strong decision-making and professional lobby for legislative and practice commitments for community-based approaches in both health and social care. Without such support, from funding to training, it is highly unlikely that there would now be a pool of grassroots practitioners – and even some user initiatives – that are strongly committed to, and actually practice, inclusive education, organize community-based housing for people with long-term mental health problems, or foster care for children without parental care.

But what do all these efforts mean for people who use services? The services one receives still largely depend on where one lives. In one of the poorer cantons in the Federation of Bosnia and Herzegovina, a war-disabled veteran with a head injury and mental health problems may only receive from his local Centre for Social Work KM12[5] (approximately EUR6) per month to support his family of four, while in the richer cantons (for example, Sarajevo Canton) the amount is approximately ten times as large. If a young family is struggling to care for their child, the state is still more likely to place that child in residential care – especially if there is a big facility nearby that they need to fill, than to provide the service user with the funding to cope during the time of crisis. As a struggling young parent, you may simply require assistance in facilitating access to potential employers, but social workers in the Centres for Social Work frequently lack skills or vision for such problem-solving approaches. At the moment, the best one may hope for is to be offered a symbolic cash handout or psychological counselling to cope with crisis.

WHERE NEXT?

In January 2006, a Social Policy Conference was organized by DFID, the World Bank, the EC Delegation in BiH, IBHI and the ministries in charge of social policy at entity level. At the conference, the resident representative of the World Bank, Dirk Reinermann stated 'We want reforms and we want them now!' as part of a somewhat predictable 'there is no alternative' argument. Kasza states that:

> Foreign models are not always borrowed; they are sometimes imposed by force. When this happens, a country may end up with policies that do not reflect the thinking or values of its policy actors, yet these policies may endure thanks to the vested interests that tend to develop around welfare programmes and the inertia that sometimes afflicts big, complex policies in any field. (Kasza, 2002: 280)

164   *Social policy and international interventions in South East Europe*

This does not mean that imposed policies are bad or neglect the needs of service users. Quite the contrary. Dümling (2004: 273–4) offers a relevant comment in regard to the Romanian experiences with similar initiatives, but which is easily applicable to the current reform context in BiH.

> Some (projects and initiatives) certainly have a positive impact on the local communities and the destiny of individuals. However, they do not necessarily promote social change considering the Romanian society as a whole . . . The projects hardly start with people themselves, but are conditioned by Western grant guidelines, as if economic and social change can be imported within two or three years. (Dümling, 2004: 273–4)

Most relevantly, the mid-term framework for substantial reforms can also be contested. Kasza (2002) also notes that the 'changes' and 'reforms' in social policy, as well as other policy realms, reflect complex contributions of different stakeholders to the policy-making process over a 50- or even 100-year period. 'After decades of modification and tinkering, today's policies are the cumulative work of different governments and sometimes different forms of government, and they represent responses to a variety of historical circumstances. As a result, few policies we analyse today are likely to reflect any one set of practical concerns or values' (ibid.: 273).

This issue is relevant in two ways – local decision-makers should have the most responsibility, and any influence of supranational actors should be met by a qualified response from their local counterparts, taking into consideration the needs and interests of the citizens they represent, which is far from the case in BiH. Secondly, if BiH decision-makers would work according to the needs of citizens and for the kinds of public policies required in this country, rather than for personal gain or the benefit of neighbouring countries due to nationalist interests, then long-term strategies and plans would not be as difficult to implement, as the experience of current short- to mid-term initiatives and strategies suggests.

NOTES

1. For example, after the opening of the renovated Old Bridge in Mostar (bombed by Croat forces during the war) in mid-2004, a new tourist guide was issued. In the guide, one can find out all about who built the bridge, when and why. One can also find out when it was renovated and opened. One cannot, however, find out why the bridge needed renovation in the first place. All this takes place, while a big cross still stands erected on a mountain overlooking Mostar, at the point from which the Croatian tanks bombed the town during the war in the early 1990s.
2. From www.oscebih.org/documents/19-eng.pdf.
3. For benefit of readers with some knowledge of South-Slavic languages, some examples include: human development – *humani razvoj*; millennium goals – *milenijski golovi*. One

particularly amusing example is the Project Document for Finnish government funded Support to Social Sector Project (SSSP), where a local translator assumed that 'Social' stands for 'Societal', hence translating the entire 40+ pages document as if it was the project dealing with reform of BiH society.
4. Including education, health, agriculture, forestry, water management, ecology, infrastructure, energy, industry, anti-mine activities and the information technology sector.
5. KM – Convertible Mark, the BiH currency (1 euro = 1.95KM).

REFERENCES

BiH Council of Ministers (Vijeće ministara) (2004), *Srednjoročna razvojna strategija BiH 2004–2007 (mid-term Development Strategy for BiH 2004–2007)*, Bosna i Hercegovina, Vijeće Ministara, Jedinica za ekonomsko planiranje i implementaciju srednjoročne razvojne strategije (Bosnia and Herzegovina, council of ministers, Economic Policy and Planning Unit), http://www.PRSP.ba/strategija_bos.html (accessed April 2005).
Birks Sinclair, Independent Bureau for Humanitarian Issues (IBHI) and European Institute of Social Services (EISS) (unpublished), 'UK Department for International Development BiH: reforming the systems and structures of central and local social policy regimes', consultation document, Contract Number CNTR 00 1629A, Consolidated municipal level review and analysis, 11 October 2002.
Cabinet Office (2003), *Trying It Out: The Role of 'Pilots' in Policy-making. Report of a Review of Government Pilots*, www.policyhub.gov.uk/docs/rop.pdf (accessed November 2006).
Dümling, B. (2004), 'Country notes: the impact of Western social workers in Romania – a fine line between empowerment and disempowerment', *Social Work & Society*, **2** (2), 270–78.
Economic Policy and Planning Unit (EPPU) (2004), *Implementacija mjera iz srednjoročne razvojne strategije BiH (PRSP) – Progres report za period Avgust 2003–Novembar 2004 (Implementation of Measures from the Mid-term Development Strategy BiH (PRSP) – Progress Report for the Period August 2003–November 2004)*, Sarajevo: EPPU, December.
Federal Office for Statistics (FOS), BiH Agency for Statistics (BHAS) and Republika Srpska Institute for Statistics (RSIS) (2005), *Living in BiH Panel Study Final Report: Wave 4*, Sarajevo, May.
Gagnon, V.P. (2002), 'International NGOs in Bosnia-Herzegovina: attempting to build civil society', in S. Mendelson and J. Glenn (eds), *The Power and Limits of NGOs: A Critical Look at Building Democracy in Eastern Europe and Eurasia*, New York: Columbia University Press, pp. 207–64.
Hadžibegić, A. (1999), 'Lokalne službe socijalne zaštite u FBiH danas i perspektive razvoja' ('Local social service departments in the federation of Bosnia and Herzegovina today and their development perspectives'), in V. Kljajić (ed.), *Socijalni rad na pragu 21. stoljeća (Social Work at the Eve of the 21st Century)*, Sarajevo: Univerzitet u Sarajevu, Fakultet političkih nauka, Centar za socijalna istraživanja, Odsjek za socijalni rad (University of Sarajevo, Faculty of Political Sciences, Centre for Social Research at the Department of Social Work), pp. 112–17.

HealthNet International and SweBiH (2000), *Assessment: Community Mental Health Care in the Federation of Bosnia & Herzegovina*, Sarajevo: HealthNet International.

International Crisis Group (ICG) (1998), *Whither Bosnia? ICG Balkans Report No 43*, September, www.intl-crisis.group.org (accessed November 2000).

International Council of Voluntary Agencies (ICVA) (2002), 'Istraživanje – Odnos NVO sektora u BiH i ostalih učesnika u razvoju' ('Research – relations between the NGO sector in BiH and other developmental stakeholders'), in ICVA (ed.), *Pogledi na NVO sektor u BiH* (*Views of the NGO Sector in BiH*), Sarajevo: ICVA, pp. 22–38.

Kasza, G.J. (2002), 'The illusion of welfare "regimes"', *Journal of Social Policy*, **31** (2), 271–87.

Kljajić, V. (1999), 'Društveni trendovi i osiromašenje – izazovi politike socijalne zaštite u BiH' ('Social Trends and Impoverishment – Challenges for Social Welfare Policy in BiH'), in *Socijalni rad na pragu 21. stoljeća* (*Social Work at the Eve of the 21st Century*), Sarajevo: Univerzitet u Sarajevu, Fakultet političkih nauka, Centar za socijalna istraživanja, Odsjek za socijalni rad (University of Sarajevo, Faculty of Political Sciences, Centre for Social Research at the Department of Social Work), pp. 34–54.

Lendvai, N. and P. Stubbs (forthcoming), 'Policies as translation: situating transnational social policies', in S. Hodgson and Z. Irving (eds), *Policy Reconsidered: Meanings, Politics and Practices*, Bristol: Policy Press.

Office for South East Europe, European Commission and the World Bank (2005), *Finansijski tokovi prema Bosni i Hercegovini 2003–2005* (*Financial Flows towards Bosnia and Herzegovina 2003–2005*), www.eppu.ba (accessed October 2006).

Save the Children UK (2005), *Situaciona analiza: Zaštita djeca bez roditeljskog staranja u BiH* (*Situation Analysis: Protection of Children without Parental Care in Bosnia and Herzegovina*), Sarajevo: Save the Children UK.

Stubbs, P. (1997), 'Social work training in Central and Eastern Europe: some initial findings', in N. Connelly and P. Stubbs (eds), *Trends in Social Work Education Across Europe*, London: NISW/CCETSW.

Stubbs, P. (2001), ' "Socijalni sektor" ili devalviranje značaja socijalne politike? Regulatorni režim socijalnog blagostanja u Bosni I Hercegovini danas' (' "Social sector" or residual policy?'), in Ž. Papić (ed.), *Međunarodne politike podrške zemljama jugoistočne Evrope: Lekcije (ne)naučene u BiH* (*International Policies of Support to Countries of South-Eastern Europe: Lessons (Not) Learnt in Bosnia and Herzegovina*), Sarajevo: Müller, pp. 125–39.

Swedish Institute for Public Administration (SIPU) International (2004), *Evaluation of Finland's Development Cooperation with Bosnia and Herzegovina*, http://www.oecd.org/dataoecd/7/3/35182016.pdf (accessed October 2006).

United Nations High Commission for Refugees (UNHCR) (2006), *2005 Global Refugee Trends: Statistical Overview of Populations of Refugees, Asylum-seekers, Internally Displaced Persons, Stateless Persons and Other Persons of Concern to UNHCR*, http://www.unhcr.org/statistics (accessed September 2006).

Wilkinson, R. (2005), 'After the war was over', *Refugees*, **3** (140), 6–18.

9. Serbia

Mihail Arandarenko and Pavle Golicin

INTRODUCTION

The social protection regime as it exists today in Serbia offers an excellent example of an 'assemblage of political discourses' which over time produced 'hybrids, paradoxes, tensions and incompatibilities' (Clarke, 2004). This regime owes its current shape (or misshape) to the three layers of heritage – first and the most distant, that of a proud self-management socialist Yugoslavia (SFRY), which built an exemplary Bismarckian welfare state on shaky economic grounds; second, the legacy of the disastrous 1990s, when both economic and social security systems largely collapsed, but were to a degree substituted by the often bizarrely innovative, though not sustainable, policies of economic and social populism; and last, and the most recent, that created by the post-October 2000 efforts made by hasty and sometimes overconfident reformers, more than generously helped by various international actors with their own often disparate agendas.

Unlike most other chapters in this volume, we shall take the year 2000, which saw the overthrow of the Milošević authoritarian pseudo-democratic regime as the watershed year, from which the real economic and social policy reforms start. This choice is additionally justified by the fact that Serbia was under international sanctions throughout the 1990s and therefore international actors did not participate in the creation of social policy at that time. Admittedly, they still influenced it in a number of ways, most notably through the economic damage created by sanctions and by the military intervention in spring 1999.

The rest of this chapter is organized as follows. In the second section we briefly describe the two different social policy legacies – first, communist, built since the 1950s through the late 1980s, and second, populist, built in the 1990s. The third section briefly looks at political parties, their ideologies and at political developments, especially after October 2000. The fourth section lists the main actors of international advice and maps out their main interests and involvements. The fifth and central section looks in some detail at reforms in specific large policy areas, but also attempts to explain how the sectorally divided interplay between policy-makers and international organizations, often additionally influenced by the involvement of local or foreign interest groups, resulted in a highly inconsistent social policy regime. The sixth section summarizes the main points we wanted to make throughout this chapter.

LEGACY

Social policy of Yugoslavia under communist rule (1945–91), especially in its mature phase, basically adopted a Bismarckian social insurance model and adjusted it to the ideological preferences of the new regime. Gradually, a dual system of social protection was built, with 'self-management' workers having multiple privileges based on social insurance, but also with an outer belt of social rights available to other citizens that were based on universal or means-tested entitlements. These included universal child allowance, income or means-tested social assistance, literacy and basic education programmes, and so on.

This system was accompanied by the 'socially sensitive' price policy – controlled and often depressed prices of food and below-cost prices of utilities and energy. Pensions were generous because of a favourable dependency ratio. Unemployment was relatively high, mostly because of a huge transfer from agricultural to industrial employment. A liberal economic emigration policy since the mid-1960s helped ease the pressure on social enterprises, but they still tended to employ surplus labour. However, the foreign debt crisis that marked the 1980s revealed that the system which was sometimes referred to as the 'Yugoslav miracle' was based on shaky economic ground and needed to be thoroughly reformed. The discussion whether it would be possible within the boundaries of self-management socialism was abruptly interrupted by the fall of the Berlin wall and, even more dramatically, the violent dissolution of Yugoslavia in the 1990s.

In Serbia a new populist regime of Slobodan Milošević established in 1987 won democratic legitimacy at the first multi-party elections in 1990. Soon the country become deeply immersed in the wars for Yugoslav succession and entered a cycle of deep economic crisis, international sanctions and hyperinflation. In late 1993 the entire system collapsed – hyperinflation was growing hour by hour, average monthly wages sunk to 10 dollars, and average pension was half that number (cf. Dinkic, 1995). The stabilization programme introduced in early 1994 marked the return to relative monetary stability, but the entire system of social protection was never to recover to financial sustainability.

The response of the regime was typical. Formal rights were not cut; there was no attempt to adjust the system to new economic reality which implied a GDP of some 40 per cent of its pre-war size. In the field of social insurance it meant the gradual amassing of arrears to the beneficiaries. In the labour area, a ban on firing employees during the sanctions was introduced, as a populist measure aimed at the support of workers and trade unions. Still, many workers were sent on paid forced leave, and many were formally working without pay. For all of them, and for almost all new entrants into the job market, the informal economy represented the only viable option.

Informality also entered the formal labour market, with massive tax evasion to which the authorities turned a blind eye, although these practices further eroded the basis from which the pensions and social entitlements were to be financed. The regime elite actively supported this development, with the leading politicians as well as security and business elite members organizing 'unofficial' markets of cigarettes, oil and basic necessities, amassing large fortunes in the process. The encouragement of 'exit' options like the informal economy or economic emigration was also a part of a strategy to dissolve any attempts at organized social and political protests (cf. Arandarenko, 2001).

POLITICAL PARTIES AND POLITICAL DEVELOPMENTS SINCE 2000

After a decade of political, economic and social struggle enhanced by the series of cruel wars for Yugoslav succession, Milošević eventually lost popular support at the elections in September 2000. Reluctant to leave power peacefully, his regime was finally overthrown on the streets of Belgrade on 5 October 2000. In the immediate aftermath of these events, a wide coalition called the Democratic Opposition of Serbia (DOS) took over the most important reigns of power in Serbia. The DOS was actually a conglomerate of 18 parties and movements with diverse political and (if any) socio-economic agendas. After elections in December 2000 the DOS formed a new government, which was dominated by the strong personality of then Prime Minister Djindjic, but also by the constant clashes between his Democratic Party (DS) and another most powerful party, Democratic Party of Serbia (DSS), led by then Yugoslav president Vojislav Kostunica.

The DOS did have a programme of radical economic reforms borrowed from another influential opposition group called G17 Plus. The programme was a standard neo-liberal reform package coupled with stronger emphasis on social justice and social dialogue. However, as with most general reform agendas, the programme did not go into technical details, nor was it really possible without insider insight into the real economic and social situation, which is a privilege of incumbent governments. But the economic and social portfolios were populated mostly by experts originating from yet another think thank, the Economics Institute. They all were immediately overwhelmed by the disastrous legacy of prolonged misrule and at first had to act as firefighters, for example, caring about energy supply, securing emergency assistance, pensions, salaries for public servants, and so on. Expert members of the government had a significant previous exposure to co-operating with international financial organizations, the UN and bilateral agencies, and soon established excellent partner relations with them.

Still, some far-reaching strategic decisions were made hastily, and without enough care to secure overall consistency and social balance of reforms. Decisions made early are perhaps the most crucial for further reform moves, since they largely reduce the availability of further options; and yet, they appear to be based on little reliable information and are hence easily influenced by the prejudices and ideologies of reform strategists, or advice and experiences which may be available quite randomly. This is a general curse of radical reforms for which Serbia offers another convincing illustration.

It would be very hard to classify the economic and welfare ideologies of DOS members or those of other Serbian parties along the usual right–left, conservative–social democratic spectrum. During the 2000s there have been quite significant movements and swaps of positions along this spectrum, with the DS belonging officially to Socialist International but advocating fast and uncompromised reforms; and the DSS belonging to the camp of popular parties, but advocating slower and more labour-friendly reforms. Furthermore, programmes and rhetoric, on the one, and real actions, on the other, may differ significantly; and in some policy areas decision-making processes have tended to be highly personalized and had little to do with the party programmes or agreed general reform agendas.

Also it should be noted that all three post-Milošević governments until 2006 (two DOS governments of Djindjic, and, after his murder in March 2003, of Zivkovic; as well as the Kostunica government formed in early 2004) were coalition governments within which complex games and horse-trading further blur attempts to discern the ideology of the parties. While the expert-led ministries within the DOS governments still retained a certain level of co-ordination, this is less the case with the DSS-led Kostunica minority government, in which each ministry is controlled from top to bottom by one of the four coalition parties. However, the DSS-led government still faced powerful continuity impetuses as a result of strong inertia, simply in the forms of draft laws prepared, reform strategies adopted and international commitments taken. One telling example of the force of inertia is the episode with economic patriotism promoted by the

G17 Plus party (in charge of important economic ministries within the Kostunica government) in 2004 as an attempted Keynesian-inspired revision of the neo-liberal agenda. Another is the attempted revision of questionable privatization deals as a fulfilment of anti-corruption electoral promises of the DSS. Both attempts caused a fierce reaction from IFIs and were consequently abandoned.

The lack of a consistent economic and social policy reform agenda did not prevent the Serbian economy from experiencing dynamic growth in the period 2001–2006. It is beyond the ambition of this overview to discuss the counter-factual reality and long-term growth rates implied by an alternative and more consistent set of policies. However, there is another strong indicator of the problematic nature of the reforms – the surprising success of the dinosaur parties of the old regime. They remained mostly unreformed and with only slightly moderated populist rhetoric. They now appeal in the first place to losers in transition, and their relative success (particularly that of Serbian Radical Party – SRS) despite their uninspiring populism is telling of the level of dissatisfaction of the population with the reforms.

INTERNATIONAL ACTORS IN THE AREA OF SOCIAL POLICY REFORM

Sectoral Involvement of International Actors

The international actors' involvement in social policy reforms in Serbia mostly followed the lines of change in the aftermath of collapse of the Berlin wall, which included economization, privatization, diversification of service providers and a human-rights based approach (HRBA). Although the adoption of the above market-led policies puts emphasis on productivity and profitability as the way to overcome the perceived deficiencies of the state sector in delivery of public services, there are certain drawbacks associated with these policies that range from challenges in implementation to its destructive impact on state capacity to deliver social services (UNDP, 2006).

Among international actors the most influential have been the two leading international financial institutions – the World Bank and the IMF. After granting Serbia access to International Development Agency (IDA) funds aimed at the least developed countries, the World Bank organized its assistance and policy advice within the Poverty Reduction Strategy Paper framework. This turned out to be a double blessing – while grants and favourable credits are fine, lumping Serbia together with sub-Saharan countries meant that her European tradition and future would not be recognized and appreciated enough. This has largely been corrected in the interaction with the government and with the full realization that national wealth is far above the official current product, but at the (crucial) beginning of the reform process the World Bank tended to tailor its advice to a quite unreliable development benchmark of below $1000 GDP per capita.

The European Union (with the EC Delegation representing the political wing and the European Agency for Reconstruction the technical assistance wing) showed little interest in counteracting the World Bank's domination. This is understandable, given the very limited requirements for social policy alignments at the early stages of the EU integration process (Arandarenko, 2003; 2004). The Stabilization and Association Process is largely limited to the areas of trade and capital movements, which means that social policy issues are left aside at the time when the countries need them the most (European Economic and Social Committee, 2000). Still, the EAR has been very instrumental in implementing projects aimed at improvements in social infrastructure, most notably in health and education.

The UNDP largely perceived its role as helping to build local capacity in social development, in line with the approach which cares about development, about fighting poverty and about creating a more equitable world. It was also instrumental in gathering various bilateral donors around different ambitious development projects worked out in close partnership with the government. Having little financial resources of its own, in most of the cases the UNDP followed the agenda of its international partners/donors which supported the projects. The UN/UNDP was, however, less successful in its effort to nationalize the UN MDGs and to offer them as a strategic framework alongside the World Bank's PRSP and, however rudimentary, the EU Social *Acquis* frameworks.

The ILO attempted to have an impact in its traditional areas, including labour standards, labour legislation, social dialogue and tripartism, and pensions. However, it was effectively excluded from the advice during initial changes in labour legislation in 2001 and had to limit its intervention to supporting the development of social dialogue and tripartism. Its suspicion toward the introduction of the second pension pillar coincided with the government's suspicion, but was not crucial for the final decision to keep the reformed pay-as-you-go system.

Finally, among the actors influencing social policy creation there has been a significant number of bilateral development organizations such as USAID, DFID and many others. The United States Agency for International Development, as an agency with considerable funds and a firm and clear agenda, has tended to act autonomously, and to find its own niches, such as local community development and support to small private businesses in the context of anti-poverty action, practically independently of government priorities. The Department for International Development, on the other hand, with an almost equally strong agenda but matched by much less funds has tended to forge strategic alliances with the donors with less technical capacity but considerable funds, such as Norway. Smaller agencies, such as the Canadian, Swedish, Swiss, Austrian, Italian, Japanese and so on have been more prone to work jointly with the World Bank or UNDP.

Donor Co-ordination

Although some form of donor co-ordination has existed almost from the very start, it has rarely been successful. At the request of the donor community, it has been partially institutionalized by the government through the Ministry of International Economic Relations, but everybody naturally wanted to meet and negotiate directly with some key local persons and line ministries. Local 'clients' are also tempted to increase their requests for assistance, because of long and uncertain granting procedures, but also in search of more relaxed donors and more generous budgets. Central prioritization but also fads and fashions among the programmes of international agencies tend to crowd out certain intervention areas and to leave almost neglected other very legitimate entry points.

At one point between the governments of Zivkovic and Kostunica in late 2003/early 2004 international organizations indeed felt like 'owners' of Serbian reforms and at the initiative of the WB and the German Association for Technical Assistance (GTZ) developed a laundry list of required reforms which was submitted to the new government. Although a sign of deep mistrust toward the reform orientation and capability of the new government, this was still a useful move and the new government was willing to show its reform credentials by rather rapidly adopting draft laws such as a bankruptcy law, a value added tax law, a procurement law, and so on, largely prepared by the previous government, as well as by implementing reforms required from the donors' list.

MAIN DEVELOPMENTS AND AREAS OF SOCIAL POLICY REFORM

Emergency Assistance and the Division of Reform Responsibilities

Immediately after October 2000 activities related to social policy followed the double-track course. The first track was crisis management, directed toward the stabilization of the system of social protection as well as the pension system and the provision of emergency assistance to the impoverished population. Activities within this track consisted of gradual repayment of pension and welfare arrears (for child allowances, cash benefits, foster care allowances, veteran disability allowances, and so on) accrued during the 1990s; establishment of regular payments of social assistance benefits; improvement of the conditions in residential institutions, and so on. While the donor funds were mostly used for paying welfare arrears, the new government committed itself to securing regular payments of current social benefits, which was achieved during 2001, while the pension arrears were eliminated in 2003. Simultaneously, the 'One-off Fund' was established at the republic level, through which, during the first two years, additional donor and budgetary funds were channelled toward the poorest and the most vulnerable (Matkovic and Simic, 2005).

The second track consisted of the formulation and implementation of reforms. Since March 2001, reforms in the areas of pension insurance and social assistance systems were co-ordinated by the Ministry of Social Affairs (MoSA), and those in the area of labour and employment by the Ministry of Labour and Employment (MoLE). The Ministry of Finance, as everywhere, was also very much involved; the Ministry of Health was, of course, responsible for health sector reform.

The Reform of Social Protection System

Formulation of reforms in the area of social policy was driven by the ideas and strategic goals defined by the then minister herself (Matkovic, 2001), as well as by the moderate(d) neo-liberal ideas of her colleagues from the Centre for Liberal and Democratic Studies (CLDS) think tank (cf. Mijatovic, 2001). However, it was also very much inclusive and large number of experts participated at several national and regional conferences which were held in 2001 in order to reach professional consensus on reform directions. The MoSA was also the driving force behind the preparation of the PRSP during 2002 and 2003, which incorporated and extended many of the ideas already developed within the process of social policy reform formulation (Vukovic, 2005). Reforms of social services included the establishment of the Fund for Financing Associations of Disabled Persons in 2002, and the Social Innovation Fund (SIF) in 2003, as mechanisms of the social welfare system reform which supported projects at local level and the development of new alternative services.

Donors' assistance was used to better target beneficiaries and to test welfare criteria through pilot projects (DFID and WB). Most of the donors followed the activities of the government, however, donors' co-ordination was insufficient, which put an additional burden on the government, which was without sufficient capacity for international co-operation.

The reform of the social welfare system was based on the objectives identified in the PRSP, which was approved in October 2003. The government nominated UNDP to take the lead role in facilitating inclusion of civil society organizations in the formulation of the PRSP document. The Strategy for the Development of the Social Welfare System was launched by the Kostunica government in 2005, building upon priorities set in the PRSP. In many ways, Serbia has a fully developed social protection system including insurance-based pensions and unemployment benefits, social assistance and child allowances, and an increasingly diverse array of social services (World Bank, 2006b).

Case Study of the Social Innovation Fund

In order to analyse the results of the reform/pilot projects, the example of the SIF is chosen here to map out the main driving forces of the social protection system reform in Serbia, the institutional sequencing in this area, the process of finding the appropriate social welfare mix, and the roles of EU/EAR and UNDP as multilateral donors in tandem whose contribution in design, establishment and functioning of SIF was crucial.

The SIF[1] was designed in 2003 by the MoSA and UNDP, and supported by the EAR, the Norwegian government and others. Its creators used the best experiences of the social investment funds founded by the World Bank, at the same time avoiding problems that WB funds have been facing, such as selection of projects, decision-making process, allocation of resources to organizations and beneficiaries, and maintenance of services. Unlike the WB focus on financial transfers, the SIF was designed to focus on services.

The SIF tried to ensure adequate institutional sequencing in provision of social services by promoting partnership at local level. The EAR/UNDP saw decentralization as a chance to bring services closer to clients and to strengthen capacity of local governments and civil society as service providers to plan and deliver services as well as to monitor its impact. A necessary attention was also given to the quality and sustainability of service provision. The idea was not to dismantle the state structure of social assistance but to form a parallel commercialized system. This was one of the main challenges as, according to the dominant social development discourse, new actors are usually seen as more responsive and rights-based than the public sector. Consequently, this leads to a substantial erosion of the role of public provision, resistance to planning and national direction, and a move towards a project-culture rather than needs-based provision.

Instead the SIF aimed to improve and develop local social services, contributing to a functioning, accountable and inclusive system of social welfare in Serbia (Social Innovation Fund, 2005). In trying to achieve the appropriate social welfare mix, EAR and UNDP set partnerships between Centres for Social Work (CSWs) and civil society organizations as one of the main criteria for selection of SIF local projects.

The SIF is itself a partnership between the agencies involved as well as between the international development partners and the government, and therefore it models the spirit of partnership at all levels. Since 2004, the SIF has supported 139 projects and started community-based care in 59 municipalities. Within the new call for proposals launched in July 2006, transformation of residential institutions has been identified as the first priority. In order to be eligible for funding, four partners have to create a consortium, including a CSW, a residential institution, a local self-government and a civil society organization.

Labour Market Reform

While initially, during the interim government (October 2000–March 2001) social policy, labour and employment were under the same roof, since March 2001 they have been split into two separate ministries. However, the newly formed MoLE did not have enough internal capacity (starting from the minister, a rather inexperienced trade union activist with no policy exposure) to lead the development of a consistent and comprehensive reform agenda, nor was it interested in assembling local expertise in the manner of MoSA. Instead, the formulation of reforms was left largely to the guidance of experts from international financial institutions.

The labour market situation at the beginning of the reform process was characterized by clear signs of striking inefficiency, which included high and growing unemployment, slow but steady decline in formal employment coupled with growing hoarded labour in the public and 'social' sectors, a very rigid formal labour market, low wages and widespread wage arrears, as well as widespread informal employment as last resort for many labour force members (Arandarenko, 2002). It was clear that a thorough reform was needed and that the reform of labour market institutions and employment policy, in turn, would have to be aligned to the general direction of market reforms.

However, as was largely the case elsewhere in transition countries, the main directions of economic reforms were designed without really looking at the labour market features as either one of the key endogenous variables within the economic system or as a constraint to certain strategic policy directions. In Serbia, for example, it was decided that sales privatization was to be the single method of privatization, despite the warnings that such an approach would imply very high unemployment levels over a prolonged period of time.

As elsewhere, the reform strategists conceived labour market reforms as subsidiary and basically exogenous.

> Envisaged labor market reform should improve the business environment and *facilitate economic restructuring* . . . The new legislation will a) guarantee core labour standards . . . b) streamline and reduce minimum statutory benefits for employment termination and employment; c) liberalize hiring procedures and allow for flexibility in the modality of employment; d) liberalize wage determination, except for the minimum wage; and e) bring statutory minimum leave and maternity benefits to levels affordable to the majority of the economy. (Government of the Republic of Serbia, 2001)

The New Labour Code was adopted in December 2001, along the lines promised by the government in the above paragraph. It was discussed with trade unions within the newly established Socio-economic Council and, despite widespread dissatisfaction among their members, all three main confederations were at one point ready to support a compromise law jointly agreed with the government and employers. However, after some unilateral last-minute changes in favour of yet more flexibility, two major confederations left the Socio-economic Council in protest and, although they returned a couple of months later, it seems that the social dialogue has ever since been largely compromised as a vehicle for consensual reform of labour market institutions and employment policy (Arandarenko and Stojiljkovic, 2006).

The tide has turned a bit with the establishment of the Kostunica government in early 2004. The new minister decided to introduce a new, 'more balanced' and 'Europeanized' labour code, despite the fierce protests from foreign investors and employers' organizations, and the IFIs. The strongest criticism focused on the re-establishment of mandatory collective bargaining, over-protection of union leaders, over-generosity of mandatory severance packages, budgetary consequences of solidarity packages for redundant workers in bankrupt firms, as well as on the introduction of a two-level appeal procedure for firing an employee for reasons of non-performance. At the end, after a typical late-night crisis session of government members with the World Bank representatives, a somewhat watered down version of the original proposal was passed by the National Assembly in early 2005.

Despite the battles over both post-2000 labour codes, it seems that they actually brought about very little difference 'on the ground'. On the one hand, their enforcement has been rather weak or at least quite uneven among the firms.[2] On the other, the labour market is also regulated autonomously by collective agreements and/or by 'inertia' factors, such as financial constraints, concession bargaining resulting in long-term implicit contracts, customs, gift exchanges, and so on.

The most recent World Bank assessment of the Serbian labour market (World Bank, 2006a) sees the changes made by the 2005 Labour Code as important, but not introducing fundamental reforms. The overall conclusion from the analysis of formal rules is that Serbia's labour market regulations are not particularly rigid compared with those of other countries in the region of South East Europe and in the OECD. Employment protection legislation (EPL) indexes for Serbia, recently calculated by the OECD and the World Bank with slightly different methodologies and comparator countries, consistently show Serbia in the middle of the distribution of countries by the strictness of regulation. Moreover, limited inspection capacity undoubtedly reduces the extent to which labour legislation actually affects labour market outcomes, improving further Serbia's relative position.

Labour Taxation Reform

The main goals of the labour taxation reform in 2001 were to broaden the tax base, lower the tax wedge and, given the weakness of tax administration, prevent by design any leakage of wage tax and social contributions revenues. The gross wage became a universal base for calculation of all taxes and social security contributions. A flat wage income tax, without a zero tax bracket, of 14 per cent on gross wage was introduced. At the same time, mandatory minimum social security contributions were introduced, at first even differentiated by level of education.

These rules produced a very peculiar and actually unique (in modern Europe) feature of the Serbian labour taxation system in the period 2001–2006 – its pronounced regressivity. The scope and consistency of regressivity could be best captured by looking at the tax wedges at different wage levels, calculated using the OECD/EUROSTAT methodology. The tax wedge for a low wage earner receiving 33 per cent of the average wage was 47.1 per cent; for a worker receiving the average wage it was 42.2 per cent, while it was down to 34.5 per cent for a wage eight times higher than the average wage (even after accounting for annual personal income tax).

The real question is not how it was possible to install this unheard of system (2001 was still the time of extraordinary politics), but rather how come this issue never really reached electoral, public or policy debate. The system was introduced amid lukewarm trade union protests, but was praised by the IFIs and much of the expert community. Its prominent Ramseyan[3] features were not even mentioned in the otherwise very elaborate PRSP, although regressive wage taxes hurt all those who should be the primary concern of PRS – the working poor, long-term and less well educated unemployed, lower-paid and vulnerable categories such as youth, women, Roma, people with disabilities, refugees/internally displaced persons, but also entire low-wage labour-intensive industries such as textile and food processing as well as depressed and underdeveloped regions.

The most striking elements of regressivity were removed in 2007 with the introduction of a rather decent zero-tax bracket of 60 000 dinars annually. But this was almost a side result of a decision of the Ministry of Finance to lower the wage tax revenues in order to cut the budgetary surplus. In parallel, the World Bank belatedly advised and supported such a move. The IMF indeed never realized that Serbia's wage tax system was regressive – in its international database Serbia is mistakenly among the countries that have so-called flat-progressive tax, falsely implying the existence of a zero-tax bracket. As for the public debate, the new change went almost unnoticed; only the former Finance Minister, responsible for the described Ramseyan reform, as if taking part in a bizarre travesty, warned that the proposed changes might introduce regressivity into the tax system!

Reform of the Pension System

Difficulties in financing pensions in Serbia arose in the mid-1980s and culminated in the 1990s. The pattern was typical of populist economic policy – preservation of high formal rights, refusal to consider any comprehensive reform of the system; and consequent inability to pay the pensions from insurance contributions within the unreformed PAYG system. In 2000 so called 'large debt' stood at 2.5 monthly pension payments for pensioners within the employee fund (some 80 per cent of all pensioners) and at 23 monthly pensions within the farmers fund (Matkovic, 2005)!

With the ageing of the population, an unfavourable and deteriorating dependence ratio and pension expenditures reaching 15 per cent of GDP, it was clear that an uncompromised reform was required. At that point a strategic disagreement between the then Minister of Social Affairs and the World Bank advisers occurred. The minister was of the opinion that PAYG should remain the backbone of the system, while the bank advisers were strongly in favour of introduction of a three-pillar system, with the growing central role of the so-called second pillar, that is, mandatory private insurance based on competitive capitalized funds. After a series of discussions, the minister got the upper hand, and the bank's advisers got a consolation in the form of development of voluntary pension insurance (so-called third pillar).

From the aspect of financial consolidation, two most important changes in 2001 were the extension of the minimum retirement age (from 55 to 58 for women and from 60 to 63 for men) and change in the indexation formula for pensions, from following wage increases only, to following a combined index of wage and cost-of-living increases. In addition, the minimum pension was lowered, and some entitlements abolished. New pensions are now calculated on the basis of entire contributions, not only on the basis of ten 'best' years. Coverage for mandatory payment of pension contributions has been extended to service and other flexible contracts. Access to disability pensions, a source of much abuse in the previous period, has been restricted, and serious efforts made to fight corruption in this area.

It is interesting that, seeing the consistency of pension reforms and the determination of reformers, the World Bank backed down and in 2003 stated that 'bold changes in the pension system in Serbia, implemented on two occasions, during 2001 and 2003, are among the most important achievements in the overall reform programme' (World Bank, 2003). Indeed, the PAYG reform secured mid-term sustainability of the system and significantly cut the share of pension expenditures in GDP from almost 15 per cent in 2000 to around 11 per cent in 2005, without significantly worsening the relative economic position of pensioners.

However, in 2005, as part of a wider bargaining agenda with the IMF, who were in general dissatisfied with the high public spending, the government had to introduce yet another set of changes to the Pension Law, again extending minimum retirement age and changing the indexation formula in favour of cost-of-living increases.

Reform of the Health System

The reform of the health sector started in 2002, significantly later than in the other social policy sectors. The features of the health sector in Serbia have been, on the one hand, a wide scope of rights, stipulated also in the Constitution, and their limited actual availability, on the other.

Despite considerable funds allocated to health care, which are estimated at some 10 per cent of GDP (Matkovic and Simic, 2005), the health system is faced with constant financing problems due to the low level of GDP, inherited debts, lack of financial discipline in collecting contributions, and so on. Approximately 150 euros per citizen is allocated annually for health-care expenditures, which is five to six times less than optimally needed. Moreover, 'out of pocket' expenditures remain unaffordable due to the low level of standard of living, especially for vulnerable groups.

The cornerstone of the public finance system in the health sector has been the Republican Health Insurance Fund (HIF). As a national institution for compulsory health insurance, HIF provides, through the network of mostly public health institutions, services for 7.5 million citizens.

Apart from the lack of fiscal sustainability, that is, the gap between HIF revenues and expenditures, the lack of capacity and readiness of HIF to undertake reforms additionally delayed the reform process in the 1990s. The HIF was always politically extremely important due to its high budget[4] and turnover. The astonishing facts that the audit of HIF had not been done for ten years during the 1990s and that ten out of 12 HIF directors were at one point put in prison speak for themselves!

Choosing the appropriate benefit package and public–private mix of financing and delivery of health-care services remain, as in all other social services systems, among the most important challenges. The position of the private health sector also needs to be clarified, especially as it has been without proper control and under the influence of the powerful doctors' lobby.

The World Bank, and to a lesser extent the EU, followed the policy of hard cross-sector conditionality in provision of their support to reform processes. For instance, the World Bank used its power to link its further assistance in the energy sector with the support for the reform of the health system.

Another important lesson learned in the reform process is that careful institutional sequencing and operating/legislative framework is needed for ensuring access to affordable and effective care. Such an overarching approach was used by the World Bank through the Social Protection and Economic Assistance Grant (SPEAG) and the Health Care projects, which created an important breakthrough toward a sustainable, performance-oriented health-care system in Serbia. Besides supporting the adequate legislative framework (Law on Health Protection, Law on Medicines and Medical Devices, and so on), parallel foci were given to the development of a master plan for the health-care provider network and to the introduction of standards and a 'positive list' of medicines at the market.

The EU has also been an important partner in the reform by providing support through EAR projects in the amount of approximately 90 million euros. However, the EU member states have defended their interest by introducing 'rules of origin' conditionality for the EU assistance. In practice, this meant that each country insisted on 'home-made' medical equipment, which did not help the process of standardization and raised the cost of putting the equipment into operation.

The UN/UNDP followed the lines of the MDGs, by providing support for combating HIV/AIDS through the UN Global Fund. Some bilateral actors pursued to a degree a 'beggar-your-neighbour' policy. Donations were sometimes seen by donor countries as a chance for getting rid of large stocks of medicines and medical equipment, hence creating even more distortions in the market in Serbia.

SUMMARY AND CONCLUSIONS: A CROWDED PLAYGROUND

Interplay, often random, of diverse local actors with a wide variety of international actors within a matrix of rather separated social policy areas, explains to a large degree a wide variety of outcomes, uneven success of sectoral social policy reforms and their overall inconsistency. This inconsistency, ranging from the anachronistically far-right reform of income taxation, through the moderately neo-liberal reform of labour market institutions, to the neo-Bismarckian reform of the pension system, could best be seen by looking at the Table 9.1.

Among the local actors who matter most are the personalities of key reform strategists and policy-makers, the local knowledge and expertise available, the administrative and managerial capacity to implement the designed reforms, and, prominently on the negative side, the influence of interest groups and lobbies. We have seen that all governments since 2000 were broad and weak coalitions made up of ideologically diverse parties which were as a rule awarded ministerial posts as spoils. Weakness and uncertainty of someone's position do not square well with strategic thinking and desirable far-sightedness; rather, they tend to facilitate rent-seeking and opportunistic behaviour. In some instances the strong and determined personality of an expert minister indeed made the difference, but these examples are not often encountered.

Similar diversity in terms of agendas and the quality of actors and persons involved could be found among the international actors. Just as competing parties, international financial and social development organizations may have explicitly or implicitly rival agendas. Their key decision-makers and/or representatives, just as other humans, tend to be dispersed along the bell curve distribution, from rather disinterested bureaucrats using the rigid template approach, to dedicated emphatic top managers, ready to tailor their institutional approach to the real needs of the country. Centrally defined assistance priorities of some countries may fit perfectly with the real needs of a recipient country, but also could be a perfect misfit. Some interventions may be led by the hidden agendas of business or consultancy lobbies, some may entirely miss an agenda; both are equally harmful.

The described randomness only emphasizes a general paradox of transition, fully applicable to its social policy segment – reforms done at the beginning when the actors are inexperienced, knowledge is very scant, problems perhaps misidentified, statistics erroneous, impact assessment analysis impossible to be done, and so on will exercise the strongest influence on the general stream of reforms. At later stages, the various aspects of the system

Table 9.1 Interplay of international and local actors and sectoral outcomes in the social policy arena in Serbia

	WB/IMF	EU (EC/EAR)	UN (UNDP, UNICEF)	ILO	Bilateral agencies	Local actors involved	Outcomes
Strategic frameworks	PRSP	Social Acquis	MDGs, human development approach	Decent work, flexicurity		Government MoSA	Localized variant of Social Development Agenda
Labour market institutions and policies	Labour market flexibility, restructuring and active policies for surplus labour; critical influence on Labour Code 2001	Freedom of movement, equal pay for equal work	Capacity-building, active LM projects, vulnerable groups	Labour standards, social dialogue; some influence on Labour Code 2005	Active labour market projects, support to vulnerable groups	2001 – MoLE, weak minister; no effective social dialogue 2005 – MoLE and unions	2001 – neo-liberal labour market institutions 2005 – moderated
Income taxation reform	Flat income tax, removal of tax reliefs, minimum contribution base					Ministry of Finance	Anachronistic, extremely right-wing regressive system of wage taxation
Social assistance	Emergency assistance,	Emergency assistance,	Capacity-building, local social services,		Emergency assistance,	MoSA (until 2004) and	Hybrid of traditional

Table 9.1 (continued)

	WB/IMF	EU (EC/EAR)	UN (UNDP, UNICEF)	ILO	Bilateral agencies	Local actors involved	Outcomes
	overall reform design, social assistance instruments (MOP)	infrastructure projects, local social services	deinstitutional-ization, child allowances (UNICEF)		local social services support to strategic reforms (DFID)	MOLESP (2004–), civil society	(CSWs, MOP) and social development-based system
Pensions	2001 – WB – advocacy of III pillar system 2005 – IMF – pressure for further restrictions			Advocacy of reformed PAYG	Emergency assistance	MoSA, social partners (until 2004)	Reformed PAYG (Bismarckian) system
Health	Overall reform design, master plan for the health care provider network	Medication management, health care IS, supply of safe blood; hospitals' reconstruction	Capacity-building, HIV/AIDS, inclusion of vulnerable groups		Emergency assistance, medicines and equipment donations	Ministry of Health, doctors' lobby groups	Reforms delayed; some rationalization achieved but it limited access of poor to medical services

will probably converge to a more consistent whole, but through the costly and perhaps unavoidable process of trails and errors.

NOTES

1. Overall value of SIF programme is 12.3 million euros for the period 2003–2009. Total EU support of 4.9 million euros was supplemented with the governmental funds in the amount of approximately 2 million euros for local projects for the period 2003–2006. In addition, around 1.4 million euros is expected for the period 2007–2008. The government of Norway also provided 3 million euros for the periods 2003–2004 and 2006–2009, while DFID provided 1 million euros for the period 2006–2009.
2. Interestingly, firms in the process of privatization face almost no legal pressure if they do not fulfil their most basic business obligations (for example, if they do not pay wages) since by law they cannot go bankrupt until the privatization procedure is completed. Also, small private firms often practise the policy of double paycheques – minimum wage paid alongside with taxes and contributions, and the difference to agreed upon take-home salary paid in cash with no further taxes.
3. British economist Ramsey proposed a rule for optimal income taxation according to which the two individuals' personal income tax rates should be inversely related to their personal labour market supply elasticities. Since the labour market supply elasticity of individuals increases at sufficiently high wage rate levels, or in the presence of non-labour income, it follows that the wealthier person needs to be taxed at a lower rate that the poorer person who has less flexibility when making labour supply decisions (Hillman, 2003).
4. For the first ten months in 2006, the HIF revenues were 96 billion dinars (approximately 1.2 billion euros) while expenditures were 88 billion dinars.

REFERENCES

Arandarenko, M. (2001), 'Waiting for the workers: explaining labor quiescence in Serbia', in St. Crowley and D. Ost (eds), *Workers After Workers' States: Labour and Polities in Postcommunist Eastern Europe*, Lanham, MO: Rowman & Littlefield, pp. 159–80.

Arandarenko, M. (2002), 'Serbia', in I. Kausch (ed.), *Employment and Labour Market Policy in South East Europe*, Belgrade: Friedrich Ebert Stiftung, pp. 159–77.

Arandarenko, M. (2003), 'The development of social policy in Serbia and Montenegro', *SCEPP AIA Report*, no. 6.

Arandarenko, M. (2004), 'International advice and labor market institutions in South East Europe', *Global Social Policy*, **4** (1), 27–53.

Arandarenko, M. and Z. Stojiljkovic (2006), 'Social dialogue in Serbia: promise unfulfilled', paper presented at Industrial Relations in Europe Conference (IREC), Ljubljana, 31 August–2 September.

Clarke, J. (2004), *Changing Welfare, Changing States*, London: Sage.

Dinkic, M. (1995), *Economics of Destruction: The Great Robbery of the People*, Belgrade: Stubovi culture.

European Economic and Social Committee (2000), *Engaged in Enlargement, Task Force Enlargement*, Brussels: European Economic and Social Committee Publication Unit.

Government of the Republic of Serbia (2001), Letter of intent to IMF, http://
www.imf.org/external/np/loi/2001/yug/01/ (accessed 6 May 2007).
Hillman, A.L. (2003), *Public Finance and Public Policy*, Cambridge: Cambridge
University Press.
Matkovic, G. (2001), 'The reforms of social sector' (Serbian language), in Z. Valic
and B. Mijatovic (eds), *The Strategy of Reforms*, CLDS, Beograd: Goragraf,
pp. 33–9.
Matkovic, G. (2005), 'Reform of pension and disability system', in B. Begovic and
B. Mijatovic (eds), *Four Years of Transition*, CLDS, Beograd: Goragraf,
pp. 329–37.
Matkovic, G. and S. Simic (2005), 'The social infrastructure reform', in B. Begovic
and B. Mijatovic (eds), *Four Years of Transition*, CLDS, Beograd: Goragraf,
pp. 347–63.
Mijatovic, B. (2001), 'The principles of a new social policy', in Z. Valic and
B. Mijatovic, *The Strategy of Reforms*, CLDS, Beograd: Goragraf, pp. 59–71.
Social Innovation Fund (2005), 'Achieving changes through partnership', mimeo.
United Nations Development Programme (UNDP) (2006), 'Can privatization and
commercialization of public services help achieve the MDGs? An assessment',
International Poverty Centre, Working Paper No. 22.
Vukovic, D. (2005), *Social Security and Social Rights* (in Serbian), Belgrade:
Faculty of Political Sciences, University of Belgrade.
World Bank (2003), 'Serbia and Montenegro: recent progress on structural reforms',
11 November, http://siteresources.worldbank.org/INTSERBIA/Resources/ SaM_
Recent_Progress_on_Structural_Reforms.pdf (accessed 6 May 2007).
World Bank (2006a), *Serbia: Labour Market Assessment*, report no. 36576-YU
(draft version), June.
World Bank (2006b), *Serbia Social Assistance and Child Protection Note*, report
no. 35954-YU, 20 June, http://siteresources.worldbank.org/INTSERBIA/
Resources/ Serbia_social_assistance.pdf (accessed 6 May 2007).

10. Albania

Arlinda Ymeraj

OUTCOMES OF THE TRANSITION IN ALBANIA

Albania recently embarked on another major step towards integration into Europe, with the signature of the Stabilization and Association Agreement with the European Union on 12 June 2006. However Albania is one of the poorest countries of Europe, with GDP per capita of US$2575 in 2004 (Republic of Albania, 2005: 11). As such, it is first challenged by the need to reduce poverty in absolute terms, and second by the need to alleviate social and regional disparities as well as by the need to improve human rights.

Albania, the youngest country in Europe, with an average age of 29 years, where 46 per cent of the 3.1 million population is below 24 years of age has experienced a thorough and rapid transformation. Since the fall of the communist regime in 1991, the country has embarked on a new path aimed at establishing democracy through the protection of individual rights and raising living standards through a free market economy. Despite its wealth in natural resources, remarkable annual economic growth from 5 to 6 per cent and sustainable macroeconomic stability, Albania remains one of the poorest countries of Europe.

The country spent 45 years, from 1945 until 1990, under an oppressive, authoritarian political system, from which it has been slowly emerging for the past 14 years. Albania has been considered the 'least developed European country by any yardstick' (Marmullaku, 1975: 52). Its poor economic legacy and the difficulties of the transition period have left the country unstable and have led to economic and social disparity among the people and regions of the country.

Unlike the most developed Eastern European countries, the new members of the European Union, which did not experience radical economic changes in the past, Albania's economy was drastically transformed. The first outcome of the reforms in Albania was the closure of inefficient state enterprises (almost 80 per cent of industrial companies), which led to massive unemployment of around 30 per cent. Shock therapy involving price and trade liberalization affected the structure of the economy and the production of goods. As a result, industrial production fell from 41.3 per cent of GDP in 1989 to 19.2 of GDP in 2004 (NIS, 2002; 2004: 367), agricultural production decreased from 35 per cent in 1990 to 24.7 per cent in 2004, while the services sector became the most important sector of the economy contributing 56 per cent of GDP.

Until 1989, the labour force consisted of the entire economically active population. Unemployment was an officially unknown phenomenon, although in reality it stood at 7 per cent. Economic restructuring after the 1990s was followed by a decrease in the demand for labour together with the emigration of about one-quarter of the working-age population, with qualified people comprising around half of these. National Institute of Statistics (INSTAT) data show that the participation in labour force for the year 2005 (INSTAT, 2005a) was only 57.8 per cent of which only 86 per cent had jobs, whereas in 1989 the participation in the labour force was 93 per cent of which 100 per cent had jobs.

Despite its massive incidence in the previous system poverty was officially recognized only after 1991. According to the *Living Standard Measurement Survey* of 2005 (INSTAT, 2005b), poverty in Albania is a multidimensional phenomenon, reflected in low or very low level of the incomes of the poor (18 per cent of the Albanians live on less than US$2 a day, while 3.8 per cent live on less than US$1 a day); higher disease rate and lack of appropriate medical services (the infant mortality, mortality rate of children aged under 5 and maternal mortality are relatively high compared with other countries of the region); illiteracy or low level of schooling (only 88 per cent of the population aged under 15 is able to write and read); low voice in government decision-making institutions as well as social exclusion (75 per cent of the poor families experience acute social problems).

Poverty has led to social exclusion and deep regional disparities. Rural areas and the mountain region have been found to be consistently poorer, according to all definitions of poverty. Rates of poverty in rural areas are almost 70 per cent higher than in Tirana, the capital. A significant proportion of this population is excluded for one reason or another from access to social service and employment benefits, as these services are available only in the towns. With people migrating away from rural areas, the quality and availability of education, social protection and health-care services in those areas have significantly decreased. Infant mortality rates in some parts of the north-east are three times the national average. It is likely that for many households social exclusion, the lack of access to basic services and lack of infrastructure are factors reducing their ability to lift themselves above the poverty line.

At the beginning of the transition, with the support of Bretton Woods institutions, a legal framework was established to ensure the smooth transition from state to private ownership as well as to introduce the rules of the market economy. Despite the compliance with international standards, the legal framework was not sufficient to ensure the sustainable development of the economy. Other crucial social and behavioural constraints hampered the formal economy and labour market development. At the end of 1996, the economic situation in the country dramatically worsened. This grew more evident in the beginning of 1997, with the financial collapse of a variety of informal investment and banking schemes – known as 'pyramid' schemes – that led the country into a new economic collapse and a period of a severe unrest. Incredibly, these schemes attracted, within a few years, the life savings of one-third of Albania's population – about US$1.2 billion (Malaj and Mema, 1998: 17). In many ways this was the second total economic collapse of the country within a space of a few years.

The poor economic performance has been fuelled by weak governance and a high level of corruption. This remains a serious problem for the development of private companies. Bribes are included in the product or service costs. According to the NGO Transparency International, Albania ranks 108th out of 145 countries on the Corruption Perception Index (CPI) 2004 with a CPI of 2.5. Corruption denies the poor, the marginalized and the least well educated members of society the social, economic and political benefits that are due to them.

Summarizing this analysis of the positive and negative outcomes of transition in Albania, we emphasize that macroeconomic stability has been maintained since 2002. Monetary and financial policies have contributed to ensuring a relatively low rate of inflation of 3–6 per cent. The overall budget deficit including grants declined and the total public debt to GDP ratio fell from nearly 67 per cent to about 54.5 per cent in 2005. Nonetheless, the efficiency of public spending remains low, particularly in the social sectors. Expenditures on priority areas have often fallen short of the stated objectives unde0r the National Strategy for Socio-Economic Development (NSSED) (World Bank, 2006a: 3). In three key social sectors – health (2.4 per cent of GDP), education (3.5 per cent of GDP), and social protection (6 per cent of GDP) – Albania ranks the lowest in allocation of resources among European countries, even among Eastern European countries.

OPENING ALBANIAN BORDERS

Massive emigration from Albania since the beginning of the process of transition in the early 1990s is one of the largest in the world on the basis of both its relative size and its economic impact. In a period of less than 15 years Albania, a country of a little more than 3 million inhabitants 'lost' a quarter of its population to emigration, mainly to Greece and Italy. Migration has had many effects on the economic and social development of the country. Here we provide some basic information on two crucial phenomena related to migration, namely, remittances and loss of human capital.

Remittances: A Positive Outcome of Migration

It is quite difficult to make an accurate and realistic assessment of the remittance flows to Albania. The Bank of Albania registers only remittances transferred through the official networks, that is, through the banking system and money transfer companies. Remittances transferred through informal channels (mostly money hand-carried by emigrants themselves when they travel to Albania, or through friends, acquaintances or paid couriers) can only be estimated. A study on remittances (IOM, 2005: 24) shows that 68.6 per cent of migrants send their income to Albania, but only 22.6 per cent of them use formal channels, such as the banking system (IOM, 2005: 25). It is widely accepted that remittances of Albanian emigrants have been a crucial factor for the financial survival of the country during the last decade. The amount of remittances is estimated to be at 13.7 per cent of GDP during 2004, with a record of 1028 million euros considerably higher than foreign direct investments, official development assistance (ODA) and exports (IOM, 2005: 54).

Despite the fact that remittances have not had an impact on the economic development of the country, they have played a key role in alleviating poverty in Albanian households. Earning remittances through emigration is seen by most Albanians as the most effective way of coping with the country's very difficult economic conditions at the individual and household level (De Soto et al., 2002: 39). The first priority for remittances is the basic survival needs of the family and an improvement in the quality of accommodation and facilities. Other priorities are related to the improvement of social relationships of the family or to finance and invest in the educational future of children.

However, policies aimed at transforming income from remittances into sustainable productive capacity are still missing. The same survey proves that 56 per cent of long-term migrants would like to return to Albania and invest (IOM, 2005: 36), but they neither find 'fertile ground' nor a reliable legal framework. Ensuring improved access to a banking system and lower remittance transfer costs, channelling remittances towards the micro-credit system combining with the social assistance policy, mobilizing emigrants' savings and targeting these into profitable investments are some policy actions that could pave the way towards a sustainable development.

Loss of Human Capital: A Negative Outcome of Migration

Emigration has impacted strongly on Albanian demography. Quite apart from the loss of around one-fifth of the country's population due to emigration between the censuses of 1989 and 2001, longer-term demographic effects should also be noted. One result of emigration can be detected in the annual statistics on births, which show a rapid decline since 1990 due to the absence of young males from the households.

Labour is the most important export of Albania. The massive emigration of Albanians includes a considerable part of the economically active (working-age) section of the population. In 1995 for example, only five years after the opening of borders, the number of emigrants represented 26 per cent of the population of working age (15–64-years-old), 35 per cent of the work force and 43 per cent of the employed population. The census showed that about three-quarters of the Albanian emigrants were young males (INSTAT, 2001). Fifty per cent of Albanian migrants are estimated to be professionals (Martin, 2003). The permanent or temporary loss of human capital has damaged the development of the country. The largest flows of emigrants originate in the countryside, where the economic situation is considerably worse than in the urban areas. Employment opportunities are scarce in rural areas, and agriculture is not considered a profitable activity, especially in the more remote areas where agricultural land is in short supply.

Key social problems arising from migration of mainly young males are family separations and the abandonment of many older people. Many women are separated from their emigrant husbands and partners. Children suffer, too, from the absence of their fathers. But perhaps the most serious problem concerns older people who have lost their family and social support. Although Albanian custom obliges the youngest son (and his wife) to take care of his parents in their old age, this tradition is breaking down through emigration. Abandoned by their emigrant children and with declining social support and pensions in the new neo-liberal Albania, many older people, especially in isolated rural areas, are becoming lonely 'orphan pensioners' (De Soto et al., 2002: 46).

SOCIAL POLICY IN ALBANIA DURING THE LAST DECADE

As in other countries of Eastern Europe, a reformed social protection system was needed in Albania to alleviate the shock of transition from a central to a market economy. Despite the fact that elements of social policy have existed before the 1990s, the institutions of the Albanian 'welfare state' are largely established from scratch. The social protection system in Albania includes four components: social assistance concerned with poverty alleviation, social insurance, labour market development and social care programmes. For the purpose of this chapter we analyse in detail only social assistance and labour market development components and make a brief reference to social insurance and within that pensions policy.

The poverty alleviation component focuses on providing cash assistance to persons to guarantee a minimum standard of living. The system is based on three principles: subsidiary (insured persons are excluded from coverage), maintenance of living standards and provision of non-contribution benefits (Tomesh, 2001). Labour market development provides unemployment benefits, vocational and professional training, counselling, market research and job placement services. The social insurance system inherited from the past provides for pensions and other benefits but covers at present only about 36 per cent of the population.

Social Assistance

The programme of poverty alleviation, named Social Assistance (SA) or *Ndihma ekonomika* (Economic Assistance) was set up from scratch in 1993. Law no. 7710 dated 18 May 1993 on 'Social assistance and care' is the main Act that forms the basis of the system. This law determines the system of social assistance and welfare that offers support to the Albanian households (in general) and citizens (in particular) that are totally without, or have insufficient, income or means of support. Where necessary and possible, public social welfare services are provided rather than social assistance benefit, or as a supplement to the letter. The law provides a means-tested cash benefit granted on a family-by-family basis. Given the specific conditions that exist in Albania (limited state budget, strong informal economy, tradition of living with parents, limited possibilities for Albanian institutions to exchange information and monitor the scheme), the protection of the household rather than the individual was considered the most appropriate approach.

The social assistance benefit is not based on a national absolute or relative poverty line. The poverty line applicable when providing social assistance benefit is set administratively. The programme is administered through the network of local governments (communes in the countryside and municipalities in the towns). Having no opportunity to finance the scheme through local taxation (the law on financial decentralization has not yet been approved), the public social assistance scheme is financed by the state budget through the block grant allocation mechanism. The programme is designed to function under the conditions of a limited budget. This means that under current legislation only the upper ceiling of monthly benefits is defined. Social administrators and local government councils retain the right to use their discretion in calculating the level of SA benefit for every household, taking into account family size and structure and the economic and social condition of the household.

Social assistance expenditures have declined as a percentage of GDP from 1.4 per cent in 1993, to 0.5 per cent in 2005, even though the number of beneficiaries has not decreased at the same rate. The monthly amount of the social assistance benefit is insufficient to allow recipients to access services that would create opportunities for them to get out of poverty, such as vocational and professional training or higher levels of education. Research work (NACSS, 2003a; 2003b) on the social assistance system performance confirms that the existing system of social assistance does not help to alleviate poverty. It neither supports households to solve their critical economic and social needs nor protects poor people from social exclusion. The social assistance policy is not capable of reducing inequalities among households and social groups.

Labour Market Developments

During the past decade, the legal framework with respect to labour market development and employment protection (Labour Code in 1995, Labour Promotion Law in 1995 and Vocational and Education Training Law in 2002) has been completed with provisions for an unemployment insurance scheme, labour services and labour promotion programmes, trade union recognition and vocational training.

At the same time, with the deregulation of the labour market the Albanian government replaced state control over labour demand and supply by setting up a process involving social partners (initially trade unions and, later, employers' organizations). Despite the adoption of a comprehensive legal framework to promote employment, the effectiveness of implementation of active labour market policies in the context of generalized collapse of outputs is uncertain. The high demand for jobs and the low supply of jobs is the main problem with the labour market (Kolpeja, 2005).

During the last 16 years of 'transition', the level of unemployment in Albania has been higher than in other countries in transition. The level is officially given as 11–14 per cent, but it is likely to be as high as 28 per cent. As unemployment (especially long term) is a certain 'entrance ticket' to poverty, not surprisingly there has been an increase in the level of poverty and a worsening position for disadvantaged social groups. This situation has been exacerbated by uncontrolled migration from rural to urban areas, especially to Tirana. As a result a new labour force has emerged, which, due to its lack of skills and professionalism, can search for a job only in the informal sector.

The creation of jobs in the country has not been able to keep up with population growth. While the latter, after 1992, increased by 2.9 per cent there were 16 per cent fewer jobs available a decade later. Most of any growth in employment was in the agriculture sector, which increased by 31 per cent (in 2005), indicating a high level of rural sub-employment and hidden unemployment. Meanwhile, employment in the public sector contracted by 68 per cent in that period. Although the number of people working in the private sector doubled, the figure still represented only 19 per cent of total employment (not including the agricultural sector) in 1991. Even though growth was seen in the agriculture and service sector, industry was still very far below even its pre-1991 levels. The implementation of active labour market policies went beyond the financial resources of Albania as they are too costly and require too much administrative capacity. Therefore, during the first years of transition, the labour market policies were 'passive' rather than 'active', mainly providing unemployment benefit payment and cash transfers for poor households. However, despite the decrease in funding of passive policies versus the slight increase of active ones, the evidence shows that the rate of unemployment is still high.

Social Insurance and Pensions

Unlike the cases of the social assistance system and the labour market policy described above, developments in pension policy have not started a new system from scratch. Reforms have been initiated within the context of the continuing Poverty Reduction Support Credits programme funded by the World Bank. These reforms have not sought to rebuild the pension system on new principles by replacing the inherited PAYG system with privately managed and invested defined contributions. Such a proposal was unlikely to be seen as sensible in the context of the collapse in trust of savings schemes following the pyramid-selling scandal as a result of which all Albanian savings were wiped out. Instead piecemeal reforms to the Bismarckian-style scheme have been undertaken.

The objectives of World Bank intervention were to improve sustainability of the pension system, and improve the efficiency of pension administration. According to the bank's report of the 3rd Poverty Reduction Support Credit (World Bank, 2006b), these objectives were largely achieved. As part of pension policy reform, a phased, five-year increase in the retirement age was introduced, starting in July 2002. Payroll contributions, which were (and still are) very high, were reduced by 4 percentage points. Benefits were reduced for those who retired early. The functioning of the Social Insurance Institute (SII) was made more transparent and efficient, professional auditing of its financial statements adopted, and steps taken to transfer social insurance collections from the SII to the General Tax Department. Outcome indicators show an improvement in the dependency ratio from 1.06 pensioners per contributor in 2001 to 0.86 in 2004, and an increase from 31 to 36 per cent in the share of the working-age population (18 through to retirement age) contributing to pension. The pension programme was also said to have had a significant impact on poverty reduction – the poverty rate among urban pension recipients in 2005 was 14 per cent with the pension, but would have been 39 per cent without the pension; for rural pensions, the corresponding figures are 23 and 39 per cent. Also, the poverty rates for pensioner-headed families declined from 26 per cent in 2002 to as low as 11 per cent in 2005. The urban pension deficit of the pension system has declined by 0.27 percentage points of GDP from 2002–2005, from 1.34 per cent of GDP in 2002, to 1.07 per cent; the rural deficit stayed constant.

DEVELOPMENTS AND ACTORS IN OFFICIAL DEVELOPMENT ASSISTANCE

The opening up of the country in 1991 was accompanied by the establish-ment of relationships with the UN, the Bretton Woods institutions and the diplomatic mission of the European Community. Indeed, since 1991, the main strategic development programmes of Albania have been designed in close co-operation with international actors. Thanks to the Kosovo crisis of 1999, the presence and size of donors' financial assistance in Albania increased considerably. The share of loans and aid allocated to institutional and civil society capacity-building also increased after 1999.

Before 1999, the World Bank had been the most active donor, especially in the provision of assistance for policy reform and institutional capacity-building. In reforming the social sectors the World Bank provided the most significant support, whereas the contribution of the few other donors had focused on their own service delivery. Thus two major World Bank projects contributed to the building up from scratch of the social policy institutions discussed earlier. The Social Safety Net Development (SSND – US$4.2 billion) and the Labour Market Development (LMD – US$1.5 billion) pro-jects were launched in 1993 in the framework of the first Country Assistance Strategy of the WB, with funds being disbursed from 1993 to 1997.

The SSND project was aimed at consolidating fundamental reform of social insurance and social assistance programmes through policy development; strengthening the institutions; and strengthening and developing research and statistical activities to support social policy formulation. The LMD project addressed the need for the provision of cash benefits in a critical stage of transition (1991–92) and designed the policy framework for the operationalization of a modern and functional employment services system. The main counterpart for both projects was the Ministry of Labour and Social Affairs and its offices at regional and local level.

After 1999, the donors' approach changed. First, donors were predisposed to co-ordinate actions among themselves and harmonize efforts for channelling the assistance in the most appropriate way. Second, bilateral and multilateral programmes of co-operation tended to be in full agreement with the country's strategic priorities. As a result of these changes, a group of the main donors, under WB guidance, was set up in December 2000. This group, which was composed of representatives from WB, IMF, UNDP, UK (DFID), USAID, Germany, Italy, Holland, Canada and OSCE, designed a plan of action to discuss the Growth and Poverty Reduction Strategy (GPRS) (PRSP) process and the donors' role in it. The donors contributed to the GPRS process, supporting it financially or providing technical assistance and research analysis. At the same time ODA was increasingly focused on supporting government activities. Sixty-eight per cent of the aid is now in support of the government sector (Ministry of Finance of the Republic of Albania, 2006).

The GPRS, completed by the government of Albania in 2001, expressed Albania's long-term vision of European integration and was intended to complement the Stabilization and Association Process (SAP). The GPRS, which was subsequently renamed the National Strategy for Social and Economic Development (NSSED), demonstrated the country's serious effort to use a comprehensive national medium-term development strategy to move from managing short-term crises to creating the conditions that promote long-term growth and poverty reduction. However, it is noted in the World Bank's own report of its third Poverty Reduction Support Credit that the government's NSSED was perceived as being written by the bank and owned only by the Ministry of Finance and not other line ministries.

The reformulated version of the NSSED in 2004 emphasizes the creation of an enabling business environment and promotion of employment opportunities for the poor, increased investments in health and education, and empowerment of the poor through greater involvement in the political process. The strategy includes policies aimed both at providing short-term help for those in need and longer-term assistance to help people reach their full potential. It recognizes the vulnerability of women, youth and the aged, together with regional and educational disparities.

Still, a substantial amount of financial aid was invested in the economic sector, while the social sector remained under-resourced. Education and health had been largely ignored as the government emphasized macroeconomic progress. In general, the social sector lacks adequate attention from donors. However, after 2004, the government's attention has shifted from economic and infrastructure development to socio-economic growth. Therefore, donors have revised their strategic priorities from humanitarian assistance into development support. The World Bank's Country Assistance Strategy for 2006–2009 complements this by aiming to increase access of the poor in rural areas to quality basic education, to improve access to and quality of government health services, to improve water provision and to continue to ensure the sustainability of the social security fund (World Bank, 2006a).

In terms of other donors and international actors, mention must be made of the European Union, whose assistance to Albania started in 1991 through the PHARE programme. Since 2001, the Community Assistance for Reconstruction, Development and Stabilization programme has been the main EC financial instrument for co-operation in the Balkan countries. Since the establishment of the CARDS programme in 2001, €240 million has been made available to Albania in technical assistance. The main area of work has been justice and home affairs (€96 million), followed by economic development (€84 million) and administrative capacity-building (€48 million) (EC, 2006).

Albania joined the United Nations in 1955. Following the collapse of the communist regime, UN humanitarian and development agencies were invited to help Albania and its people progress jointly towards peace, prosperity and equality. The UN agencies in Albania have pledged to uphold the principles of the UN Charter – bringing together Albanian citizens and government and international citizens in the spirit of solidarity, to improve life for those suffering from poverty and inequality, and to protect the vulnerable. The UN system, with its 12 organizations and close to 300 staff in Albania, is working closely with the people and the government of Albania, and its national and international development partners, to produce tangible results in the country's progress towards the MDGs, and the government's development objectives, including EU integration. Rooted in the UN Charter, all the UN organizations' work is dedicated to promoting human rights as well as the crucial development issues highlighted by international conventions and summits. The UNDP is the co-ordinating agency among the UN agencies. To date, the UN agencies have provided around US$600 million, covering all key sectors. However, only around 30 per cent of financial aid is direct cash assistance to government, while the 70 per cent is disbursed through NGOs leading to a welfare mix involving a large number of non-state actors. The role of UNICEF has increased over the years, both quantitatively and qualitatively. It is leading a partnership with the government of Albania, European Commission and the Swedish International Development Agency (SIDA) to reform the juvenile justice system. It has also continued to broker for social business between the public and private sectors through the Youth Albanian Parcel Service (YAPS) Foundation, a project that helps disadvantaged young people to be reintegrated into labour market and social life, and provides substantial assistance in creating mechanisms that helps prevention of HIV/AIDS.

Among bilateral donors is USAID, which has been operating in Albania since 1992, providing assistance to increasing economic growth and agricultural development through private investment. It also supports democratic reform and health reform. The SIDA concentrates its efforts on supporting public administration, democracy and human rights, rural development, health, environment, trade and industry. The goal of the Norwegian Agency for Development Co-operation (NORAD) is to promote regional stability and economic growth through good governance, democratization and development of public institutions.

INTEGRATING DONORS' POLICY AGENDAS WITH GOVERNMENT STRATEGIC PRIORITIES

One consequence of this range of external interventions is that at present, there are three main parallel policy agendas shaping government policy: the NSSED 2005–2008, led by the government; the SAA, led by the EU, and the MDGs, led by the UN. Integrating the three policy agendas into one policy document is of particular importance, for government and donors alike. As a result, the government is now in the process of revising the NSSED (which will then be called National Strategy for Development and Integration – NSDI) and the UN is working with the national authorities as well as other donors to ensure the MDGs are further integrated and aligned with EU accession parameters.

The Albanian government is integrating existing policy frameworks into a single medium-term development plan and has made significant progress towards implementing external assistance more efficiently through an Integrated Planning System (IPS). The IPS links programming, implementation, budgeting, monitoring and evaluation. This will facilitate aid co-ordination, not least as aid will be tailored to the government's structures and capacities. In November 2005, the government established a new

Department of Strategy and Donor Co-ordination within the Council of Ministers, which underscores the government's increased leadership in the area of donor co-ordination.

As the National Strategy for Development and Integration establishes a framework of seven-year sectoral and cross-sectoral strategies, it provides an opportunity for joint UN advocacy and/or technical support in areas where agencies' mandates connect and where co-ordination already exists, such as gender, HIV/AIDS and poverty reduction. The planning framework and cycle also allows for more effective and timely engagement of non-resident UN specialized agencies and other programmes.

A Donor Technical Secretariat (DTS), composed of four multilateral agencies (EU, OSCE, UNDP and the World Bank), will continue to facilitate co-ordination among donors, including key bilaterals, and support national leadership in this area. A multi-donor programme has been established to build the capacity of the new Department of Strategy and Donor Co-ordination and to provide a management information system to support the IPS.

THE IMPACT OF FOREIGN AID ON IMPROVING THE SOCIAL WELL-BEING OF PEOPLE

The level of official development assistance is relatively high, at about 5 per cent of GDP. Both fiscal and external balance therefore depends to a considerable extent on donor aid. However, Albania's external and domestic debt indicators have improved considerably over time. Overall public debt has been declining from 71 per cent in 2000 to 56.6 per cent of GDP at end-2004 (WB, 2006a). Besides the figures, it is important to mention that the Official Development Assistance is spread across all sectors. While the presence of the EU, the World Bank and the IMF is higher in public sector reforms, economic management, social sector and infrastructure, the UN and other governments' donations are highly involved in private sector development, environment, governance and decentralization. Nevertheless, the investment in social sectors still remains among the lowest in the region.

Since 2002, three progress reports of NSSED have been published. However, measuring the impact that the NSSED has had on the improvement of people's lives is difficult. The critical issue remains the lack of an adequate monitoring and evaluation system, based on output indicators rather than process or input indicators. Lack of standards and benchmarks for implementation is the second area of concern. While progress has been made in legislation and policy development to improve social protection, health and education in Albania, implementation of these laws and policies lag behind. One of the missing links between policy formulation and its implementation is the absence of by-laws, standards and protocols of care, which should be based on international standards.

What has been reported so far clearly shows that Albania, as a country which has placed the prospect of European integration at the top of the political agenda, is still in need of foreign assistance. The donor community has the advantage of having the financial potential, technical expertise and professional capacity to participate in the development process. From the donors' point of view, taking the decision to invest in any field seems easy to justify: there is a long list of priorities addressing the human rights and needs of excluded social groups. Nevertheless, the question is not only one of spending money. The assessment of the effectiveness of policies and actions depends on concrete results, as long as the ultimate goal of social investment is to improve the social status of society. It is not yet clear about the improvements in social well-being produced by the capital flow of ODA, despite macroeconomic progress. For this to happen, the building of functional partnerships among donors and between donors and government to qualitatively reform the social protection sector is still of vital importance. Nicholas Barr argues that 'enhancing transition countries' human resources – making labour markets more effective, improving education and training, reducing unemployment and poverty, and promoting better health – is fundamental to the reforms' (Barr, 2005). In this context, a part of the burden for reform falls on the social policy as a mechanism to avoid social exclusion and develop social capital, as an engine which gives power, voice and freedom to the poor.

CONCLUSIONS: THE FUTURE OF SOCIAL POLICY DEVELOPMENT IN ALBANIA

On 1 May 2004, eight former communist countries joined the EU. Bulgaria and Romania are now also members. The others in the region try hard to achieve it. European Union accession for Albania can be a reality. This means that a new social policy agenda should be designed, a policy which empowers human rights and provides equal opportunities to any individual. In addition to pursuing pro-poor policies, this means there needs to be support for positive reforms that will directly improve the well-being of poor families; in particular, to assist chronically poor families in breaking poverty cycles, by enhancing human and physical assets. Key public services, in particular social security programmes, play a vital role in minimizing the adverse effects of economic reform and prevent families from falling further into poverty and being excluded (Waddington, 2004).

According to Briggs (1961: 228; Zamagni, 1997), the welfare state is a state in which the organized power of the state is equally used, through policies and institutions, as an effort to alleviate the negative outcomes of market forces in three directions: first, providing a minimal standard of income to families and individuals; second, guaranteeing a level of security, especially in critical situations like sickness, retirement and unemployment; and third, providing quality social services to all citizens. Considering the theoretical and practical arguments developed here, we can state that Albania was and still is in need of developing the social protection mechanisms required of a welfare state.

In designing and implementing social policies, all actors should participate. This means that the management of the mechanism should be totally decentralized. Strengthening collaboration with business, non-government partners and communities, creating fertile ground for civil society to actively participate would promote the poor to be part of social development. It would also stimulate all forms of social interaction and encourage people to shift from their situation, serving as a tool to develop social capital, at least among the poorest strata.

It is no accident that these reforms are called 'transition reforms'. The old system cannot be destroyed immediately: the process of evolution must follow in a natural and gradual way, substituting old relationships slowly only when new relations are created. The socialist system came to power through violence, damaging all previous societal values, whereas the new system aims to respect all human rights and cannot be based on an externally imposed transformation. Whether or not the government is willing and able to respect this principle, whether it is capable of understanding domestic conditions and reacting to them, depends on the government itself as well as on the level of responsibility of the people. So we come full circle. The legal institutions, public services, government and state mirror the attitudes of the people and their respective representatives, chosen by the people themselves. But the most important element of this circle is the relationship between state and citizen, because it affects the well-being of people, which should be, and can be, better if both state and citizens work towards it.

REFERENCES

Barr, N. (2005), *Labour Markets and Social Policy in Central and Eastern Europe: The Accession and Beyond*, New York: IBRD.
Briggs, A. (1961), 'The welfare state in historical perspective', *Archives Europeenes de sociologie*, **282**, 221–59.
De Soto, H. G., P. Gordon, Z. Sinojmeri and T. Gedeshi (2002), *Poverty in Albania: A Qualitative Assessment*, Washington, DC: World Bank.

European Commission (EC) (2006), *Albania 2005*, progress report, Brussels: EC.
INSTAT (National Institute of Statistics) (2001), *Census of Population and Dwellings*, Tirana: INSTAT.
INSTAT (National Institute of Statistics) (2005a), *Labour Market Survey*, Tirana: INSTAT.
INSTAT (National Institute of Statistics) (2005b), *Living Standard Measurement Survey, Preliminary Report (draft)*, Tirana: INSTAT.
International Organization of Migration (IOM) (2005), *Competing for Remittances in Albania*, prepared for IOM Tirana, 29 June by N. Zwager, I. Gedeshi, E. Germenji and C. Nikas, Tirana: IOM.
Kolpeja, V. (2005), Active Labour Market Development in Albania, mimeo, Tirana.
Malaj, A. and F. Mema (1998), 'Features and effects of the informal financial market', *Economy and Transition*, **5**, Tirana: University of Tirana, Faculty of Economics.
Marmullaku, R. (1975), *Albania and the Albanians*, London: C. Hurt & Co.
Martin, P. L. (2003), 'Highly skilled labor migration', International Institute for Labour Studies, Geneva, May.
Ministry of Finance of the Republic of Albania (2006), *The 2006 Survey on Monitoring the Paris Declaration*, Tirana: Ministry of Finance of the Republic of Albania.
National Albanian Centre for Social Studies (NACSS) (2003a), 'The role of the social assistance mechanism in reducing poverty', *Economy and Transition*, **4**, 30–42.
National Albanian Centre for Social Studies (NACSS) (2003b), *Reducing Social Exclusion through the Mechanism of Social Assistance: Albania*, Tirana: National Albanian Centre for Social Studies.
National Institute of Statistics (NIS) (2002), *Living Standard Measurement Survey*, Tirana: NIS.
National Institute of Statistics (NIS) (2004), *Statistical Yearbook*, Tirana: NIS.
Republic of Albania (2005), *Progress Report for the Implementation of the National Strategy for Socio-Economic Development during 2004*, Ministry of Finance, Republic of Albania, June.
Tomesh, I. (2001), *Social Rights and Policies*, lectures delivered during the summer school, 'Social policies in the post-communist countries', Tirana, 7 July.
United Nations (UN) (2005), *United Nations Development Assistance Framework*, Tirana: UN.
Waddington, H. (2004), *Linking Economic Policy to Childhood Poverty: A Review of the Evidence on Growth, Trade Reform and Macroeconomic Policy*, CHIP Report No. 7, Childhood Research and Policy Centre, London: CHIP.
World Bank (2006a), *Country Assistance Strategy 2006–2009*, Report No. 34329, Washington, DC: World Bank.
World Bank (2006b), *Report on 3rd Poverty Reduction Support Credit*, IDA-40060, Report No. 36524, Washington, DC: World Bank.
Zamagni, S. (1997), *Economia civile come forza di civilizzacione della societa italiana*, Milan: Mondadori.

11. KOSOVO

Fred Cocozzelli

INTRODUCTION

The development of post-conflict social welfare programmes in Kosovo is perhaps the most extreme example of external intervention in policy formation among the cases being examined. Coming as part of an exceptionally comprehensive international mission that was not only mandated for relief and reconstruction, but effectively assumed sovereignty over the province, external actors were unequivocally dominant, allowing local actors to emerge only slowly and often under the direct tutelage of the internationals. Specifically, social policy-making in the period after the NATO air-strikes of spring 1999, relied heavily on two forces. The first was international relief and reconstruction agencies whose strategic priority was initially emergency response and, subsequently, disengagement. The preference for operations designed to respond to the immediate post-conflict emergency as opposed to longer-term social and economic development had an important impact on the final policy outcome. The second force was donor agencies, and their hired consultants who focused most intently on creating the conditions for a market economy and viewed social policy warily as a potential interference (Héthy, 2005: 33). Kosovan popular actors, from organized labour and capital to political parties and social movement organizations, were not an influential part of the initial policy formation process.

THE RECENT POLITICAL HISTORY OF KOSOVO

Kosovo was an important site of contention in the former Yugoslavia. Although an integral part of the Republic of Serbia, the demographic make-up of the province had skewed disproportionately towards Kosovo Albanians (Lydall, 1989: 190–91; Hammel and Stevanovic, 2002), while continuing to be an important part of the Serbian national discourse of identity (Bieber, 2002; Dragović-Soso, 2002: 124–7). The paradox of Serbian territory with a large majority of Albanian residents was problematic in Federal

Yugoslavia with its legal distinctions between nations and nationalities. To accommodate the contradiction, Kosovo, along with Vojvodina, a majority Hungarian province, was made an autonomous region of the Republic of Serbia in 1974 (Magaš, 1993: 19). This arrangement was almost universally unsatisfactory, perceived by Serbs as an unfair constraint on Serbia, and by Albanians as a denial of full rights within the Yugoslav federal system.

As Yugoslavia entered the painful process of dissolution in the late 1980s, the contradiction of Kosovo was at the centre of the debates that were fraying the federal structures. A milestone on the path to crisis was the curtailing of the province's autonomy in March 1989 (Clark, 2000: 49–52), which escalated tensions between the Serbian and Albanian communities. In July 1990, a majority of Albanian members of the provincial Assembly voted to declare Kosovo a republic within Yugoslavia (Clark, 2000: 73; Judah, 2000: 65). In response, the Kosovo Assembly was promptly dissolved by the Serbian government. Defying the dissolution order, the Albanian members of the assembly met in September 1990 and declared the province independent (Clark, 2000: 73). A year later, they met again to call for a referendum on independence. Unofficial and unsanctioned, the vote amounted to a poll of the Albanian population of Kosovo, revealing a community that overwhelmingly opted for independence from a rapidly disintegrating Yugoslavia (Clark, 2000: 82).

Having declared independence, but without the means to enforce it, the Albanian Kosovo community went about building the 'Republic of Kosova' as a state within a state. The following May, semi-clandestine elections were held for parliament and a president. The overwhelming winner was Ibrahim Rugova and his political party, the Democratic League of Kosovo (LDK) (Clark, 2000: 83; March and Sil, 1999: 5). The parallel regime effectively organized Kosovan Albanian society outside Yugoslav state authority and successfully built up an international network of support, but it was limited in its ability to achieve independence for the province. In terms of social policy, the parallel regime was especially important because, under its guidance, a civil-society based social assistance and social services network was constructed. Organized primarily by the Mother Teresa Society (MTS), the network operated in close co-ordination with, but independently from, the Republic of Kosova institutions. This network played a vital role in the post-conflict relief operations, but was largely excluded from the eventual state-based social welfare institutional settlement after 1999.

When the international community's 1995 efforts to resolve the Bosnian war failed to address Kosovo, Albanian Kosovan criticism of LDK leadership grew (Clark, 2000: 123; O'Neill, 2002: 22; Vickers, 1998: 290). By this time more militant Kosovo Albanian organizations began agitating for violent resistance to the Belgrade regime. The Kosovo Liberation Army (KLA), which had already been active in small attacks and assassinations, began to step up its operations until, by 1998, they were waging a significant insurgency in the province. Like the LDK and the parallel regime, the KLA devoted significant attention to building an international network to raise money, provide weapons and build political support. By early 1999, the fighting was intense and international pressure was being put on Belgrade to bring the situation under control peacefully.

When US and European diplomatic intervention in February 1999 failed to conclude an agreement to end the violence, the crisis intensified. On 24 March, NATO forces began a campaign of air-strikes against Serbia. On 3 June, Yugoslavia agreed to withdraw from Kosovo, and on 10 June, the UN Security Council passed Resolution 1244 mandating the creation of a UN Interim Administration Mission in Kosovo (UNMIK). The UN mission was authorized to perform all civilian administrative functions. In co-ordination with the deployment of UNMIK, a Kosovo Force (KFOR) was launched by NATO to provide a security presence. Between UNMIK and KFOR, Kosovo became an international protectorate.

The Economic and Social Situation

In all respects Kosovo was the poorest and least developed part of Federal Yugoslavia. Despite federal development assistance to the province, improvements were slow and catching-up almost non-existent (Magaš, 1993: 19). With the overall decline in the Yugoslav economy in the 1980s, the situation in Kosovo worsened. In 1960 the per capita GDP of Kosovo was one-fifth that of the wealthiest republic, Slovenia (Allcock, 2000: 84). In 1979, Kosovo's per capita output was less than one-third of the national average (Lydall, 1984: 175). Unemployment figures rose from 18.6 per cent in 1971 to 27.5 per cent in 1981 (Tomc, 1988: 71). In addition to a generally weak economy, persistent ethnic inequalities compounded local tensions. One study from 1984 found that, although Serbs and Montenegrins made up 15 per cent of the population, they held 30 per cent of all state jobs in the province (Malcolm, 1999: 337). A 2000 IMF assessment of the economic background of the province stated, 'While pre-war statistics on the economy are incomplete and unreliable, they paint a picture of an economy that was already in serious decline' (Corker et al., 2001: 3).

This bleak legacy was made worse by the destruction wrought by the conflict, leaving the province in economic turmoil. Extraordinarily high unemployment, dependence on remittance incomes, poverty and lack of resources characterized the post-conflict economic situation. Estimates from 2000 put remittance income, from the large diaspora, at approximately

US$1500 annually per family (Corker et al., 2001: 23). Remittance levels have since dropped and in 2004 the figure was approximately US$560 annually per family (Statistical Office of Kosovo, 2005). Despite this, remittances remain the second most important source of family income.

Theoretically taking Kosovo as an independent state, it would be the poorest country in the Balkans, with a per capita GDP of €950 in 2003 (UNDP Kosovo, 2004: 15). Estimating the Human Development Index for Kosovo gives a value of 0.734, placing in at the bottom of the rankings for the region. It would also have the lowest national GDP per capita at purchasing power parity, as well as the lowest life expectancy in the Balkans. Poverty remains a central fact of life, with approximately 37 per cent of the population in poverty, and slightly more than 15 per cent of the population in extreme poverty (World Bank, 2005: 17). This marks a decrease in the overall poverty level from about 50 per cent, but an increase in extreme poverty from 11.9 per cent compared with 2001 figures (World Bank, 2001: 10).

Lack of productive employment is a persistent problem. Overall unemployment was estimated at 49 per cent in 2003; taking into consideration informal labour dropped the rate to 38 per cent. Unemployment of women and young people (16–24 years of age) was considerably higher, 63.6 per cent and 71.6 per cent respectively. Rural unemployment was estimated at 54.5 per cent and urban unemployment, 43.6 per cent (RIINVEST, 2003). Since 2003, rather than estimating unemployment rates, the Ministry of Labour and Social Welfare has been recording the number of job seekers registered with employment offices. By December 2005 there were almost 320 000 registered job seekers (RIINVEST, 2006).

SOCIAL POLICY FORMATION IN KOSOVO

Recent social policy formation in Kosovo has gone through three distinct phases. The first coincides with the intensification of the conflict and immediate post-conflict crisis. This phase was largely an emergency response, dominated by international NGOs, and which lasted from 1998 to August 2000. The second phase was the transition from emergency humanitarian aid to a UN-sponsored social assistance programme which became the foundation of the new welfare regime. The transition was led by UNMIK and a consortium of international NGOs, relief agencies and donor governments. Local NGO participation was limited to those organizations that had been involved in emergency food distribution. Social policy formation entered a third phase when local institutions assumed responsibilities with the establishment of the first post-conflict Kosovan government in 2002.

This period has been dominated by the establishment of traditional social policy programming such as old-age pensions, disability and unemployment insurance, and social services, and the institutionalization of the social assistance programme. Policy formation continued to rely heavily on international input, increasingly in the form of consultants.

The Emergency Phase

With the Security Council's adoption of Resolution 1244 on 10 June 1999, the UN took administrative responsibility for Kosovo. Immediately following this, there was a massive population movement as approximately 850 000 Kosovo Albanian refugees who had fled the province during the conflict returned. Additionally, thousands of Kosovo Serbs, fearing persecution, left for Serbia proper. Prior to the air-strikes, international relief NGOs had been active inside Kosovo. During the crisis they moved to neighbouring countries to respond to the refugee flow. In the immediate post-conflict period these agencies launched a massive operation for the return and resettlement of refugees, delivering food, medicine and reconstruction supplies.

Working with partner agencies, the UN High Commissioner for Refugees, which was initially the lead agency responding to the refugee crisis, established a systematic approach to relief operations. In the food sector, its primary implementing partner was the World Food Programme (WFP), which maintained a commodity pipeline to supply food items for distribution. In addition, the US NGOs, Catholic Relief Services and Mercy Corps International managed a second pipeline from the United States Agency for International Development/Food For Peace (FFP) programme that had originally been established to respond to IDPs in Kosovo in 1998. The WFP and FFP pipelines were integrated and managed in co-ordination. This distribution network became part of the organizational foundation for the later social assistance programmes.

The post-conflict humanitarian assistance programme involved distribution to as much of the population as possible. The programme was an extraordinarily complex logistical exercise that required co-ordination at a variety of levels, and created localized nodes of power. At the village or neighbourhood level, the network had direct interaction with the political dynamic. Local distribution agents fulfilled a basic welfare need, and assumed a high level of social and political importance in the community. Surprisingly, the network that was built in the immediate post-conflict period was not part of either the prior Yugoslav state social welfare network, nor the later UNMIK established network, but instead remained mostly in the private NGO sphere.

Commodity aid distribution networks are opportunities for mobilization. Local distribution partners (LDPs) needed large numbers of people for their operations. The LDPs were expected to gather volunteers to unload and distribute commodities. In the majority of cases the LDP was a chapter of the Mother Teresa Society. Occasionally, a branch of either the Red Cross of Kosova, or a local ad hoc 'Emergency Committee' was chosen as the LDP. In the Serbian communities, the Yugoslav Red Cross was the most common LDP, but the Serbian Orthodox Church was also active. In no case was the LDP a representative of the municipal authorities, or the old state social welfare system, such as the Centre for Social Work. With UNMIK still in the process of deployment, members of the KLA-led provisional government, to which the INGO community was reluctant to offer any level of recognition, were presenting themselves as the municipal authorities. As for the CSWs, prior to the intervention, the INGO community preferred to work with civil society organizations rather than state agencies, so there was little or no history of co-operation. In addition to distributing rations, the LDPs maintained beneficiary lists, adding and subtracting names as necessary, and communicating this information to their INGO partner. The process raised the profile and authority of the LDP in the community.

After a peak in summer 1999, donors reduced the level of food aid. This process introduced targeting and means-testing into the evolving social welfare system. Reductions began in October 1999 with monthly distributions dropping from 1 300 000 to 900 000 beneficiaries per month (Development Researchers' Network, 2002: 9). In regions that had suffered the most severe destruction, reductions were in the range of 15 per cent to 20 per cent; in regions that had little or no war damage, reductions approached 40 per cent. In order to effectively target the reduced food aid, a system of beneficiary categorization was adopted. This had a long-term impact because targeting became the model for differentiated social assistance benefits later. It also later undermined the position of the LDPs in their communities.

Although it was clear to the INGOs and UNMIK that the need for food aid was declining, initial reductions generated anxiety among the population because it coincided with what should have been the harvest period. Since the conflict had peaked during the spring planting season, and the air-strikes had continued through the summer growing season, there was no crop for autumn 1999. Through the LDPs, beneficiaries stated their concern that food stocks would not last through the winter. Donors were reluctant to lessen the reductions since they were already concerned that aid was having a damaging affect on the commodity markets. These concerns were ultimately unfounded, with no reports of food shortages during the winter of 1999–2000. Beneficiary resistance did, however, make implementing the reductions more difficult.

Resistance to the food aid reductions and the categorization among Kosovan NGOs and local authorities was broad. It was as pronounced in Albanian and Serbian communities as it was in other minority areas. It also crossed institutional boundaries. Emergency councils, MTS branches, Albanian and Serbian Red Cross offices all expressed resistance to the cuts. Activists shared concerns that removing anyone from the beneficiary list, regardless of need, would be construed as selective and arbitrary. Some activists refused to distribute based on the reductions and either warehoused the aid while trying to negotiate smaller reductions locally, or distributed to the same number of beneficiaries at reduced ration rates. The food aid cuts made these organizations acutely aware of their political vulnerability. By making wholesale distributions they were unanimously popular, but reductions were certain to anger some of the population and open their operations to criticism.

Once the context shifted from emergency response to targeted need-based assistance, the role of LDPs began to become closer to that of social welfare agencies. These organizations were not public agencies and did not have the political capacity, or legitimacy, to implement such programmes. Activists argued that their organizations were built on the ideal of equitable distributions throughout the community. Being an LDP had made them the most visible service provider in the locality, and the blanket distributions had made the organizations almost invulnerable to political criticism. Beneficiary categorization was problematic because it introduced a kind of means-testing into the system. Activists had to evaluate beneficiary resources and determine where they fitted into the categorization scheme. The room for manipulation, as well as for accusations of corruption, was much greater.

Despite the resistance, the international community insisted on more substantial reductions, which were implemented in April 2000. This second round of reductions occurred in mid-spring, when it was clear that the agricultural base was recovering. The LDPs continued to resist the cuts, but with less support from the beneficiary population. The decreasing food aid reflected the evaluation that despite the destruction of the conflict, Kosovo maintained significant resources. The risk of negatively interfering in the agricultural and commodity markets was becoming a greater concern to international actors. By the beginning of 2000, the international donors involved in the relief operations began to prioritize exit strategies.

The Transition from Emergency Relief to Social Assistance

During this same period of winter 1999–2000, UNMIK's administrative structures were formalized. At the outset UNMIK had been organized around four 'pillars': Pillar I – Humanitarian Assistance; Pillar II – Civil Administration; Pillar III – Democratization and Institution Building; and Pillar IV – Economic Development. Pillar I, which had been led by UNHCR, was dissolved and operations in this sector were subsumed under either Economic Development or Civil Administration. The administrative departments of UNMIK's Joint Interim Administration Structure (JIAS), which was the governing arrangement that had been negotiated with local political actors, also underwent formalization. The JIAS Department of Health and Social Welfare (DHSW) was created in this process.

The DHSW had responsibility for existing state social welfare institutions, including the CSWs in each municipality, the Institute for Social Policy, a residential mental health facility, and a home for the elderly. At the beginning of 2000, the DHSW was tasked with the formation of a new social assistance scheme. The idea of using the INGO food distribution network as the foundation for the reconstruction of a social welfare network was first discussed informally in February 2000. As UNHCR contemplated the phasing down of its major operations, and UNMIK considered its options for addressing the problem of providing a livelihood to those who were dependent on assistance, discussions explored policy alternatives. The first formal efforts were driven by a multi-agency Transition Task Force organized in late March 2000 and chaired by a representative of UNMIK's DHSW. In addition, the Task Force was composed of representatives from WFP, UNHCR, USAID/FFP, the INGOs active in food distribution, and the larger Kosovo Albanian LDPs. By June 2000, the Transition Task Force had designed a new social assistance programme to be implemented by the end of summer. The actual implementation was a high-pressure and fast-paced affair, owing more to the practices of humanitarian NGOs and their ethos of rapid response than a traditional social services exercise. It was later referred to as the 'legendary period' by the UNMIK Director of the Department of Labour and Social Welfare (Héthy, 2005: 154).

Initially the social assistance scheme was to be an entirely cash based programme, with beneficiaries receiving vouchers redeemable at a branch of the Banking and Payments Authority of Kosovo (BPK). The Task Force decided, however, to include a food basket for a variety of reasons. Although it complicated the logistics, it increased the impact of the assistance package by guaranteeing at least a basic level of nourishment. The inclusion of a food basket also meant that the substantial resources of INGOs in the food distribution network could be directed toward assisting the transition. Finally, including the food basket meant that the LDPs, who at this point had the most detailed and comprehensive beneficiary lists, would play a role in the transition.

The first project of the Transition Task Force was the creation of an operating framework to define the roles and responsibilities of the institutional actors involved. Since the social welfare scheme was an UNMIK programme, the DHSW had primary responsibility. The implementation partners (IPs) and LDPs were to offer support throughout the process, provide critical participation at the planning level and use their resources in the field to facilitate implementation. The LDPs expressed concern that the programme would eventually lead to their exclusion from an official social welfare role as the CSWs took on greater responsibility. This concern was well founded and largely came to be borne out.

The social assistance programme provided assistance to a family, rather than an individual. A family was defined as no more than three vertical generations, that is, parent, children and grandparents. The programme had two categories of beneficiaries. A Category I family was one in which all members were incapable of work. In order for a family to be eligible for Category I assistance, every member was to fit into one of four subcategories (JIAS, 2000):

1. under 15 or under 18 and still in full time education;
2. over 65 (male and female);
3. disabled and incapable of work (with a certificate from a doctor – this can be physical or mental handicap); or
4. the only able-bodied adult in the household looking after at least one child under the age of 10.

Category II was originally composed of '[h]ouseholds where there are people who are able to work but at the moment are not able to find paid work' (DHSW, 2000: 2) When implementation of Category I began, beneficiary numbers exceeded expectations, and Category II was delayed. When Category II was put into operation a rule was added that limited the benefits to families in which there was at least one child under 5 years old and/or an orphan under the age of 15. This prevented it from becoming an unemployment insurance benefit, which was not considered financially tenable at the time.

The initial household benefits had a maximum of 120DM per month (approximately €60). The benefits were calculated as follows (JIAS, 2000):

- 15DM per family;
- 50DM for the first person or applicant;
- 25DM per second member; and
- 10DM per additional family member.

In addition to the cash benefit, Category I households received a basic food ration consisting of 12 kg of flour, 1 litre of oil and 1 kg of beans per person per month. Beneficiaries received two vouchers from the CSW. One was for the cash benefit, redeemable at the municipal branch of the BPK. The second voucher was for the food ration and was redeemable with the LDP. The food ration was not included in Category II benefits.

The social assistance scheme was a workable exit strategy for the international aid agencies, but as social policy the programme had a number of problems. The USAID/FFP were able to shut their commodity pipeline in March 2001. The following month, food benefits ended for families on social assistance. A year later, WFP phased out the last of the food distribution and ended its programming. The major limitation of the programme as policy was a result of how it had been developed. Despite the participation of some LDPs, the Transition Task Force lacked significant local input. This limited the potential sustainability of the programme itself, and its impact in building social welfare institutions. The policy-making process was driven by expatriate humanitarian workers and NGO personnel, and largely excluded popular political actors who could later play an important role in legitimizing the programme among Kosovans. In terms of its impact on institution-building, the example of the Institute for Social Policy (ISP) is illustrative. Although the ISP had been founded as a resource for social policy information, it was not present in the design of the programme, denying the institute a major opportunity for capacity-building. This was especially damaging since it had been deeply politicized during the course of the conflict and early involvement would have brought with it much needed attention from international agencies and donors. This attention to the ISP only came later.

At the policy-making level the dominance of external actors was established. The local participation that did occur was limited and subordinated to the larger international agencies, who had greater access to staff, financial resources and expertise. The local organizations who were members of the Task Force were selected by the internationals, and none could make a claim of popular representation. The social policy that was developed was implemented by decree. This pattern continued after the transition phase (Héthy, 2005: 68). This process contributed to the later popular conception of the social welfare programme as an 'UNMIK project'.

Social Policy under the PISG

In May 2001 the Constitutional Framework for Provisional Self-Government in Kosovo established the legal basis for a provincial government. Approving the Constitutional Framework set in motion the reorganization of the JIAS administrative departments into ministries and transitional departments that would correspond to the new government. The first of two legal instruments used to this end was UNMIK Regulation 2001/19, 'On the Executive Branch of the Provisional Institutions of Self-Government in Kosovo', promulgated on 13 September 2001, giving form to the Office of Prime Minister as well as the other ministries. The Ministry of Labour and Social Welfare (MLSW) was created and given responsibility to develop and implement relevant legislation, and direct and supervise labour and social welfare institutions. The ministry is organized into the Department of Labour and Employment (DLE) and the Department of Social Welfare (DSW). The second legal instrument was UNMIK Administrative Direction 2001/14 of 4 October 2001 which reorganized the JIAS administrative departments into the transitional departments, including the Department of Labour and Social Welfare. Notably, social welfare was detached from the Department of Health where it had been placed in the JIAS and merged with the Department of Labour and Employment. Once the Provisional Government was elected, the transitional departments would transfer to the ministries.

The administrative structure of the new Kosovo government was given the unwieldy title of the Provisional Institutions for Self-Government (PISG). Following elections in November 2001, a government was formed in February 2002, and a Kosovan Minister of Labour and Social Welfare was designated. The major tasks facing the social welfare sector at the time were to revise the social assistance programme, which was the primary assistance programme in the province, and to construct a new pension system.

Despite the elections and the formation of a government, the pattern of international dominance over social policy-making continued. Between spring and winter 2001, a regulation on pensions was drafted, primarily under the direction of the World Bank and a consultant from USAID. The regulation was promulgated in December 2001 as UNMIK Regulation 2001/35, after the November elections, but before the February 2002 formation of the first government (Héthy, 2005: 164), apparently in order to ensure a workable scheme free of local political involvement and bargaining. Only the details such as the date of introduction and the benefit rate were left to the newly elected Kosovo Assembly (Héthy, 2005: 172). Since the assumption of responsibility by the PISG, this pattern largely continued with the first significant piece of social legislation to pass the Kosovo Assembly, the revised social assistance scheme (UNMIK Regulation, 2003/15, promulgated with Regulation, 2003/28). The social assistance scheme, passed in August 2003, provided a legal foundation for the system that had been put in place during the emergency phase. Although more inclusively prepared than the law on pensions, the drafting of the law on social assistance was still primarily directed by international UN staff working in the MLSW. Kosovans in the ministry were too overwhelmed by the transition of administrative authority to take a lead role.

The Kosovo Social Protection Project (KSPP), jointly financed by the World Bank and the UK's Department for International Development (DFID), launched in July 2001, was the main support project in the sector. Originally scheduled to run until February 2004, the KSPP was extended first to February 2005, and then to August 2006. The KSPP was designed around four objectives: strengthening the social welfare system; upgrading social welfare infrastructure; capacity-building for CSW staff, and support to pensions administration activities (MLSW, 2002: 4). The timing of the project had an effect on its impact. Being launched in summer 2001, at the end of the JIAS period but before the establishment of the PISG Ministry, the project was caught in the confused dynamic of the transition. With the attention of local Kosovan staff absorbed in the process of administrative organization, international consultants and UNMIK staff appropriated a larger role in the policy-making process. More successfully, infrastructure improvements were significant, resulting in either substantial renovations, or new construction of a majority of CSWs. Efforts regarding capacity-building were focused on establishing a social work programme at the University of Prishtinë, and introducing case management into the CSWs, yielding mixed results. The sustainability of the University of Prishtinë programme is suspect, but case management has been officially adopted by the CSWs. The KSPP input into the design of the pensions' scheme was largely overshadowed by USAID. Oddly, the overall effect was both of lasting impact in terms of establishing social policies that would be in a position to become entrenched, and of fleeting impact in terms of social policy-making practices.

The latest aspect of social policy formation under the PISG involves the decentralization of authority in the province. Decentralization in the social welfare sector is occurring both within the Ministry of Labour and Social Welfare, as well as within the larger governing structures. The decentralization process in Kosovo has been seen as an important aspect of bringing local governance 'in line with modern European practice' (Council of Europe, 2003: 40). The relevant UNMIK regulation (2000/45) states that municipalities are responsible for 'social services and housing'. Acting on this, responsibility for some aspects of social welfare programming are being shifted to the municipalities. The social assistance scheme, however, has remained a province-wide programme and is not being decentralized.

The Social Assistance Scheme

The Kosovo social protection system is still dominated by the social assistance programme both in terms of budgetary costs and number of beneficiaries. The scheme is effectively the same programme that had been developed during the transition with some changes to the application criteria, the maximum size of beneficiary families and the appeals process. Rates of payment were also increased slightly and the entire programme was legally codified (Héthy, 2005: 159–60). The upper and lower age limit on dependent children was broadened, and disabled and elderly dependants were recognized for Category I families. Single-parent families with children up to age 15 became eligible; and the definition of a full-time caregiver expanded to include adults caring for children under 5, family members with permanent disabilities and persons over 65 who require full-time care. Financial criteria were reformed to recognize the increased formalization of the economy. The scheme distinguished between two kinds of assets, reckonable (property, business activities, bank deposits, cash holdings, income from all sources, remittances or pensions from abroad, rent and income in kind), and non-reckonable (basic pension, future disability pension, other official welfare payments, grants, certain loans and home produce for consumption). The maximum number of family members factored into payment was expanded from five to seven. The appeals process was clarified, and a separate independent commission for appeals was authorized. Finally, the highest rate of payment was increased to €75, and a mechanism for future adjustments in line with changes in the Consumer Price Index was established (MLSW, 2003). In all, these changes were more a matter of reinforcing the original social assistance programme than full reforms.

The social assistance scheme was largely considered a success for UNMIK. In December 2005, the programme served 178 121 beneficiaries, or 42 052 families (SOK, 2006). These numbers have seen a decline over the five years of implementation with a peak of 198 739 recipients in July 2001 (SOK, 2004). Using data from the DSW, the estimated average yearly social assistance payment is approximately €672. This average payment has a replacement rate of 26 per cent of the estimated average yearly wage. Regarding minority coverage, internal DSW documents estimate that 17.5 per cent or about 8900 families are from minority communities. Although there were complaints that the criteria are too strict and the financial award is insufficient, there have been relatively few complaints of discrimination. The strongest criticisms regarding minorities claimed that the system did not address the concerns of discrete minorities living in enclaves, but rather promoted a generalized Kosovo-wide perspective that dismissed localized problems.

Municipalities that are majority Serbian or have significant Serbian enclaves pose special implementation problems. The initial concern revolved around delivering services to minority enclaves within municipalities where a different ethnic group comprised the majority. For the most part, the DSW has dealt with enclaves through using local 'sub-branch' offices. At the time of the original implementation, this was considered primarily a security concern. The greater problem eventually turned out to be that the CSWs in the Serbian areas, especially in the north, but also the sub-branches in the enclaves, engage with the Prishtinë-centred UNMIK/PISG social welfare institutions on their own terms, creating a parallel system. More often than not in the Serbian communities, instructions and guidance from Belgrade are given a higher priority than those from Prishtinë. This Kosovo Serbian parallel system has emerged with former state institutions of Serbia remaining under the de facto authority of Belgrade. For both the social workers and the recipients of these services and benefits, this system creates a prioritization and hierarchy of citizenship that acts against the efforts to create a non-ethnicized Kosovan identity. This problem is reinforced by both the prior success of the Albanian parallel regime, and the lack of popular participation in the early process of social policy formation in post-conflict Kosovo.

Pensions

The Kosovo pension was established with the passage of UNMIK Regulation 2001/35 in December 2001. The pension in Kosovo is composed of four parts, two mandatory and two optional. The mandatory programmes are a Basic Pension and Individual Savings Pensions. Supplementary Employer Pensions and Supplementary Individual Pensions are optional. The Basic Pension is 'paid by the Pension Administration to all persons habitually residing in Kosovo and who have reached Pension Age' (UNMIK, Reg. 2001/35 Sec. 2.4). The Basic Pension was originally budgeted in July 2002 at €28 per month per pensioner, and was ostensibly based on a food basket of 2100 calories per day per adult (Héthy, 2005: 173). The Basic Pension was raised to €35 per month in January 2003. At that rate, the Basic Pension achieves an estimated wage replacement rate of roughly 16 per cent. The Basic Pension is a universal programme paid out at the same level to all Kosovans regardless of work history. The universality of the Basic Pension abrogates some of the local history of highly ethnicized labour contention that has resulted in employment gaps for many individuals, from all ethnic communities.

The Individual Savings Pension is a contributory system where both the employer and the employee are required to contribute a minimum of 5 per cent of total annual wages to an Individual Account. Employers and employees may voluntarily contribute up to an additional 10 per cent of annual wages, for a total of 15 per cent each (UNMIK, Reg. 2001/35 Sec. 2.7). Upon reaching pension age (65), the Individual Account is used to purchase an approved Savings Pension Annuity from a private insurance company (Sec. 12.1). There is no minimum contribution period for the pension, however, if there is €2000 or less in the Individual Account the beneficiary receives the amount as a lump sum rather than being obligated to purchase an annuity (Sec. 12.15). The Individual Savings Pension is an entirely new system. It implies no claim on contributions made to the prior Yugoslav pension system. It is not universal and applies only to those Kosovans in the formal work sector. Benefits will be differentiated by contributions and work history.

The two optional pensions are the Supplementary Employer Pension Funds and the Supplementary Individual Pensions. Supplementary Employer Pension Funds may be set up by employers as a benefit for employees. They are licensed and regulated by the Pensions Department of the BPK (Sec. 13.2). These pension funds must be open to all employees, although they may be restricted by occupational categories (Sec. 14.7). A set number of years of employment may be required for participation in the Pension Fund, but it may not exceed five years (Sec. 14.10). Supplementary Individual Pensions are also licensed and regulated by the Pensions Department of the BPK. These pensions are established directly between individuals and their financial institution. Neither Supplementary Employer Pension Funds, nor Supplementary Individual Pensions have begun paying out.

In the near term the only active pension programme is the Basic Pension. In June 2003 there were 100 981 Basic Pension beneficiaries (MLSW, Social Welfare Payments Division 2003b). The Kosovo Basic Pension compares unfavourably to pension programmes in the region in terms of level of benefits and the replacement rate of average annual wages. The Kosovo Basic Pension is distinguished in the region, however, as a universal system that does not require employee or employer contribution, or prior work history.

Future policy formulation regarding pensions has been more regularised with the passage of the pension law. The law (UNMIK, Reg. 2001/35) establishes a Pension Policy Working Group, comprising 'the Head of the DLSW, the Managing Director of the BPK, the Head of the Central Fiscal Authority, other relevant members of the Economic and Fiscal Council, their designees, and others appointed by the SRSG'. This arrangement should promote greater accountability in pension policy formation as it clarifies which government officials are most directly responsible for the policies.

CONCLUSION: DETERMINING THE CHARACTERISTICS OF THE EMERGING KOSOVO SOCIAL WELFARE REGIME

Based on the social assistance programme and the pension scheme, the social welfare regime developing in Kosovo could best be described as almost a caricature of a 'liberal regime' according to Esping-Anderson's (1990: 26–7) typology. The social assistance scheme features strict qualification criteria, means-testing and modest benefits. The impact of the scheme is further limited by implementation that is divided along ethnic lines. The parallel administration that has developed in Serbian areas of Kosovo undermines claims of a non-ethnicized system. The social assistance scheme will likely encourage ethnic and economic stratification, and will regulate welfare as a safety net rather than a social right.

The Basic Pension, as a citizens' pension, is more universalistic. However, the benefits are so meagre that it is almost certain to be overtaken by the contributory schemes of the Pension Law, which are not universal. Instead, these contributory schemes will reproduce the disparities and inequalities of wage differentials. The extreme modesty of the Basic Pension benefit, as indicated by the low replacement rate, suggests that it will become a safety net of last resort for the elderly poor. A stratified system will emerge with Basic Pensioners at the bottom. The market promotion inherent in the other parts of the Kosovan pensions scheme will drive the emerging pension regime away from a corporatist model, towards an even more pronounced liberal model than the social assistance scheme.

This chapter has focused on the formation of specific policies related to the provision of social welfare in Kosovo, namely, the social assistance scheme and the old-age pension. Two large areas of social policy, namely, labour and employment, and health, have been excluded from the analysis. To a degree this exclusion reflects the compartmentalized, neo-liberal, approach to social policy that was employed in Kosovo. Héthy's (2005: 203–9) account of the resistance offered by UN headquarters in New York to the efforts of the Department of Labour to draft a comprehensive labour law is illustrative of the pressures not to approach social policy broadly as a core part of economic reconstruction.

In some ways the social welfare regime that is emerging in Kosovo is a quintessential example of globalized social policy. The public institutions of Kosovo are extraordinarily weak due to the particularities of how the dynamics of contention played out in the province. For the majority Kosovo Albanian community, the prior Yugoslav institutions were delegitimized by the oppressive actions of the Belgrade regime. In their place, a semi-official parallel regime was established that was unable successfully to make the full claim of sovereignty. Under UNMIK, the Serbian community launched their own parallel institutions. Without policy-making institutions that are representative of the Kosovo public, the province is left to be buffeted by powerful global trends as articulated by international actors such as the World Bank, or donor governments such as the USA or the UK. Even taking into consideration increasing local accountability, the international community bears a major responsibility for the type of social welfare regime enshrined in Kosovo today.

REFERENCES

Allcock, J. (2000), *Explaining Yugoslavia*, New York: Columbia University Press.

Bieber, F. (2002), 'Nationalist mobilisation and stories of Serb suffering: the Kosovo myth from the 600th anniversary to the present', *Rethinking History*, **6** (1), 95–110.

Clark, H. (2000), *Civil Resistance in Kosovo*, London: Pluto Press.

Corker, R., D. Rehm and K. Kostial (2001), *Kosovo: Macroeconomic Issues and Fiscal Sustainability*, Washington, DC: International Monetary Fund.

Council of Europe, Decentralization Mission (2003), *Reform of Local Self-Government and Public Administration in Kosovo: final Recommendation, SG/Inf*, Strasbourg: COE.

Department of Health and Social Welfare (DHSW) (2000), *Transition to Social Assistance from Emergency Aid Information Pack*, Prishtinë: DHSW.

Development Researchers' Network (DNR) (2002), *WFP/UNHCR Food Assessment in Kosovo – March 2002*, Rome, Italy: DNR.

Dragović-Soso, J. (2002), '*Saviours of the Nation': Serbia's Intellectual Opposition and the Revival of Nationalism*, Montreal: McGill-Queen's University Press.

Esping-Anderson, G. (1990), *The Three Worlds of Welfare Capitalism*, Princeton, NJ: Princeton University Press.

Hammel, E.A. and M. Stevanovic (2002), 'The migration of Serbs and Albanians within and between inner Serbia and Kosovo c. 1930–1981', *Centre for Slavic and East European Studies Newsletter Spring 2002 Special Supplement*, University of California, Berkeley.

Héthy, L. (2005), *Kosovo Mission: Reconstructing the Labour and Social Welfare System (1999–2003)*, Brussels: European Trade Union Institute.

Joint Interim Administration Structure (JIAS) – Social Welfare (2000), *Social Assistance Scheme Manual*, Prishtinë: JIAS.

Lydall, H. (1984), *Yugoslav Socialism*, Oxford: Oxford University Press.

Lydall, H. (1989), *Yugoslavia in Crisis*, Oxford: Oxford University Press.

Magaš, B. (1993), *The Destruction of Yugoslavia: Tracking the Breakup 1980–92*, New York: Verso Books.

Malcolm, N. (1999), *Kosovo: A Short History*, New York: New York University Press.

March, A. and R. Sil (1999), 'The "Republic of Kosova" (1989–1999) and the resolution of ethno-separatist conflict: rethinking "sovereignty" in the post-cold war era', Working Paper, Columbia University, Columbia International Affairs Online (CIAO), http://www.ciaonet.org/wps/sir01/index.html (accessed 11 May 2007).

Ministry of Labour and Social Welfare (MLSW) (2002), *Kosovo Social Protection: Funded by the World Bank and DFID, Description of Project Activities*, December, Prishtinë, mimeo.

Ministry of Labour and Social Welfare (MLSW) (2003), *Explanatory Memorandum: Draft Law on the Social Assistance Scheme in Kosovo*, Prishtinë: MLSW.

Ministry of Labour and Social Welfare (MLSW), Social Welfare Payments Division (2003), *Summary Report*, Prishtinë: MLSW.

O'Neill, W. (2002), *Kosovo: An Unfinished Peace*, Boulder: Lynne Reiner.

RIINVEST (2003), *Early Warning Report, Kosovo*, Report 3, January–April 2003 Prishtinë: RIINVEST/UNDP Kosovo/USAID Kosovo.

RIINVEST (2006), *Early Warning Report, Kosovo*, Report 12, October–December 2005, Prishtinë: RIINVEST/UNDP Kosovo/USAID Kosovo.

Statistical Office of Kosovo (SOK) (2004), *Statistical Data on Social Welfare in Kosovo*, Prishtinë: SOK.

Statistical Office of Kosovo (SOK) (2005), *Number of Beneficiaries of Social Assistance and Pensions in Kosovo in 2004*, Prishtinë: SOK.

Statistical Office of Kosovo (SOK) (2006), *Series 5: Social Statistics – Social Welfare Statistics in Kosovo 2005*, Prishtinë: SOK.

Tomc, G. (1988), 'Classes, party elites, and ethnic groups', in D. Rusinow (ed.), *Yugoslavia: Fractured Federalism*, Washington, DC: Wilson Centre Press.

United Nations Development Programme (UNDP) Kosovo (2004), *Human Development Report: Kosovo 2004, The Rise of the Citizen: Challenges and Choices*, Prishtinë: UNDP Kosovo.

United Nations Interim Administration Mission in Kosovo (UNMIK) Regulation (2000), *On the Municipal Administration in Kosovo*, 2000/45.

United Nations Interim Administration Mission in Kosovo (UNMIK) Regulation (2001), *On Pensions in Kosovo*, 2001/35.

United Nations Interim Administration Mission in Kosovo (UNMIK) Regulation (2003), *On the Promulgation of the Law Adopted by the Assembly of Kosovo on the Social Assistance Scheme in Kosovo*, 2003/28.

Vickers, M. (1998), *Between Serb and Albanian: A History of Kosovo*, New York: Columbia University Press.

World Bank (2005), *Kosovo Poverty Assessment: Promoting Opportunity, Security, and Participation for All*, Washington, DC: World Bank.

World Bank (2001), *Kosovo Poverty Assessment*, Washington, DC: World Bank.

12.   Conclusions

Bob Deacon, Noémi Lendvai and Paul Stubbs

INTRODUCTION

This book has brought together three fields of study: that concerned with the role of international actors and their influence on national policies; changes taking place to social policies in the context of globalization, transnationalism and Europeanization; and the political transformations taking place in South Eastern Europe. It has reported the results of empirical investigations into recent changes in social policy in the region and the ways in which transnational actors are influencing these changes.

We divide this concluding chapter into three sections. The first summarizes the actual developments in social policy in the countries of the region and the several and diverse ways in which international actors have, to varying degrees, been influential. We then draw some analytical conclusions arguing how the case studies lead to changes in the ways social scientists should make sense of: the role of international actors engaged in transnational policy-making including that of the EU; the role and nature of states in this 'multi-level and multi-actor' process; and the prospects for social policy and the diversity of welfare regimes. Finally, we make suggestions about the kind of research that is needed to advance understanding in these interrelated areas.

INTERNATIONAL ACTORS AND SOCIAL POLICY IN SOUTH EAST EUROPE

Answering the questions posed in Chapter 1 in the light of the case studies in Chapters 3 to 11 and taking account of the reflections upon Europeanization in Chapter 2 allows us to begin to piece together the key themes and the complex variations in the presence, nature and influence of international actors on the making of social policy. Based on these answers, we can draw more fundamental conclusions about the nature of the making of social policy in SEE, conceived as a complex product of transnational and domestic legacies, trends and processes. The review of the case studies also reveals some of the limitations of the comparative case study method for understanding transnational policy-making, a point to which we return at the end of this chapter.

The Variability of Social Policy 'Choices' and 'Accidents'

In terms of the variability of the social policy 'choices' being made by different countries in SEE in the spheres of social protection, social services, pensions, health and labour market policies, a number of things are apparent. In some fields there is almost uniformity in the direction of social policy reforms. In others there is diversity. Labour market policy has shifted in the direction of flexibilization and activation accompanying the informalization of the market everywhere. Compensatory unemployment benefits have been reduced or made more conditional. In terms of pension policy, however, while the dominant trend, pushed hard by the World Bank, has been towards the establishment of a multi-pillar system involving the erosion or reduction in importance of the PAYG state system in favour of the increased importance of an individualized, privately invested and managed defined contribution pension, this trend is not universal and has been resisted in Slovenia, Serbia, Bosnia-Herzegovina, Albania and, it would seem, in Turkey too. In Kosovo an unusual mixture has emerged of private savings being held by the state and used on retirement to buy an annuity if there are sufficient funds available, with a fall-back state guarantee. Reforms in health care have been less dramatic and more variable but almost always involve a push to partial privatization or marketization, but at the same time there are moves to try to ensure universal access in a resource-constrained environment. Some form of safety net social assistance scheme has emerged everywhere, often with local variation in the adequacy of the amounts provided and variable eligibility conditions. The major, although far from complete, trend in social services has been away from institutional care to other forms of support, including foster care and community-based support. Long-established Centres for Social Work in the post-Yugoslav countries are now being strengthened, having been sidelined in the emergency post-war humanitarian phase of relief in some countries. They now operate within an enlarged welfare mix alongside INGO and NGO players. In this sense welfare parallelism has emerged especially in those countries affected by the wars. The concept of and concern, at least formally, with social exclusion and inclusion echoes imported Euro-speak. Indeed, one feature of the shift in social policies in the region is the reframing of social policy issues away from traditional sector policies and clear policy choices within them to a more discursive concern with social problems associated with women, older people, young people and children. In turn this has led to a projectization of social policy concerned with minorities, human rights, empowerment, participatory poverty assessments, social exclusion and discrimination. At the same time there has been a shift from a traditional state socialist obsession with defectology involving special education and institutional care towards inclusive care.

One aspect of social policy change noted in the Serbian chapter, but applicable elsewhere, is the sometimes accidental or arbitrary nature of the 'choices' made. Some policy shifts, especially in the early days of transition, depended on a particular constellation of consultants and ministers working in the absence of any public political discourse or concern about social policy choices. We return to this theme of the relationship between external and internal actors and the politics of social policy reform later.

A Range of International Actors Scrambling for Influence; the World Bank Remains Dominant but the Neo-liberal Project is Contested, Partial and Unfinished

In answer to our question concerning how complete the neo-liberal project in social policy has been in the region, we can conclude that it is not complete as resistance to the privatization of pensions has been shown in a number of countries and there has been only partial marketization of some health services (see Table 12.3). In some cases such as Turkey, external intervention has been concerned to universalize services and benefits formerly available to a privileged few. In the health sector most interventions have been concerned to set up an independent public health insurance fund to protect it from state plunder. However liberalization is extensively under way in terms of the activation of the labour market. The EU has not been a bulwark against the liberalizing trend as we note below.

In addition to the presence of the World Bank, the EU and the UN agencies including the UNDP, ILO and UNICEF, the region is marked by a proliferation of actors, some of which are completely new and largely incomparable with any other bodies elsewhere, and all of which contribute, explicitly or implicitly, to a crowded arena of policy advice, project implementation, and strategic alliance-building in social policy. Table 12.1 captures the presence of these actors in different countries.

In terms of the unusual actors at the regional level, the most important of these has been the Stability Pact for South Eastern Europe, established in 1999. After sustained lobbying by a range of actors, an Initiative for Social Cohesion (ISC) was established in 2000 within Working Table II on Economic Reconstruction, Development and Co-operation. Its overall objective was 'to address social issues that affect the daily lives of citizens of

Table 12.1 International actor presence and significance in the region

	Relationship to EU See Chapter 2 for details	Lending category/ status	World Bank pension loan	World Bank PRSP prepared	ILO presence mentioned	Bilateral donors	Other forms of intervention
Slovenia	Member	None – high income	NO	NO	YES		C of E stability pact (donor)
Croatia	Candidate	IBRD	YES	NO	NO	DFID Japanese	INGOs
Serbia	SAA negotiations called off	Blend	NO	Yes but abandoned	YES	DFID, USAID, GTZ Norway etc.	
Bulgaria	Member	IBRD	YES	NO	YES	DFID	C of E
Romania	Member	IBRD	YES	NO	YES	USAID DFID	Children's INGOs
BiH	Negotiations for SAA	Blend	NO	Yes (MTDS)	NO	DFID	OHR
Macedonia	Candidate	IBRD	YES	Yes but abandoned	NO	USAID	C of E stability pact
Kosovo	Not a country	Grants only (not a country)	Grants	No (KDP)	NO	DFID	UNMIK
Albania	SAA signed	Blend	YES	YES (GPRS)	NO	USAID, Italy, SIDA, NORAD	INGOs
Turkey	Candidate	IBRD	YES	YES	NO?	???	

the countries of SEE through regional approaches in the field of health, social protection, employment policy and vocational training, social dialogue and housing' (ISC, 2002: 2). In a series of meetings in 2001, when the co-chairs were taken by the governments of France and Serbia and Montenegro (then FRY – the Federal Republic of Yugoslavia), the main priorities for the coming years were to: improve health policy; strengthen social protection systems; develop social dialogue; enhance employability; stimulate new housing policies; and monitor and co-ordinate social policy development related projects (ISC, 2002). Leading roles were taken by the ILO, the Council of Europe, the European Trade Union Confederation, and the World Health Organization, with funding from a range of donors, including most prominently Switzerland and the Council of Europe.

The lofty aims of the initiative have gone largely unnoticed and have had little impact outside a small circle of cognoscenti. As the Stability Pact prepares to transform itself into a regional co-operation initiative, the overview of the ISC states that its activities 'will continue in the form of networks that have been established among the relevant actors' (Stability Pact, 2006: 6). The three areas mentioned are health, employment and social dialogue, with no reference to social protection. In fact, as a spin-off from the ISC, the Council of Europe has established the Social Institutions Support Programme, with a main office in Skopje in the Western Balkan/CARDS region, to support the modernization of social policies and institutions, and to promote regional social security coordination. This programme is mainly funded by the European Commission, and co-funded and managed by the Council of Europe's Directorate General of Social Cohesion (DG III). The programme has contributed to the creation of a network of social security professionals and set the basis for regional co-operation in the field of social security. However, the Zagreb declaration following a Ministerial Conference on Social Security Co-ordination in the Western Balkans (Social Institutions Support Programme, 2006) has had little impact. As noted in the Macedonia chapter, the activities of the Centre are 'by and large of academic or/and networking character, thus having no (or at least very negligible) general impact'.

However, more significantly in Bosnia-Herzegovina, through the Office of the High Representative (OHR) and in Kosovo, through the UN-administration (UNMIK), as well as through NATO-led peace-keeping missions (SFOR and KFOR), a new kind of ad hoc protectorate governance exists. Interestingly, while in BiH, initially post-war, relatively little emphasis was placed on social policy issues, this was not the case later in Kosovo. Both chapters warn of the dangers, in terms of the absence of any public sphere for debating social policy choices, of these protectorate and semi-protectorate arrangements.

Overall, the book shows that there is a bewildering array of international actors and their representatives, some of whom 'wear more than one hat', all competing to shape the social policy of the region. Indeed, in this context new intemediaries and brokers emerge with major implications for transparency and ownership. At the very least, as some of the case studies show, some country's social affairs ministries have been left confused and disempowered in these processes. Indeed, it is not unknown for different donors to be working with different ministries on similar themes, from divergent perspectives, at the same time. What all of this often means is that the real centre of social policy development is determined within the fiscal envelopes of the Ministry of Finance, much constrained by the condition-alities of the IMF and World Bank.

In terms of our second question – where, why, how and when have certain international actors been influential? – a number of answers are evident. In general where the economy and the state has been weaker (even taken over as a protectorate) and where 'civil society' or the 'public sphere' appears less active, then the role of international actors has been that much stronger. The variation in the region is from Slovenia at one extreme where 'inter-national actors were obliged to respect Slovenian conditions' to Kosovo at the other extreme in which 'the development of post-conflict social welfare programmes . . . is perhaps the most extreme example of external intervention in policy formation'. Here 'Kosovar popular actors, from organized labour and capital, to political parties and social movement organizations were not an influential part of the initial policy formation process'. Albania after the pyramid selling debacle comes a close second. In the countries involved in the wars of Yugoslav succession, the subse-quent post-war stabilization process created opportunities for IO involve-ment and INGO involvement on a large scale, often in ways that distorted subsequent developments in national social policy.

In terms of the major external players, the World Bank is cited every-where as having, or attempting to have, the greatest influence on social policy using loan conditionality or cross-conditionality with the IMF to secure change. A country's status with regard to eligibility to borrow cheaply from the IDA arm of the World Bank is a factor here, with Albania, Bosnia-Herzegovina and Serbia eligible for IDA as a result of low incomes, but deemed financially creditworthy. Kosovo, since it is not a state, is eligible only for grants, not loans. Croatia, Macedonia and Turkey qualify for non-concessional loans through the IBRD as do Slovenia, Bulgaria and Romania.[1] The ILO, while it is mentioned in a number of chapters, appears to have played something of a minor role, although it is now involved in pro-ducing regional and country overviews of key social policy issues, including social services (Fultz and Tracy, 2004) and social security spending (ILO,

2005). The two UN agencies with an extensive country presence are UNDP and UNICEF. The United Nation Development Programme is a significant actor, often in conjunction with bilateral donors, although its efforts to inject MDG concerns into the PRSP appear to have met with mixed results. Its Human Development Reports remain influential. The United Nations Children's Fund has an operational presence linked to state obligations under the Convention on the Rights of the Child and has a high profile on child protection reform. The TransMONEE programme has been an important source of data and analysis on regional trends affecting children. Nevertheless, it barely features as a key reform actor in the case studies in this book.

Among the bilaterals, the UK's DFID has been active everywhere, often in conjunction with the World Bank. In addition, the Scandinavians, particularly Finland, Sweden and Norway, are involved in supporting social policy initiatives. USAID has had significant inputs into some reforms, notably in pensions and the labour market but is now slowly withdrawing. In Bosnia-Herzegovina and Kosovo, in particular, a group of primarily US-based INGOs, including CARE, Catholic Relief Services and Mercy Corps International, more renowned for their emergency relief programmes, ventured into the sphere of social policy, particularly CARE. The British-based consultancy company Birks Sinclair and Associates Limited has been involved, mainly on DFID-funded programmes, in a number of countries.

Variable Relation to an 'Indifferent' EU Minimizes and Delays the Europeanization of Social Policy

Often coming late in the day after the World Bank has set the social policy reform agenda is the European Union which, in the case of Turkey for example, has 'little interest in counterbalancing the IMF/World Bank'. In the case of Macedonia it was reported that there was 'minimal intervention by the European Union, in the period until 2004, towards steering the country's social policy direction closer to the "European social model"'. Furthermore 'the absence of any concrete EU social policy prescription, created an additional gap, which altogether enabled the current neo-liberal social policy orientation in Macedonia to take hold'. The chapters on Bulgaria and Romania, Slovenia and, in particular, Croatia note the significance of the process of drawing up Joint Inclusion Memoranda as injecting a new dynamic into social policy thinking and, to an extent, programming. At this point, we can conclude that the European Union's main contribution to the social policy of the countries of the region sometimes appears have been the generation of a discourse if not (yet) a practice of social inclusion. More generally, the EU has contributed to the process noted earlier whereby traditional domains of social policy have been deconstructed and new domains have emerged.

In terms of social policy, the variable relationship to the EU matters, as it presents a variety of very different modalities and frameworks, all with their own particular problems. While EU membership involves signing up to and realizing in practice a somewhat limited set of legal social policy requirements: health and safety regulations, equal treatment of men and women, transferability of social security rights, and a system of social protection, this leaves a lot of room for policy choice. At the level of rhetoric, the EU exhorts the countries of the region to establish a social dimension to their market economies. In practice many authors (de la Porte and Pochet, 2002; Deacon et al., 1997; Ferge, 2002; Vaughan-Whitehead, 2003) have observed previously that there has been very limited influence from the EU on social policy in Eastern Europe. There have been exceptions to this, as in the negative opinions regarding Bulgaria and Romania with regard to children in institutions and street children, and more widely in terms of the question of the treatment of minorities where the EU has 'shown some teeth' in the accession negotiations (Ferge, 2002). This may yet prove to be an important issue, of course, in relation to other SEE applicant countries in the context of concerns about human rights and, in particular, the rights of minorities.

In terms of EU assistance, what appears to occur is that the social *acquis* are emphasized least for those countries which, perhaps, need them most – the poorest countries, for whom EU membership is more distant. For many of these countries the EU's external assistance agenda, and its various aid and reconstruction programmes, bear at best only a passing connection to the social *acquis*. In short, the EU's relationship with much of the region of South Eastern Europe is dominated, still, by a reconstruction and development agenda, heavily bureaucratized and delayed in its implementation, in which social policy concerns are rarely or haphazardly stressed. This is the case with the CARDS programme in the Western Balkans (cf. Stubbs, 2004) and appears to be the case within the specific context of the European Agency for Reconstruction which is responsible for the main EC assistance programmes in Serbia and Montenegro, Kosovo and Macedonia. There is little room to be optimistic that the newer Instrument of Pre-Accession Assistance for the countries of the Western Balkans will offer more coherence or greater emphasis on social policy issues in this regard. Hence, we would assert that the EU and models of a social Europe are absent from centre stage in most of the key debates and technical assistance programmes of the EU regarding policy reform in South Eastern Europe.

Most crucially, the 'Europeanization', or to be more precise the 'EU-ization', of South Eastern Europe takes place in a much more complex and hybrid way than the institutionalist literature on Europeanization often seems to suggest. On the one hand, EU-ization represents a very uneven and incoherent process, in which the EU has a variety of external assistance agendas which do not correspond to its own agenda (most notably the social *acquis* and the revised Lisbon agenda). On the other hand, EU-ization of South Eastern Europe has to be understood in the context of 'multilateral donor tandem' and in the context of an ambivalent competition/co-operation between the World Bank and the EU. While South Eastern Europe is the newest region of 'Europe in waiting' (Clarke, 2005a), its contemporary policy debates are dominated, shaped and projected by the World Bank rather than the EU.

The competition/co-operation between the EU and the World Bank takes many shapes and forms. Often the two agencies offer very different 'technologies of involvement' and 'technologies of enumeration'. From the point of view of social policy, the World Bank has a strong and often pervasive 'structural adjustment' framework, which addresses key social policy areas, such as pensions, social assistance and health. On similar 'core' issues, the EU largely remains silent (as in Croatia, Romania, Bulgaria or Macedonia) or plays a co-ordinating, but not a decisive role (as in Slovenia). A second important difference in their approach is that while the EU seems to be using 'soft' technologies such as supporting and monitoring the adoption of the regulatory framework of the *acquis*, the World Bank is relying on 'hard conditionalities' reinforced by structural loans (Table 12.2). As noted in Chapter 1, notwithstanding the existence of a joint EU/World Bank office for the region, the World Bank often appears to pay lip service to, or indeed to misunderstand, EU social policy processes, in programmes and adjustment loans. Also, of course, the World

Table 12.2   European Union and World Bank modes of influence compared

	EU	World Bank
Regulatory frameworks/ legal standards/ framework legislations	*Acquis communitaire*	–
Policy-making/ agenda-setting	Ambivalent 'reform' agenda – political and economic criteria	Structural adjustment agenda
Projects/programmes/ funds	Soft, but bureaucratized funds (CARDS, PHARE, IPA, etc.) with little social policy agenda	Loans, 'hard' funds attached to core social policy agenda

Bank's insistence on the importance of absolute poverty lines stands in contrast to the emphasis on relative poverty by the EU.

However, a number of cases reveal important similarities between the two agencies. First, as we learned from the Croatian chapter, often key international actors such as the World Bank and the EU are forced to pool from the same social policy 'experts' and rely on the same consultants. Second, we see similar practices of enframing used through a series of 'data', 'report' and 'knowledge' production throughout South Eastern Europe, whereby important studies, reports and databases are developed to be acted upon. In this regard, a careful analysis of key documents produced by the World Bank and the EU show surprising textual (cut and paste) similarities. The Romanian case shows how the EU's Open Method of Co-ordination for social inclusion (OMC/inclusion) as soft governance stands hand in hand with a World Bank loan of US$57 million for promoting the aims set by the OMC process. In that sense the World Bank in SEE follows its policy developed in Central Eastern European countries in the late 1990s, where the World Bank discourse from transitional structural adjustment moved towards helping further adjustment in order to support these countries in their integration to the European Union

To sum up, the Europeanization of South Eastern Europe has three important and unique characteristics. First, it represents a very incoherent set of influence and practices, which bear little resonance with the agenda of the EU integration itself. Second, while for many Europeanization implies the adoption and promotion of 'Social Europe' and represents a counterbalance to Americanization, or neo-liberalization, the chapters show a far more complex picture. Finally, as much as very diverse socio-economic and cultural contexts would require a differentiated approach by the EU, the EU itself remains largely indifferent and shows little learning capacity. Paradoxically, while one of the core agendas of the EU is to enhance the learning capacity of institutions in the candidate and aspirant states, there is little evidence of the development of these capacities in the way the EU conducts the accession processes. This not only significantly weakens the influence of the EU in this crowded economic and social transnational space, but may prove to hinder the EU integration of the region in the future.

Diverse Institutional and Cultural Legacies Mediate External Influences

In terms of our question about diverse institutional and cultural legacies mediating the impact of external actors, a number of points can be made. First, the common legacy among all of the countries was that of the quite similar state socialist (Bulgaria, Romania, Albania), Bismarckian (former

Yugoslavia) or 'Inegalitarian corporatist' (Turkey) (formal) work-related welfare state with social security benefits reflecting certain privileged work categories. This was combined with a state commitment to universal health and education in all countries except Turkey. In terms of social care, institutionalization and defectology reigned supreme. The Bismarckian legacy was overridden in Kosovo and the state-socialist legacy, except in the pension field, collapsed along with the economy in Albania. In Kosovo totally and in Albania partly the external actors began, in effect from scratch, to invent social policies. On the other hand, the Bismarckian legacy in Slovenia and Serbia and even in post-war Bosnia-Herzegovina was entrenched enough to provide an institutional obstacle to change. This is less the case in Croatia and Macedonia, at least with regard to pension reform. In Romania and Bulgaria the legacy delayed the impact of the neo-liberal agenda. In Turkey the World Bank has rather been concerned not to overthrow the corporatist legacy but to universalize its provisions and remove some of the worst elements of inequity in its operation. In general a commitment to universal health and education has not been challenged by external actors, although marketized ways of ensuring it are being introduced. There were uneven legacies in terms of the presence or absence of a long-term and long-established professional class of social workers. This class which was well established in the former Yugoslavia and, in part, in Bulgaria and Romania, was associated with institutional care which became challenged in the post-communist transition and is being replaced by care in the community and social inclusion, at least in theory.

Our questions concerning culture and confessional practice in the SEE region present us with not only the Catholic and hence Bismarckian inclined, but liberal influenced, Croatia and Slovenia, but also Orthodox and initially Bismarckian Serbia, Macedonia and Bulgaria, and an Islamic-influenced Turkey, Albania and parts of Bosnia-Herzegovina. None of the case studies suggest that these cultural contexts were significant in terms of promoting or resisting neo-liberal social policy ideas. In most of the texts, international actors combine with secular elites to reproduce secularized, supposedly 'modern' social policy. The role of religious-based international organizations, including various Islamic charities, often based in Saudi Arabia, Caritas and International Orthodox Christian Charities has not been mentioned in the case studies. Our view is that this is a complex product of realities on the ground and the way in which social policy issues have become framed so as to discount cultural factors. More work is clearly needed, then, to explore this complex issue, within a more open frame.

The related set of questions we posed concerned the ethnicization of social life in much of the region, through wars, forced migrations and the interest of one state in contiguous diasporas elsewhere, does receive some attention in the case studies. There is, clearly, a clustering of ethnicized questions and ethnicized claims-making in social policy in Bosnia-Herzegovina, Croatia, Serbia, Albania, Kosovo, Macedonia and Turkey. The significance of disjunctions between formal citizenship, place of residence and belonging, leading to the invoking of cross-border solidarities and ethnicized welfare claims-making is relevant in Croatia, Serbia, Kosovo, Macedonia and Bosnia-Herzegovina. However, they have not been addressed as central issues by most of the chapters' authors. In part, this may be because a national- or country-based comparative methodology is not best suited to capture cross-border processes. The intellectual and data frames used are not conducive to revealing answers: in this sense, national frames are both too small and too large. In addition, of course, technical questions of the transfer of entitlements when states break up are complicated by the slow and contested unfinished processes of state-building, migration, return and resettlement. Nevertheless the parallel Serbian-directed provisions for Serbs in parts of Kosovo is noted and the reported decision to build a new pension system in Kosovo which makes no claims upon the former Yugoslavian pension 'fund' was clearly driven by political pragmatism. In Bosnia-Herzegovina both entities have retained the former Yugoslav PAYG schemes, but because of differential economic growth in the two entities they now pay out at different rates leading to residence claims which do not match where people actually live and to legal class actions by those in Republika Srpska to claim benefits at the level of those in the other entity. One consequence of the wars has been the significance of veterans' 'claims-making' distorting social protection and benefit allocation priorities, especially in Bosnia-Herzegovina and Croatia, which the World Bank appears powerless to tackle. Examples of 'enclave welfare' entailing a notion of 'community citizenship' or 'ethnic membership entitlements' were noted in Macedonia in terms of the Albanian community.

It can be argued that a supposed 'normal' focus on the development of collective social rights and duties (the stuff of social policy) could be seen as lending support to collective but ethnicized claims. Now it might be suggested that this ethnic exclusivity is, itself, 'normal' and was the story of the development of social rights in even the most advanced social democratic states of Europe, and is a stage of historical development which is only now giving way to the realities of complex multicultural and multi-identity societies. Dimitrijević (1997) however, for example, has argued that the focus of social policy in SEE should be on individual rather than collective rights. Certainly a rights-based approach to social policy has been a key feature of the discourse about social entitlements in the context of developing countries, and prescription for social policy in SEE has sometimes used this approach in furthering claims to social protection. The reframing of social policy as social rights was evident in the Bulgarian and Romanian chapter and elsewhere.

In addition, the role of and variety of state and sub-state agencies in reproducing exclusionary practices which cut across traditional citizenship-based claims to social rights is an important phenomenon throughout the region. The fate of the Roma in South Eastern Europe, clearly over-represented in parts of the social control elements of welfare such as children's homes and juvenile justice institutions, also gives cause for concern. In addition, wider diasporization is clearly a factor which serves to de-territorialize social policy in parts of South Eastern Europe, although sending remittances home, noted in Chapter 1, is also a phenomenon which has been little remarked upon in the case studies reported here except for Albania where the emigration of skilled workers and the level of remittances is significant. Again the comparative method might not enable a focus on these issues.

The Complex Coexistence of 'Social Policy', 'Social Development' and 'Post-conflict Reconstruction' Frames

The 'normal' transition from state socialism to welfare capitalism observed previously in Hungary, Ukraine and Bulgaria (Deacon et al., 1997) within which we might expect institutional legacies to matter has, of course, been overlayed in some countries in this book by war and various post-war settlements, internal conflict and financial collapse, all of which have impacted upon the trajectory of social policy reforms. One aspect of this has been that the region has been seen by external agencies through the lenses of development and post-war reconstruction, thus bringing to the area a development discourse and practice combined with emergency interventions which then have distorted 'normal' social policies. This means that the intellectual reference points, and therefore the discourse of policy advocates working in the region, is more complex than the clash between the EU and World Bank social policy discourses of universalism as opposed to selectivity, or regarding public versus private social provision. This is particularly important in terms of the development of social funds, explicitly in some parts of the region and implicitly in others, and the formulation of Poverty Reduction Strategy Programmes used to fashion safety nets. Gerry Redmond (2006) makes a series of points about the problematic nature of PRSPs and the tendency for these to result in policies directed at targeting the poor for special relief and facilitating small enterprise loans. Poverty Reduction Strategy Programmes appear less concerned with defending under-funded universal social protection, health and educational systems and with universal child benefits or public pension systems. It is fair to suggest that, in general terms, there is a disjuncture between the intellectual and policy worlds of development specialists and those of European social policy experts. The existence of the two paradigms in some ways reflects the ambiguity of the EU towards the region, as we discussed earlier. Is it a region on the brink of rejoining Europe within which a social policy paradigm applies, or is it a region still in the throws of post-war crisis and under-development within which a development paradigm is fitting? The book charts this clash and the development of hybrid or mixed discourses which seek to combine social development and social policy frames.

This returns us to the question we asked in Chapter 1 about whether the aid processes that were related to the post-conflict situations of the wars of Yugoslav succession are consistent with social policy-making in 'normal' times. In earlier studies of the development of social policy in Bosnia-Herzegovina (Deacon and Stubbs, 1998; Stubbs, 2001), it was shown how relief interventions have tended to operate through international and local NGOs, often subcontracted to provide services, thus forming a parallel system with little integration or functional relationship to the well-established system of public services, including Centres for Social Work, with a 50-year history. These CSWs were sometimes used as mere conduits for emergency aid and time-limited cash assistance programmes, serving to undermine further their legitimacy. These conclusions have been replicated in a number of the case studies in this book, particularly Bosnia-Herzegovina, Albania and Kosovo. Of course, throughout the region, there was an urgent need to diversify provision of services and to secure a mixed model of welfare incorporating 'new' actors such as associations of citizens, community-based organizations, local NGOs and, indeed, an emerging private sector. The problem is that, within the imported social development discourse, these actors were seen as, in and of themselves, more 'progressive', 'responsive', 'rights-based', and so on, than the public sector, leading to a substantial erosion of the role of public provision, a resistance to planning and national direction, and a move towards a project-culture rather than needs-based provision. Again, interestingly, some chapters note that a new frame is emerging in which processes from the PRSP are now fused into a more European-sounding national development planning strategy. The move from projects to strategies may, also, fall victim to the vagaries of external consultancy-led interventions.

The Shaping of Social Policy in SEE

From the discussion above we are now able to compare and contrast in summary form in Table 12.3 the extent to which the factors that we have

Table 12.3 Significance of four major factors influencing social policy

Country	Continuation of Bismarckian/corporatist/state socialist institutional legacy	Impact of war and INGO lead post-war reconstruction	Impact of neo-liberal agenda on pensions	Impact of neo-liberal agenda on labour market	Impact of neo-liberal agenda on health services	EU influence
Slovenia	YES	NO	NO	YES	NO	YES
Croatia	Partial. Not pensions	YES	YES	YES	PARTIAL	YES late
Serbia	YES	YES partially	NO	YES	NO	Emergent
Bulgaria	Being eroded	NO	YES	YES	NO?	YES
Romania	Being eroded	NO	IN PROCESS	PARTIAL	NO	YES
BiH	YES (pensions)	YES heavily	NO	NO	NO	NO
Macedonia	Eroded	PARTIAL	YES	YES	PARTIAL	Emergent
Kosovo	Replaced	YES heavily	YES in unique form	NO	NO	NO
Albania	Eroded by financial collapse	NO but collapse leads to same effect	NO	PARTIAL	NO	NO
Turkey	Unequal corporatism being universalized	NO	NO	YES	NO	Emergent

identified have been differentially important in shaping social policy in each country or territory. The four factors are:

1. Social policy institutional legacies: primarily those associated with work-based state socialist or Bismarckian/Corporatist benefits structures.
2. Neo-liberal driven interventions primarily associated with the World Bank. In Table 12.3 we distinguish between pensions, labour markets and health.
3. War and post-war reconstruction leading to a broad welfare mix and welfare parallelism.
4. Closeness to, and impact of, the European Union.

Table 12.3 shows the diversity of outcomes in the case study countries. To an extent, the pattern emerges of those countries and territories which were most disrupted by conflict, and/or which are the poorest, as well as the most developmentally advanced, for very different reasons, being relatively resistant to neo-liberal agendas. Obviously, trends towards Europeanization are only now beginning to develop for most of the region. Clearly, it is in the most disrupted societies where the proliferation of international non-governmental activity and influence is greatest.

International Actors as Agencies of Empowerment and Disempowerment

Finally in this section we turn to the series of questions posed concerning the impact of international actors on the policy-making process understood as a set of power relations. We asked what the implications were of a policy-making process involving transnational actors for national institutional follow-through and, essentially, whether international actors enrich the national policy debate and empower local actors or in fact disempower, becoming substitutes for normal politics. An absence of follow-through of legislation inspired by external actors was certainly reported strongly in the cases of Bulgaria and Romania, and suggested in Albania and other cases. Empty institutions have been created in a context of excessive legalism with EU-like legal frameworks downloaded, cut and pasted, but with little real institutional follow-through. It is important to note that the EU and other actors have recognized this and have increasingly funded capacity-building projects to compensate. The legal frameworks in Kosovo, and the constitutional framework in Bosnia-Herzegovina were, essentially, protectorate engineered. International organizations and international NGO interventions sometimes have enriched the national policy debate and empowered local actors. In Slovenia the World Bank's failed interventions raised the pension issue to a constitutional crisis but by contrast in Croatia the intervention was hardly challenged. In the case of Serbia a regressive tax law was engineered without even a debate among policy experts let alone a politicized public. The buying out of independent experts by external actors noted in Bulgaria, Romania and Macedonia often detracts from the possibility of open debate and policy contestation. In the term used in the case of Bulgaria and Romania, external actors exercise 'indirect influence by providing expertise and moulding local knowledge'. In this sense the transnationalisation of social policy-making has led in places to its depoliticization and technicization in the emerging policy spaces created by their intervention. These new policy spaces are sometimes open and permit the emergence of a new set of civil society actors, as noted in Croatia around issues of gender and child protection, but are sometimes closed down, as in Kosovo, inviting in a new technocracy who act as the new intermediaries between the international and national in policy articulation. The advice and policy-translation activities of this limited-in-number cohort of local but co-opted social policy scholars are often rendered unaccountable and untransparent.

These new SEE local actors engage with a 'new' mobile technocratic policy advising and project designing class which emerged in three broad circuits. One circuit is a socio-economic policy expertise which began in the countries of the former Soviet Union, moving to the new EU member states, including Slovenia, and Romania and Bulgaria, before emerging in other countries of South Eastern Europe. The pension reform circuit emerged in Latin America before moving to the former Soviet Union and, subsequently, to SEE. Finally, a post-conflict social development circuit moved from conflicts in the Third World to the post-Yugoslav countries before moving on to newer conflict zones. Again, a comparative case study methodology is not the best tool to grasp these processes. Another issue worthy of note is the rise of 'think tanks' as policy actors including G17+ in Serbia, which became a political party, and a range of liberal groupings, alongside regionally focused international think tanks such as the European Stability Initiative often contracted to implement policy prescriptions which they have recommended in their analytical work.

REVISITING ANALYTICAL FRAMEWORKS

Over and above our analysis of the particular ways in which external actors have been influential in the specifics of social policy in the region, we believe it is possible to draw rather more general conclusions refining our understanding about international actors, states and social policy. These insights derive from the case studies and, build on other work in other parts of the world.

International Actors

The book has illustrated the proliferation of international actors and their variability in their policy orientation (cf. Deacon, 2007). Hence, impact is also variable although we would conclude that, always and everywhere, they are relevant and, hence, that no analysis of social policy change is complete without their role being understood. The well-known World Bank neo-liberal versus EU social solidarity ideological struggle in terms of the models and contents of social policy (cf. Deacon et al., 1997) is still there but is most apparent in SEE in the pensions field. In terms of labour markets, the prescriptions of each organization are broadly similar. In health, social care and social assistance the contestations are more complex and highly mediated through outsourced technical expertise.

The study has begun to show how 'old' and 'new' kinds of international organizational structures collide, elide and coexist. Thus the traditional, predictable, stable IOs with a clear function, mandate and tools are still present, perhaps even in some contexts dominant, but a new breed of flexi, hybrid, less predictable organizations, networks, temporary coalitions and informal networks are sharing the stage. These are increasingly influential in their own right and having slow but perceptible impacts on the older traditional organizations. We are witnessing a move from a dominant international civil servant class to a mobile, flexible, short-term consultant class in need of further study.

The specific ways in which IOs relate to local players matter. They mould local knowledge and expertise, strengthening some think tanks and scholars not others. They co-opt scholars into IOs, dissolving potential criticisms and engendering a revolving-door process of a scholar becoming a deputy minister becoming a World Bank consultant, and such like. Hybrid forms of identities are also privileged as agencies search for 'internationalized locals' and 'localized internationals'. These translators and intermediaries frame the social policy choices as much as, if not more than, traditional publics, emerging civil society and, even, parliaments.

Powerful external agencies shape domains and statistical nomenclature but this of itself does not guarantee institutional, policy or practice change. Notions of 'strong' versus 'weak' conditionality oversimplify and need to be, at the very least, complemented by notions of technologies of power, disciplinary complexes and knowledge claims. A literature which shifts focus from 'governance' to 'governmentality' is, hence, relevant here, understanding emerging rationalities, knowledge claims and calculation as forms of social practice. In addition, while focusing on international actors there is still, of course, a need to note the many, varied and sometimes successful forms of domestic policy resistance, subversion or lip service, not least as local agents have 'time' on their side in a way that mobile consultants often do not (Lendvai and Stubbs, forthcoming). Finally, agency needs to be brought back in to discussions in terms of the role of particular individuals and a sense in which social policy-making may be a series of accidents, as the right (or wrong) people in the right or (wrong) or place meet other right (or wrong) people at the right (or wrong) time. Such chance encounters, most clearly addressed in the Serbia chapter, but also noted in the chapter on Bosnia-Herzegovina, can and do shift policy in ways which can and do become entrenched, especially in transition contexts.

States

In terms of states, the study has shown that states still matter but, more important, the variations in state forms, state capacity, the nature of public administration, the nature of political parties and the degree of clientelistic relations, all mediate the extent to which and the ways in which states have policy influence. Again, a structural and institutional notion of the state needs, therefore, to be complemented by discursive and agent-centred definitions. International actors need to be conceived as a part of the 'extended' state with transformational effects in some places. The traditional distinction between the internal functions of the state and the external functions of the state also tends to be eroded. Above all, then, states should not be conceived simply or exclusively as unified, cohesive macro-structures defined by their functions, but should be seen as composed of overlapping networks of agents with diverse and competing interests, projects, and agendas. Similarly, sovereignty needs to be conceived in new forms which replace traditional either/or notions. The studies show varying kinds of reformulation of sovereignty so that, in both Bosnia-Herzegovina and Kosovo, it is not the case that external actors can rule without reference to internal processes. Forms of protectorates, semi-protectorates and quasi-protectorates exist in the region, however, and their impact on social policy choices is considerable. Over and above this, a dominant rationality of 'new public management' which transforms the state into a rational, calculative, actor disciplined in the same way as an external project, seems to be present everywhere.

Social Policies

Social policy understood in terms of sectors (education, social protection, health, labour markets) and policy choices in those sectors (public or private, universal or selective) still apply and matter but the discourse of social policy is being transformed or deconstructed and reconstructed, in the process of transnational engagement. The process is uneven but involves a complex slippage from social policy to social development to social exclusion to poverty alleviation to human security to livelihoods. Social policy understood as redistribution, regulation and rights still holds good but transnational actors downplay the first in favour of the last and do not address their own role in the second. Social statistics matter, but are not disinterested. The question of whose frame is used and how it is self-validated becomes important (St Clair, 2006). Perhaps most importantly, coherent welfare regimes of the Esping-Andersen type are dissolving to be replaced by assemblages of policies which vary within states, across sectors and between them (cf. Clarke, 2004). Legacies still matter but in complex ways. The legacies themselves are complex, diverse and, in some cases, fused, involving a mix of Bismarckian, self-management socialism and state bureaucratic collectivism, for example.

FUTURE RESEARCH AGENDAS

Finally, we make a few suggestions about the implications of this study for the design of future research into the role of international influences on national, regional and global social policy-making. First, it should be clear that the comparative case study method used here is a useful tool in enabling us to understand the making of social policies in bounded terri-tories but that this needs to be complemented by more multi-level, multi-sited studies of transnational actors, organizations and processes themselves. In this book we have hinted at these processes but have not always understood them completely, precisely because our case studies have focused on national processes and not on the role of organizations such as the Stability Pact, or the advice of the same agencies or consultants across different countries. Similarly, while the study recognizes that cross-boundary solidarities, migrations and diasporas matter, they are not well covered by the comparative case study method. This book is unable to tell some of this story, precisely because of the difficulty of what might be termed 'fixed spatial methodologies' to grasp the movements which are so important in this region.

To conclude, a future research agenda could well be complemented by transnational ethnographic approaches exploring the role of policy trans-lators and intermediaries operating in the new breed of flexible, hybrid, fluid and less predictable organizations, temporary coalitions and informal policy networks. This book has also contributed to an approach which renders problematic the idea of universalizing neo-liberalism. The neo-liberal project is by no means as unchanging, all-powerful and universal as some of the critics of neo-liberalism suggest. On these lines, John Clarke has argued that, while 'neo-liberal globalization' is the dominant form of contemporary globalization, any attempt to understand it as 'a hegemonic project' has to address 'both the logics and limits of neo-liberalism, and the different ways in which people and places live with/in – and against – neo-liberalism' (Clarke, 2004: 89). He is profoundly interested, therefore, in 'uneven neo-liberalisms', varying in space and time, and able to enter 'national-popular formations' only in and through alliances, 'assemblages of political discourses' which inevitably change, shape and produce 'hybrids, paradoxes, tensions and incompatibilities' rather than 'coherent implementations of a unified discourse and plan' (ibid.: 94). Global policy ideas are always articulated in specific places and times, or as Collier and Ong would have it, 'territorialised in assemblages' which 'define new material, cultural and discursive relationships' (Collier and Ong, 2005: 4). It is ethnographic studies which can draw attention to the work of 'translators', 'brokers', 'mediators' or 'those translocal agents who mediate languages, contexts, sites and levels' (Clarke, 2005b: 8) which could complement the studies offered here.

NOTE

1. The authors are grateful to Laurie Joshua for clarification of this point.

REFERENCES

Clarke, J. (2004), *Changing Welfare, Changing States: New Directions in Social Policy*, London: Sage.

Clarke, J. (2005a), 'Reconstituting Europe: governing a European people?', in J. Newman (ed.), *Remaking Governance: Peoples, Politics and the Public Sphere*, Bristol: Policy Press, pp. 17–38.

Clarke, J. (2005b), 'What's culture got to do with it? Deconstructing welfare, state and nation', paper presented at Anthropological Approaches to Studying Welfare, Aarhus, November, http://www.hum.au.dk/ckulturf/pages/publications/jc2/culture.pdf (accessed 3 May 2007).

Collier, S. and A. Ong (2005), 'Global assemblages, anthropological problems', in A. Ong and S. Collier (eds), *Global Assemblages: Technology, Politics and Ethics as Anthropological Problems*, Oxford: Blackwell, pp. 3–21.

De la Porte, C. and P. Pochet (2002), *Building Social Europe Through the Open Method of Co-ordination*, Brussels: PIE-Peter Lang.

Deacon, B. (2007), *Global Social Policy and Governance*, London: Sage.

Deacon, B. and P. Stubbs (1998), 'International actors and social policy develop-ment in Bosnia-Herzegovina', *Journal of European Social Policy*, **8** (2), 99–115.
Deacon, B., M. Hulse and P. Stubbs (1997), *Global Social Policy: International Organisations and the Future of Welfare*, London: Sage.
Dimitrijević, V. (1997), 'Policies regarding nationality and human rights in the Balkans', paper presented to conference on Central Europe and the Balkans: Towards the European Union, Trieste, November.
Ferge, Z. (2002), 'European integration and the reform of social security in the accession countries', *European Journal of Social Quality*, **3** (1/2), 9–25.
Fultz, E. and M. Tracey (2004), *Good Practice in Social Services Delivery in South East Europe*, Budapest: ILO.
Initiative for Social Cohesion (ISC) (2002), 'Improving social policy in South Eastern Europe', Brussels: Stability Pact, mimeo.
International Labour Organization (ILO) (2005), *Social Security Spending in South East Europe: A Comparative Review*, Budapest: ILO.
Lendvai, N. and P. Stubbs (forthcoming), 'Policies as translation: situating trans-national social policies', in S. Hodgson and Z. Irving (eds), *Policy Reconsidered: Meanings, Politics and Practices*, Bristol: Policy Press.
Redmond, G. (2006), 'Poverty reduction strategies and well-being in Albania and former Yugoslavia', in M. Petmesidou and C. Papatheodorou (eds), *Poverty in Mediterranean Countries: Trends, Policies and Welfare Prospects in the New Millennium*, London: Zed Press, pp. 166–87.
Social Institutions Support Programme (2006), Ministerial conference on Social Security Co-ordination in the Western Balkans Region: Zagreb Declaration, Council of Europe, http://www.coe.int/t/dg 3/sisp%5CSource%5CZagDeclLetSign. PDF (accessed 3 May 2007).
St Clair, A. (2006), 'Global poverty: the co-production of knowledge and politics', *Global Social Policy*, **6** (1), 57–77.
Stability Pact (2006), 'Report of the special co-ordinator on regional ownership and strengthening of stability pact task forces and institutions', Brussels, Stability Pact, http://www.stabilitypact.org/rt/Annex%202%20-%20Report%20of%20the% 20Special%20Coordinator%20on%20Regional%20Ownership%20and%20Strea mlining.pdf (accessed 3 May 2007).
Stubbs, P. (2001), ' "Social sector" or the diminution of social policy? Regulating welfare regimes in contemporary Bosnia-Herzegovina', in Ž. Papic (ed.), *Policies of International Support to South Eastern European Countries: Lessons (not) Learnt from BiH*, Sarajevo: Muller, pp. 123–40.
Stubbs, P. (2004), 'Prioritising social policy and the fight against poverty and social exclusion in the western Balkans', *SEERC Bulletin*, **2**, www.seerc.info (accessed 3 May 2007).
Vaughan-Whitehead, D. (2003), *EU Enlargement Versus Social Europe?*, Cheltenham UK and Northampton, MA, USA: Edward Elgar.

Index

Titles of publications are in *italics*.

accession to EU 35–40
  Bulgaria 62–3
  Croatia 96–7, 98–9
  Romania 62–3
  see also Europeanization
Albania 10, 187–201
  aid, impact on social well-being
    199–200
  and international actors 195–8
  labour market policy 193–4
  migration 189–91
  pensions 194–5
  poverty 188
  social assistance policy 192–3
  social insurance 194–5
  social policy 191–5
  unemployment 188
Amitsis, G. 131
*Annual Progress Report on Growth
    and Jobs* (European Commission)
    31
Arandarenko, M. 145
Averting the Old Age Crisis (World
    Bank) 92, 93

Bag-Kur, Turkey 105
Barr, N. 200
Birks Sinclair and Associates Ltd 159,
    227
Bismarckian legacy 230–31
Bohle, D. 27
Böröcz, J. 28
Bosnia and Herzegovina 149–64, 225
  economy 152–3
  history 149–50
  medium-term development strategy
    162–3
  political system 151–2
  post-war period, social welfare
    157–61

poverty 152
social welfare administration 153–5
war period, social welfare 155–6
Briggs, A. 201
Bulgaria 10, 62–72
  accession to EU 36
  social policy reform 67–72
  transition and social policy 65–7

CARDS programmes
  Albania 197
  Macedonia 143, 145
Carmen, E. 27
Centres for Social Work (CSWs) 10,
    176, 184, 208, 210, 211, 212, 214,
    216, 222
  Bosnia and Herzegovina 154–5, 234
  Croatia 86, 88, 89
child care
  Bulgaria 67, 70
  Macedonia 137
  Romania 77–8
Child Protection, National
    Programme, Macedonia 144
child welfare, Bosnia and Herzegovina
    155
citizenship and ethnicity, Macedonia
    137–8
Clarke, J. 16
commodity aid distribution, Kosovo
    207–8
communist legacy, social policies,
    Serbia 168
Community Assistance for
    Reconstruction, Development and
    Stabilization, *see* CARDS
    programmes
comparative case study method
    (CCSM) 2
complex multi-lateralism 3

conditional cash transfers, Turkey
125–6
conditional social transfers 144
Convergence Programmes 34
cosmopolitan transnationalism 3
Country Assistance Strategy (CAS)
Albania 197
Slovenia 51
Croatia 85–100
accession to EU 36
demographic changes 86–7
EU and social policy 96–9
health care reform 96
pension reform 91–5
war and social welfare 86–90
Croatia: Beyond Stabilization (World
Bank) 93
cultural legacies 9–11, 230–33

Deacon, B. 1, 7, 8, 11, 23, 51, 62, 63,
64, 65, 66, 67, 79, 87, 97, 130, 131,
133, 221, 228, 233, 234, 238
decentralization
social policy, Kosovo 214
social welfare, Macedonia 136–7,
144
Democratic Opposition of Serbia
(DOS) 169
DFID (Department for International
Development) and Serbia 173
DHSW (Department of Health and
Social Welfare), Kosovo 210
diaspora strategies 7
diasporization, effect on social policy
15; *see also* migration
Dimitrijević, V. 232
Dimitrov, V. 25
disinflation programme, Turkey
124–5
donor co-ordination
Albania 198–9
Serbia 173
Donor Technical Secretariat, Albania
199
Dümling, B. 159, 164

earthquake relief, Turkey 124–5
ECHO (European Community
Humanitarian Office), assistance
to Croatia 88

economic indicators, South East
Europe 11–14
economic reforms, Serbia 169–70
economic situation
Albania 187–9
Bosnia and Herzegovina 152–3
Kosovo 205–6
Turkey 110–11
education and local government,
Macedonia 137
Elster, J. 82
Emergency Earthquake Recovery
Loan, Turkey 125
emergency relief and social policy 11,
234
Kosovo 207–9
Serbia 173–4
emigration from Albania 189–91
employment
Albania 193–4
and social policy 30–31
Turkey 108–9
employment policy, Macedonia 134–5
Estonia, employment and social policy
30–31
ethnicity
and social policy 231–2
and social welfare, Macedonia
137–8
EU, *see* European Union
European Agency for Reconstruction
(EAR) 172
European Commission *Annual
Progress Report on Growth and
Jobs* 31
European Community Humanitarian
Office (ECHO)
and Bosnia and Herzegovina
157–8
and Croatia 88
European Regional Development
Fund 31
European Union
accession, *see* accession to EU
and employment policy reform,
Macedonia 135
and health system reform, Serbia
181
membership, *see* accession to EU
and post-communist welfare 33–5

and social policy 22–6, 28–35, 227–30
   Albania 197
   Bulgaria 63–4
   Croatia 96–9
   Macedonia 136, 142–5
   Romania 64–5
   Serbia 172
   Slovenia 51–2, 56–8, 59–60
   Turkey 118–19
   Structural Funds, Italy 28
   and World Bank 229–30
Europeanization 22–40
   institutionalist approaches 23–6
   post-structuralist approaches 26–8
   of social policy 28–35
   South East Europe 35–6, 227–30

family benefit reform, Romania 79
family role in welfare regime, Turkey
   106–7
Federation of Bosnia and Herzegovina
   (FBiH) 151, 153–4
Ferrera, M. 29
Financial Supervisory Commission,
   Bulgaria 70
Finland, aid for Bosnia and
   Herzegovina 159, 161
Flaker, V. 159
flex organizations 5
food aid, Kosovo 207–9
foreign aid
   impact on social well-being, Albania
   199–200
   see also emergency relief
frontier zones 6
Fund for the Establishment of Social
   Assistance and Solidarity, Turkey
   105–6, 125

Gagnon, V.P. 156, 157
gender equality policies, Hungary 29
globalization, impact on social policy
   7–9
Gould, J. 5, 7
governance approach to
   Europeanization 23–6
government structure, Bosnia and
   Herzegovina 151–2
governmentality approach to
   Europeanization 26–8

Graziano, D. 28
Green Card scheme, Turkey 107
Greskovits, B. 27
*Growth and Jobs, Annual Progress
   Report on* (European
   Commission) 31
Growth and Poverty Reduction
   Strategy (GPRS), Albania 196
growth paradox 14
Guillén, A. 24

Haahr, J. 27
Harrison, G. 6–7
health care reform
   Bulgaria 70
   Croatia 96, 90
   Macedonia 137, 141–2
   Romania 78–9
   Serbia 180–81
   Slovenia 54–6
   Turkey 123–4
Health Insurance law, Macedonia
   141
Healthnet International (HNI) 157–8
Holman, O. 32–3
human capital loss through migration,
   Albania 191
human development indicators, Turkey
   112–15
humanitarian assistance
   Bosnia and Herzegovina 157–8
   Croatia 87–8
   Kosovo 207–9
Hungary
   gender equality policies 29
   regional and social policy recoupling
   31

ILO (International Labour
   Organization) 226
   and pension reform, Slovenia 52–3
   and social policy reform, Serbia 172
   and socio-economic policies, Turkey
   117
imagined communities 9
IMF
   and employment policy reform,
   Macedonia 134
   and social policies, Turkey 116–17,
   118–19

income inequality, Bulgaria 71
Independent Bureau of Humanitarian
    Issues (IBHI) 159
inegalitarian corporatism, Turkey 104
inequality, South East Europe 14–15
institutionalist approach to
    Europeanization 23–6
Integrated Planning System, Albania 198
international actors 3–5
    and cultural legacies 230–33
    and policy-making process 236–7,
        238–9
    and social policy 221–37
    and social policy reform, Serbia
        171–3, 182–4
    and strategic development, Albania
        195–8
International Labour Organization, *see*
    ILO
international organizations
    humanitarian assistance
        Bosnia and Herzegovina 157–8
        Croatia 87–8
        Kosovo 207–9
    and social policy
        Macedonia 132–5, 144–5
        Romania 73–6
        Turkey 116–19
    see also European Union; ILO;
        IMF; UN; UNDP; World Bank
international relations 3
Italy, EU Structural Funds 28

Jakobsson, K. 30–31
Janevska, V. 134
Jankulovska, L. 141
Jessop, B. 6
Joint Assessment Paper for
    Employment Priorities, Turkey
    118
Joint Inclusion Memorandum
    Croatia 98–9
    Turkey 118
Joint Interim Administration Structure
    (JIAS), UNMIK 210

Kasza, G.J. 163, 164
Kosovo 203–19
    economy 205–6
    emergency assistance 207–9

pensions 216–17
political history 203–6
poverty 206
social assistance 209–12
social policy, PISG 212–14
unemployment 206
Kosovo Social Protection Project
    (KSPP) 214
Krizsan, A. 29

Labour Code, Serbia 177–8
labour force loss through migration,
    Albania 191
labour force participation, Albania 188
Labour Market Development (LMD),
    Albania 195–6
labour market policies
    Albania 193–4
    Bulgaria 70
    Slovenia 46–8
labour market reform, Serbia 176–8
labour taxation reform, Serbia 178–9
Larner, W. 7
Lendvai, N. 156
Leonardi, R. 26, 30
Living in BiH: Wave 4 report (FOS,
    BHAS and RSIS) 152
local distribution partners, Kosovo
    208

Macedonia 130–46
    accession to EU 36
    decentralization 136–7
    employment 134–5, 131
    ethnicity and social welfare 137–8
    EU and social policy 136, 142–5
    health care reform 141–2
    international agents 132–5, 144–5
    pensions 139–41
    poverty 138–9
    social protection 135–7
Mandatory Fully Funded Pension
    Insurance law, Macedonia 140
MEDA programme, Turkey 118
Medium-Term Development Strategy
    (MTDS), Bosnia and Herzegovina
    162–3
Meyer, J. 4
migration
    Albania 189–91

rural–urban, Turkey 108–9
and social policy 15
Milošević regime, Serbia 168–9
Mitchell, K. 27
mixed model of social welfare, Bosnia
and Herzegovina 160
Moreno, L. 29

National Action Plan for Employment,
Macedonia 143
National Programme for Child
Protection, Macedonia 144
National Programme to Combat
Poverty and Social Exclusion,
Slovenia 56
National Programme for Social
Protection, Macedonia 144
National Strategy for Integration in
the EU, Macedonia 143–4
National Strategy for Poverty
Reduction, Macedonia 139
National Strategy for Social and
Economic Development
(NSSED), Albania 199–200
neo-liberal governmentality approach
to Europeanization 27
New Labour Code, Serbia 177
Novikova, I. 29

Ohrid Framework Agreement 136
Ostović, D. 94
Ougaard, M. 6

parallel power networks 15–16
Paraskevopolous, C. 26, 30
pension policy
Bosnia and Herzegovina 154
Bulgaria 63, 70
Kosovo 216–17
Romania 63, 78
South East Europe 222
transnational advocacy coalition
4
Turkey 105–7
pension reform
Albania 194–5
Croatia 91–5
Macedonia 139–41
Romania 78
Serbia 179–80

Slovenia 48–54
Turkey 119–23
Pension Reform Technical Assistance
project, Macedonia 140
PHARE (Poland and Hungary
Assistance for Economic
Restructuring) programme 31
Albania 197
Slovenia 51–2, 59
policy diffusion 3–4
policy-making, impact of international
actors 236–9
policy transfer 3–4
political history
Kosovo 203–6
Serbia 168–71
Turkey 111, 116
political structure, Bosnia and
Herzegovina 151–2
politics of scale 5
populist regime, social policies, Serbia
168–9
post-communist states, impact of EU
on welfare policies 33–5
post-conflict aid
Kosovo 207–9
and social policy 234
post-structuralist approaches to
Europeanization 26–8
poverty 14–15
Albania 188
Bosnia and Herzegovina 152
Kosovo 206
Macedonia 138–9
Slovenia 56–8
Turkey 110
Poverty Reduction Strategy Papers
(PRSP)
Macedonia 139
Serbia 171–2
Poverty Reduction Strategy
Programmes 233
primary health care, Macedonia 141–2
privatization of health service, Croatia
90
Programme Adjustment Loan (PAL),
Croatia 98
Provisional Institutions for Self-
Government (PISG), Kosovo
212–14

Radaelli, C. 25
Redmond, G. 233
regional policy and social policy
    re-coupling 31
regressive labour taxation, Serbia
    178–9
Reinermann, D. 163
remittances from migrants, Albania
    190
Republican Health Insurance Fund
    (HIF), Serbia 180–81
Republika Srpska 151, 153
Roma mobilization, Slovakia 29
Romania 10–11, 62–5, 72–80
    accession to EU 36
    social policy reform 64–5, 72–7
rural–urban migration, Turkey
    108–9

safeguard clauses, EU accession 63
Sassen, S. 6
Seekings, J. 104
Serbia 167–85
    communist regime 168
    emergency assistance policy 173–4
    health system reform 180–81
    international actors in social policy
        reform 171–3
    labour market reform 176–8
    labour taxation reform 178–9
    pension system reform 179–80
    political developments 169–71
    populist regime 168–9
    social policy legacies 168–9
    social policy reform 173–81
    social protection policy 174–6
Slovakian Roma mobilization 29
Slovenia 45–60
    accession to EU 35–6
    health policies 54–6
    labour market policies 46–8
    pensions policy 48–54
    poverty and social exclusion policies
        56–8
    unemployment policy 46–8
social assistance 222
    Albania 192–3
    Bulgaria 67
    Kosovo 209–12, 213–14, 214–16
    Macedonia 135–6

Romania 79
    Turkey 124–6
social care and local government,
    Macedonia 137
social exclusion, Albania 188
social inclusion policies, Slovenia 48,
    56–8
Social Innovation Fund, Serbia 175–6
Social Institutions Support
    Programme, Council of Europe
    225
    Macedonia 145
Social Insurance Institute, Albania 195
Social Insurance Institution (SSK),
    Turkey 104
social insurance, Albania 194–5
social policy
    Albania 191–5
    Bosnia and Herzegovina 153–64
    Bulgaria 65–72
    Croatia 86–100
    and employment policy 30–31
    and international actors 221–37
    Kosovo 206–17
    Macedonia 130–46
    and regional policy 31
    Romania 72–80
    Serbia 171–81
    and transnationalization 7–9, 239–40
Social Policy Conference 163
social policy legacies 230–33
    Serbia 168–9
Social Protection, National
    Programme for, Macedonia 144
social protection reform
    Macedonia 135–8
    Serbia 174–6
Social Risk Mitigation Project Loan,
    Turkey 125
Social Safety Net Development
    (SSND), Albania 195–6
social security reforms, Romania 78
social well-being, impact of foreign
    aid, Albania 199–200
socialist legacies 10–11, 230–31
socio-economic developments, Turkey
    110–11
Solidarity Fund, Turkey 105–6, 125
Solioz, C. 15
Sotiropolous, D. 24

South East Europe
  accession to EU 35–6
  as a region 9–16
  see also individual countries
sovereign frontiers 6–7
St Clair, A. 4
Stability Pact for South Eastern
    Europe 16, 223, 225
  Initiative for Social Cohesion 223,
    225
Stabilization and Association
    Agreement, Croatia 96–7
State Insurance Supervision Agency,
    Bulgaria 70
state-centrism 3
states 5–7
  role in policy-making 239
Stubbs, P. 1, 5, 66, 67, 85, 88, 91, 97,
    153, 156, 159, 221, 228, 234,
    239
Support to Social Sector Project
    (SSSP), Bosnia and Herzegovina
    159, 161
Sykes, R. 8

taxation, labour, Serbia 178–9
Teague, P. 24
Todorova, M. 9
trade unions, challenge to pension
    reform, Macedonia 140–41
Transformation of Health project,
    Turkey 123
transition process
  Albania 187–9
  effect on social policies 11
Transition Task Force, Kosovo 210,
    211
transnational policy advocacy,
    pensions 4
transnationalism 3–4
  and social policy 7–9
Turkey 11, 103–27
  health care reform 123–4
  human development indicators
    112–15
  international actors in social policies
    116–19
  pension reform 119–23
  political developments 111, 116
  social assistance 124–6

socio-economic developments
    110–11

UK DFID 227
  Bosnia and Herzegovina 159–60
UN (United Nations) 227
  aid to Albania 197–8
  and health system reform, Serbia
    181
  and Kosovo 207
  see also ILO; UNDP; UNICEF
UN Preventive Deployment Mission
    (UNPREDEP) 132–3
UNDP 227
  and Albania 197–8
  and health system reform, Serbia 181
  and social policy, Croatia 99
  and social policy reform, Serbia 172
  and socio-economic policies, Turkey
    117
unemployment policies
  Bulgaria 70
  Romania 79
  Slovenia 46–8
unemployment
  Albania 188, 193–4
  Kosovo 206
  Macedonia 131
UNHCR, assistance to Croatia 88
UNICEF 227
  and Albania 198
United Nations, *see* UN
UNMIK (UN Interim Administration
    Mission in Kosovo) 205, 209–10
USAID (United States Agency for
    International Development) 227
  and Albania 198
  and social policy reform, Serbia
    172–3

Vali, M. 31
Van der Molen, I. 29
Vaughan-Whitehead, D. 146
Vermeersch, P. 29
vocality of actors 29–30

Walters, W. 27
war
  Bosnia and Herzegovina 149–50,
    155–6

and social policies 11, 234
  Croatia 86–90
and social welfare, Bosnia and
  Herzegovina 155–6
War Victims Rehabilitation Project,
  Bosnia and Herzegovina 157
Wedel, J. 5
West, C. 30–31
Wincott, D. 35
workfare 35
World Bank 226
  Country Assistance Strategy,
    Albania 197
  and employment policy reform,
    Macedonia 134
  and health care reform
    Croatia 96
    Serbia 181
  loans, Turkey 125
  and pension reform
    Albania 194
    Croatia 91–4
    Macedonia 139–40

  Slovenia 50–51
  relationship with EU 229–30
  social assistance model,
    Macedonia 144
  and social policy reform
    Albania 195–7
    Croatia 99
    Serbia 171–2
  and socio-economic policies,
    Turkey 116–17
World Bank War Victims
  Rehabilitation Project,
  Bosnia and Herzegovina
  157
World Health Organization
  (WHO) and Slovenia 55

Yugoslav socialism 10

Zamfir, C. 81
Zaviršek, D. 159
Zentai, V. 29
Županov, J. 89